The Democracy Deficit

The
Democracy
Deficit

Taming Globalization
through Law Reform

Alfred C. Aman, Jr.

To Broker — David Held —
with respect and admiration —

Fred Aman

NEW YORK UNIVERSITY PRESS
New York and London

NEW YORK UNIVERSITY PRESS
New York and London
www.nyupress.org

Library of Congress Cataloging-in-Publication Data
Aman, Alfred C.
The democracy deficit : taming globalization through law reform /
Alfred C. Aman, Jr.
p. cm.
Includes bibliographical references and index.
ISBN 0–8147–0700–9 (cloth : alk. paper)
1. Administrative procedure.   2. Economic policy.
3. Industrial laws and legislation.   4. Globalization.
5. Law reform.   I. Title.
K3402.A95   2004
342'.066—dc22   2004010881

New York University Press books are printed on acid-free paper,
and their binding materials are chosen for strength and durability.

Manufactured in the United States of America
10 9 8 7 6 5 4 3 2 1

To Carol

Contents

Preface

This book is about globalization, politics, markets, and law in the United States. It deals specifically with the interrelationships of these concepts and the domestic institutions they involve. This book argues that the forces and processes we call globalization can be influenced, shaped, and harnessed to achieve public ends. Law, particularly domestic administrative law, has a crucial role to play in this endeavor, and much is at stake. Indeed, democracy in the twenty-first century depends on the ability of citizens to affect the policies that globalization would now seem to dictate.

How one conceptualizes globalization greatly affects one's analysis of politics, markets, and law. From the standpoint of prevailing views, the idea that law, much less domestic law, has an important role to play in governing globalization may seem to be counterintuitive. Globalization is widely understood as a phenomenon in the private sector, especially involving markets and capital flows. Globalization is often understood in largely neoliberal, economic terms, as if it were a force of nature. For some, globalization is all about competition—a competition for markets and investments that is global in scale and more intense than ever before. For individual corporations to succeed, for example, they must become more efficient, taking full advantage of new technologies and moving various components of their operations around the world, so as to lower costs and expand their markets. States are expected to follow suit by deregulating their markets, privatizing governmental services, lowering taxes, and, in the process, becoming more effective in attracting new businesses. This conception of globalization easily translates into a domestic politics of efficiency at the local level that may make it at least appear that the public sector's responses to collective problems will be costly, resulting in higher taxes. Under this view, law's most important role is to create, protect, and enforce the property rights necessary for markets to take hold and flourish, as well as to dismantle the inefficiencies of the past.

Such views of globalization encourage a political discourse that reduces all values to economic terms. They treat globalization and market processes as forces of nature, more or less like the weather—something to be harnessed, perhaps, but beyond shaping in any fundamental way. Indeed, those who see globalization this way tend to believe that attempts to control markets can only give rise to inefficiencies, red tape, and worse—some argue that powerful interests will inevitably turn such legal processes to their own private advantage, at the expense of the public at large.

As this book discusses, market discourses, viewed in this manner, have a way of dividing and conquering interests defined in terms of noneconomic values. They can disaggregate the public, in effect, and make the connections between and among social issues seem remote.[1] Market outcomes, however, are not necessarily the best justice outcomes. "Costs" are not just expenses, but expenses relative to values (monetary and otherwise). For this reason cost should not be the only factor affecting our political responses and capacities for innovation. The social values that determine costs are—or should be—central issues for public debate. Markets alone do not provide the requisite means for democratic outcomes. Globalization need not mean substituting markets for politics and law. Human beings should not be allowed to fall off the demand curve. If democracy means anything, it means that citizens can affect their own destinies through the political process.

The viewpoint of globalization that forms this book begins not in the inevitability of global markets or some form of world government but in the role of domestic law and politics in producing certain market conditions (global or otherwise). Specifically, I focus on the distinctions between the private and the public sectors, the federal and the local, and the foreign and the national. I reevaluate these distinctions to show that globalization is not something "out there," foreign and distant; rather, it is embedded in our own domestic institutions, both public and private. Today, many of what were formerly public functions are now performed by the private sector. When public responsibilities are delegated to the private sector or to what some call our emerging international branch of government, we need new institutions and new legal structures to ensure that citizens continue to have a democratic role to play. The main role of law is to create the democratic forums, flows of information, and political processes necessary for an active, effective, and creative citizenship. It is time to see globalization for what it is—institutional processes subject to influence and control at the domestic level. In the complex, interdependent world in which we now live, we still are and can remain responsible for our collective lives. This can occur only through a democracy that empowers citizen involvement and knowledge, not just economic "efficiency" defined in narrow terms. My purpose in this book is to explore the structural openings for such engagement and look forward along broad lines of legal reform.

This book has benefited greatly from the generous comments of my colleagues in a variety of contexts over the last several years—the classroom, conferences and seminars, fellowship programs, and many helpful individual conversations with colleagues and students. Professor Jost Delbrück and I have taught a seminar on globalization and the law at the Indiana University School of Law–Bloomington for ten years. We also have edited the *Indiana Journal of Global Legal Studies* since its inception in 1992. In these contexts and in our various conversations, he has offered generous comments and encouragement over the years, and I am deeply grateful, especially for his help as this book began to take shape and come to fruition. His interest in and creative contributions to the globalization literature always inspired me. I also am grateful to the IU School of Law for its research support over the years and for the comments of my students, both in the classroom and as members of the *Global Journal* staff.

I wrote most of the first draft of this book at Princeton University, as a fellow in the Law and Public Affairs Program and a visiting professor in the Woodrow Wilson School. I am deeply grateful to the director of the Law and Public Affairs Program, Chris Eisgruber, for creating such a stimulating and supportive intellectual environment for LAPA fellows. I appreciated very much the critical readings and comments from other fellows in the program, as well as other colleagues, and each of my students in my seminar. I also wish to thank, in particular, my colleagues at IU and elsewhere who have read all or parts of this book while it was taking shape: Professors John Applegate, Paul Craig, Yvonne Cripps, Robert Fischman, Dean Lauren Robel, Sir David G. T. Williams, David Williams, Susan Williams, and Elizabeth Zoller. My conversations with them over the years, their comments on drafts, not to speak of their overall encouragement and substantive help, have been enormously important to me.

This book also has benefited from my research assistants over the years, especially as we neared the conclusion of the book. Betrall Ross, a graduate student at Princeton, provided excellent, comprehensive research on a number of substantive areas dealt with in the book. I also wish especially to thank Aaron Furniss, IU School of Law, 2004, for his superb help at the very end. He always seemed able to find the unfindable footnotes, to read the manuscript with great care, and to make helpful comments, suggestions, and additions. This book would not have been possible without the superb secretarial assistance I have had over the years, including that of Jan Turner and Deborah Westerfield during my years as dean at IU, Cindy Schoeneck during my year at Princeton University, and Marjorie Young, Shellie Bayer, and Marian Conaty upon my return to IU. Their skill, judgment, and dedication added enormously to the success and enjoyment of this project. Finally, there are some "thank you's" that always seem inadequate because the inspiration one receives from some people almost defies description. This book is dedicated to my wife, Carol Greenhouse. Her deep faith in this project and in me were not only inspirational; they truly made this book a labor of love.

The Democracy Deficit

Introduction
The Domestic Face of Globalization

Can citizens govern globalization? This book argues that they can, and that the state, through the creative use of its own domestic law, has a crucial role to play in this process. I use the term "globalization" to refer to pluralistic, multicentered and dynamic processes involving interrelationships among states and nonstate entities across national boundaries.[1] Global activities differ from international activities, in that the latter occur only between and among states and state entities.[2] When we refer to globalization, the area of interrelation might be the whole world or geographically distinct regions.[3] The key element that distinguishes globalization from international affairs, then, is the dynamics of state and nonstate institutions within and across national borders.

Some of the new importance of the private sector in globalization arises from the effects of technology and the flow of capital around the world. Private decisions involving production, finance, and investment occur increasingly free of direct, individual state involvement.[4] Transnational corporations decide where it is most cost effective to locate various activities in the sometimes long value chains connected with the production and marketing of goods and services. They may locate Research & Development in one country, component assembly in another, final assembly in another, and distribution networks in yet another. They also decide how much to customize the globally conceived product for local markets.[5] Through the General Agreement of Tariffs and Trade (GATT)[6] and other multilateral agreements,[7] trade in goods also is facilitated; a substantial portion of world trade today takes place between and among divisions of the same company doing business in various locations around the globe.[8] Not only trade is transnational. The politics involved in issues such as global warming, ozone depletion, and the destruction of the rain forest involve political networks that also transcend nation states and state institutions.[9]

These factors do not mean that states are no longer important as influences on these business or environmental aspects of global problems. It does mean that the role nation states play is substantially different from that of the past. Not centered within any one nation state or group of nation states are the financial, production, and investment networks.[10] Problems such as the environment, terrorism, or public health cannot be resolved by way of individual nation state action alone.[11] And any one nation state's jurisdiction is inevitably limited in relation to such issues.[12] As a result, new bodies of global, international and domestic law are developing to deal with problems that are neither wholly domestic nor wholly international.[13] These new bodies involve new forms of power sharing and delegation. Increasingly they work in concert with transnational nonstate entities, which are now more powerful than ever before.[14] For example, transnational corporations do not dictate public policy to national governments, but the potential impact of their decisions facilitates the flow of power from states to markets, as do technologies and the integration and interdependence of increasingly global markets. As Susan Strange has noted, the "shift away from states and towards markets is probably the biggest change in the international political economy to take place in the last half of the twentieth century."[15] This shift of power reflects the changing role of and impact on domestic, state-centered law and politics on the domestic front.

Globalization complicates both the form and content of democracy. While globalization involves a host of new arrangements such as these between the public and private sector, it creates a powerful need for new forms of law responsive to these fundamental changes in states and markets.[16] For example, transnational corporations have a distinct need for dispute resolution techniques not directly linked to any one country. Elaborate and important arbitration procedures have been developing to meet these needs.[17] Similarly, human rights have been conceptualized in ways that transcend any one state's view of these issues. Local courts apply the rulings of the European Court of Human Rights, dramatically changing local law in the process.[18] Indeed, in a global world, legal pluralism is increasing, as is the capacity for and the actual growth of various forms of global law, defined primarily as the law of private actors.[19]

While individual countries and sectors within those countries shape, and are shaped by, globalization in different ways, it is probably safe to say that everywhere, globalization complicates democracy both in theory and in practice. Globalization complicates democracy in theory because the prevailing models and metaphors of globalization derive largely from a vision of capitalism that equates markets with democracy, imagining markets as an expandable lateral system in which individuals are free to participate according to their own interests and abilities. Globalization complicates democracy in practice for a host of reasons. But in the United States, the fundamental reason is that models and metaphors of law are based on a vision of state power that imagines it as a vertical hierarchy, the federal government *over or above* the states; the states *over or above* local communities; and, looking outward from the United States, transnational organizations *over* national organizations.

The market metaphors are primarily lateral, or horizontal; the power metaphors are primarily hierarchical, or vertical. The telltale signs that these imagined models are in play turn up in usages of the word "global" as if it meant "worldwide." When "global" is used to suggest homogeneity in the fields of production and consumption, this is the market metaphor at work, depicting the world as ultimately one unified market; when it is used to suggest a form of dominance, this is the power metaphor at work, conjuring up world government by law. Either way these models are highly misleading. Markets are neither self-governing nor necessarily democratic, and law must be flexible enough to accommodate a three-dimensional view of regulation, one that involves the vertical and horizontal relationships among the public and private sectors as well as the merging of these sectors.

As we shall see in subsequent chapters, putting these models into practice actually shrinks democracy, no matter how their proponents might advocate them in the name of democracy. Critics of the practices based on these models often use the phrase "democracy deficit" to refer to this effect of globalization. Democracy deficits can take many forms, depending on the institutional location and the substantive and procedural decisions involved; their vertical or horizontal nature; and the procedures to which they are compared. Democracy deficits may arise from decisions that have significant adverse effects on individuals but are inaccessible to affected citizens because they are made by jurisdictions or private entities beyond the reach of the domestic or international political structures of those affected. Such democracy deficits often are the result of negative spillovers from one jurisdiction to another, such as acid rain, or they can arise from private decisions to move capital from one part of the world to another. Representation or direct participation in the decisions that lead to these spillovers usually is not possible in jurisdictions in which affected citizens do not live and in whose political processes they cannot directly participate; nor is it even theoretically possible to participate at the international level, if there is no treaty or relevant international organization with jurisdiction over the issues involved or if the decisions causing the adverse effects are made by private entities.

Democracy deficit concerns can result from more directly vertical relationships in which decisions are made from above, for example, by supranational organizations like the European Union. In the European Union context, democracy deficit concerns often arise from the fact that some decisions in the chain of command are thought to be simply too far removed from affected citizens in a particular state.[20] Though one might argue that the power to make these decisions was, in effect, delegated by the states to the European Union, opposition to the unforeseen outcomes of these broad delegations of power often describes these outcomes as a form of democracy deficit in tension with principles of subsidiarity that argue for decision-making processes as close to the affected citizens as possible.[21] Of course, issues of domestic federalism are similar, when decisions are made at the national rather than state or local levels of government.

Still another kind of democracy deficit derives from the fact that the democratic processes used to conform domestic law to an international ruling may, in reality, be substantially less than those used to create these rules or laws in the first place. For example, pursuant to treaties negotiated within or judicial decisions rendered by the World Trade Organization (WTO), domestic law must often change to harmonize with these outcomes. The processes used appear to be democratic, but the outcome of these processes, given the prior commitments made in the treaties involved, means the outcomes usually are a foregone conclusion. The same processes used to promulgate a rule or pass a statute are employed to rescind the rule or amend the law, but the fait accompli nature of the processes used means, in reality, that the same is less. They have a rubber-stamp quality to them.[22]

Fast-track legislative processes (i.e., processes that do not allow for amendments on the floor of the House or Senate) may also contribute to a sense of a democracy deficit; they also represent a kind of fait accompli law making, since amendments are not allowed. In this case, a democracy deficit derives from there actually being fewer legislative processes involved. In this sense, the growing power of the executive branch can be seen in the fact that some major domestic issues now fall within the president's power as commander in chief or within executive foreign policy powers. Democracy deficit concerns can arise from the increased use of executive treaties or from broad-based executive orders, such as those involved with establishing military tribunals.[23]

Another accelerating source of democracy deficit is in the deterritorializing effects of globalization, both at home and abroad. For example, some decisions that have substantial impact on citizens of a country are made by organizations, either domestic or multinational organizations, that are essentially private, beyond direct democratic control or influence. Transnational actors of all kinds have a need for rules to make their operation run smoothly. The transnational aspects of their operations place them beyond the control of any one jurisdiction, and the rules and dispute resolution mechanisms that they develop are voluntary and, essentially, private in nature. Yet, these rules can and often do have transnational effects on various publics. Corporate codes of conduct governing labor conditions, voluntarily adopted, may or may not be the result of input by citizens in various countries who are concerned with child labor, low wages, or the right of freedom of association.[24] It may seem that there is no democracy deficit in such contexts, since one might not expect the decision-making processes of private actors to be democratic, beyond their own shareholders. But this assumes that our concept of public and private should remain constant, even in the face of denationalizing global forces. The horizontal nature of transnational governance creates new issues of legitimacy and democracy that go beyond individual states. We must, therefore, also go beyond state-centric approaches and habits of mind when thinking about democracy in contexts such as these.

As a matter of interpretation, democracy deficits, of course, also turn on how one conceptualizes democracy. Democracy may require more than the involvement of a legislative or executive body or the participation of a member state. It also involves concepts of legitimacy, which include opportunities for participation in decision-making processes by stakeholders whose interests may not adequately be represented by a member state. Decisions made by judicial panels at the WTO, utilizing decision-making processes that are not particularly transparent and that limit participation only to member states, are not likely to be seen as legitimate by those whose interests are not fully (or even partially) represented by formal state representation. The inevitable trade-offs that arise when free trade conflicts with environmental protection are likely to produce widespread participation demands from a range of nongovernmental organizations (NGOs) whose interests are more varied and diverse than any single state representative can be.[25] From their point of view, there is a democracy deficit if they are excluded from the relevant decision-making processes. From a broader public point of view, the quality of the decisions may suffer if the perspectives of diverse interests and parties are not considered. One might argue that such democracy deficits may exist only in the eyes of the beholders. If so, that would only underscore the point that the scope of democracy should be decided by democratic means. As Jost Delbrück has argued, "What we are now dealing with is a complex system of global, international and national governance."[26]

In this book, I will focus on the legal resources for expanding citizens' democratic engagement in, and sometimes against, globalization as governance. My focus is on domestic law. The primary purpose of this book is to develop an analysis of globalization from the domestic side. By turning the lens to globalization's domestic side, we can both advance understanding of the contemporary world and, within the United States, develop approaches to reforms that would expand and strengthen democracy in the various governmental and nongovernmental settings where policy is made and applied today. By this, I mean representation not just in the legislative and executive branches of government but also at ground level, in contexts created by deregulation and privatization. These highly varied contexts often combine elements of the public and private sector as public functions are pushed to the private sector by the application of so-called market values to an increasingly wide range of former government functions and services. This book is intended to broaden the dialogue over globalization past any simplistic "pro" and "anti" positions, and so far as law is concerned, past the terms set by debates over regulation that have dominated the discussion of globalization in the United States since the late 1970s. As we shall see, that debate is highly ideologized, especially in its construction of law and markets and in the inevitability of a zero-sum competition between these as approaches to social ordering.

Indeed, one argument some advocates of privatization offer is that the very recourse to markets and the private sector would appear to diminish the importance of law, or even render it superfluous. One of the primary reasons to opt for the market and the private sector generally, they say, is to increase efficiency. This book argues, however, that the embedded nature of globalization within American institutions of government renders this kind of either/or thinking obsolete. The public and the private sectors often merge, necessitating new approaches to law, to maintain the values of and opportunities for public debate over public matters delegated to the private sector. In many of these privatized settings—e.g., prisons, health care, education, and housing for the poor, to name just some—products and services may be provided privately, but the responsibility for their success or failure remains public. Thus, whether or what kinds of markets are appropriate in specific private contexts are questions in which the public should be involved, as they should participate in questions over the compatibility of profitability and public service. Understanding globalization from the domestic side means sorting through such rationales from the standpoint of how markets actually function in specific contexts, making service providers more subject to accountability in some instances, less in others.

Law—and administrative law, in particular—can help create conditions and opportunities necessary for meaningful politics around local and global issues affecting citizens. The first step is to develop a domestic perspective on globalization. As we shall see, "global forces" do not come from beyond our nation or beyond government, but are deeply embedded within our own domestic institutions, both public and private. Focusing on globalization from a domestic perspective—the domestic "face" of globalization—means focusing on the legal institutions and processes that are the main vehicles of globalization within the United States.

Domestic legal systems are not just affected by global processes; they are embedded within them, i.e., they are integral to them.[27] Domestic institutions, however, tend to be neglected in discussions of globalization, as if "global" meant "foreign." By looking at globalization's domestic side, we can appreciate both the effects of globalization on domestic institutions as well as the potential effects of domestic institutions, especially legal institutions, on globalization. The domestic side of globalization may be counterintuitive for those who imagine globalization primarily in terms of a free-flowing private sector. However, the interplay between globalization and domestic processes is a two-way street (and not just one street, but a whole map of streets), and understanding something of its history, institutions, and legal and political complexities from the domestic side is crucial to both analysis and reform.

In the United States today, globalization tends to be understood in terms of market pressures, as a force favoring efficiency and seemingly unfettered competition. Many regulatory policy approaches now privilege markets over law. The main regulatory reforms in ascendancy today consist of various forms of deregulation, privatization, and public/private partnerships—with the private sector often performing tasks once reserved primarily for government. Indeed, political debates about these reforms usually treat globalization as if it were synonymous with the market, and sometimes seem to be little more than ideological assertions about the virtues of markets over bureaucracy. In particular, I will focus on the problems for democracy posed by market-oriented approaches to globalization, especially insofar as those approaches assigned to the private sector are functions formerly performed by public institutions.

One premise of this book is that the primary purpose of public law, and administrative law in particular, is to ensure that citizens can influence and take responsibility for the new public-private partnerships that are the main institutional effect of globalization in the United States. This means more than providing negative rights and remedies for injustices, or even making private providers accountable for their actions. Traditionally, public law (such as administrative and constitutional law) is the law that applies primarily to governmental institutions. For this to occur, public law must supply procedures and forums to enable citizens effectively to participate in the shaping of the policies and structures of the private and semiprivate regulatory regimes that now govern what was once public. Some of these procedures and forums already exist, and others do not—although some basic principles exist in law to serve as guidelines for their invention.

Another premise of this book is that social justice and the political change it requires necessitates a proactive, future-oriented role for law. Law is not just an instrument of command or control but is also a highly flexible idiom for creation and innovation. For these reasons, I regard law as essential to the creation of a new "politics" by which concerned citizens might debate real alternatives to the means and ends of the privatized and, as we shall see below, internationalized institutional structures within which many legal and economic policies are produced today.

In the context of globalization, debates regarding the role of law typically borrow their form from debates over federalism. This means that law is seen in hierarchical terms as if power were entirely a top-down affair; a supremacy clause is tacitly assumed. Accordingly, debates over the various versions of the so-called new world order dwell primarily on issues of sovereignty. How much sovereignty do we give up by delegating decision-making authority to international organizations such as the WTO? How do we harmonize domestic law with the law as mandated by international organizations? As we shall see below, international organizations are important decision-making sites affecting citizens at the local level, and they raise important issues for domestic law. More importantly, as we shall see in later chapters, underlying this debate about the role of law in a global economy are assumptions about democracy and legitimacy.

As noted above, some theorists envision law and markets as rival forms of governance, law being the form of governance belonging to the state, and markets being the form of governance belonging to democratic society. At the risk of oversimplification, one might further describe such theories as based on an assumption that the differences between law and markets essentially involve a zero-sum relation, strengthening one implying a weakening of the other.[28] Why should this be the case? For some theorists, the answer is in the models themselves. The market, imagined as an open field of products supported or rejected by potential consumers who are free to choose for themselves, would seem to be the very image of perfect freedom. Meanwhile, law, imagined as a restrictive "product" designed by specialists, would seem to be democratic only to the extent that the lawmakers can legitimately claim to be acting on behalf of those people they represent.[29]

Some theorists tend to regard the judiciary as the least democratic branch (if not antidemocratic), since judges (including most importantly the nine justices of the Supreme Court) are not elected.[30] The idea of representation is key, and some theorists place great emphasis on election as the criterion of which an office holder's (or an institution's) claim to legitimacy might be substantiated before its constituents. From their point of view, election is a specialized indirect form of market selection and, wherever possible, government action should be replaced by the market in the more direct sense. This ideal is based on a model of pure democracy as an open market in which individuals can assert their own interests. For some theorists who hold to this view, all interests are essentially economic interests. But in this, they do not distinguish between markets and metaphorical markets—a distinction that will be important to our discussion later. Be that as it may, relative to such open competitive arenas as these theorists imagine the marketplace to be for individuals (and, by extension, corporations), formal political arenas are more limited—restrictive by definition (i.e., to office holders)—and also prone to "capture" by office holders' particular interests with respect to amassing and retaining power, as well as economic interests that seek to control these office holders.

Scenarios such as these are not difficult to find in the marketplace and in politics. Markets *are* sometimes more open than public office and politicians *are* sometimes venal or corrupt. But more fundamentally, these very theories have guided the development of markets and political institutions in the United States for twenty-five years or more. This being the case, it is especially important to note some deep flaws in these metaphors and models that define markets as if they were a general or natural state of affairs in relation to which law could be only an intrusion or diversion from efficiency.

First, markets and law are neither internally unified nor stable. Markets and law are institutions and, as for all institutions, this means that they are dynamic social processes, not monolithic entities. Even within the United States, which is only one player, albeit a powerful one, markets and legal systems are plural and internally diverse, shaped by their own mechanisms of inclusion and exclusion and prone to change.

Second, markets and law do not function in a zero-sum relation. Strengthening one does not necessarily weaken the other. Nor does enhancing a person's power as a consumer imply empowerment in democratic terms, since the former is inevitably reactive (one can only choose from among available options) and the latter is ideally proactive and deliberative, as well as electoral. Democracy is not merely about "freedom of choice" but also about participating in the creation of new options, among other things.

Third, the federal structure is not a straightforward hierarchy that increasingly distances power from the people through incrementally attenuated systems of representation but is, rather, a system for allocating powers between states and the federal government, and also for regulating the borders (including a large gray zone) between the public and private sectors.

Fourth, in the same vein, "the global" is a reference not to domination of or by foreign countries or international organizations (whether by market power or legal rules) but to the nexus of transnational institutions and processes on which the pragmatic autonomy of individual states is contingent.

The terms of current debates on these issues have been set largely by public choice theorists. In simplified form, the theory goes something like this: perhaps the democracy of the market is the best democracy of all, since collective action risks cooptation by special interests with the most to gain or to lose. But if there is to be public action, citizens should be as close to the decision makers as possible. The greater the distance, the more likely it is that special interests will prevail over the collective good. For the same reason, local community decisions are better than state decisions, and state decisions are better than national decisions. Moreover, whatever the decisions, they gain their legitimacy from procedures that adhere to formal models of democracy, that is, that depend primarily on the actions of elected legislators and executives. The state, in other words, is a formal institution, the very formality of which is the warrant of its democratic legitimacy.

There is much to be said for the skepticism that the public-choice model expresses relative to public law making. In the legislative process, there are indeed powerful interests at work, and it is in their interest to lobby as effectively as they can. But it is easy to carry this analysis too far, becoming more cynical than analytical about the ways in which public policy is made. More important, the overall thrust of this skepticism errs in imagining bright-line distinctions between states and markets, states and civil society, among states, and between states and nonstate entities. The turn to the private sector as the primary protector of the public interest not only idealizes the market but also fails as an analysis of globalization. As we shall see later, the problems of democracy deficit to be addressed in this book stem not from the cooptation of the state by private interests but—if anything—from the inverse: the infusion of the private sector by public-service functions. Nor are the solutions to the problems of globalization to be found primarily "outside the state" in civil society and markets, as if these were also distinct and separate realms of social life. Rather, we shall see that "public" and "private" are mutually intertwined and that deregulation in favor of markets is itself a potent form of legal regulation.

A strictly hierarchical conception of law perpetuates the fiction that "globalization" is "out there," like a force of nature, the result of the economy at work. In contrast, drawing on recent history, I will argue that globalization is embedded in all of our local institutions, public and private. The primary manifestations of this embeddedness are the government's use of markets and private providers to produce and distribute public goods, and the private sector's attempts to sell managerial services in markets previously restricted to public institutions. Today, the roles and functions of public and private actors are now so enmeshed as to make any bright lines between them, for purposes of addressing issues of accountability or transparency, artificial and even counterproductive. The democracy deficit results not from too much public decision making but from too little. Markets, unchecked or unfettered by law, simply do not offer the transparency and accountability necessary for a vibrant democratic society.

Rather than enter into debate about law versus markets or the virtues of the public versus the private sector, as if these were either/or issues, this book sets forth in fresh terms an agenda for domestic-law reform. By taking into account the global dynamics in which domestic institutions operate as both key players and affected parties, we can develop new approaches to law and policy. I present these in terms of some basic principles of administrative law—administrative law being the main body of law that establishes both positive and negative rights for citizens confronting questions about the relationship of states to markets. Those principles place primary emphasis on citizens having the information necessary to understand issues of public significance. I extend those principles to include the private sector, where the private sector is performing public functions, as well as to international bodies.

More than deepening public awareness and understanding, the reform agenda I propose also includes the expansion of public *participation* in shaping those issues and outcomes. Thus, I also consider political and economic forums (both old and new) available to citizens and other stakeholders for the effective and timely expression of their views and preferences, regardless of the label attached to the decision makers involved. I do not claim that the reforms I propose will answer to *all* the needs for democratizing globalization, or for calling public and private institutions to fuller account; however, they would widen the arenas for public involvement and state accountability at the institutional junctures where globalization comes home, so to speak. Law remains relevant in privatized and deregulated settings, and there is existing law to apply.

The democracy problem inherent in globalization invites a debate over more than which public institution—the court, the executive, or the legislature—is best suited to decide which legal issues. More fundamentally, it involves coming to grips with the fact that private entities carrying out public tasks must be held accountable for their performance. Market forces alone may not suffice for such purposes. Citizen responsibility for private actions requires more than deference to a single legislative decision to privatize or an executive determination to contract out governmental responsibilities. There should be regular opportunities for citizen input well beyond the initial decision to substitute markets for law. What is at stake when the state delegates power to the market and to nonstate private actors is nothing less than democracy itself.

I am optimistic about the future of democracy if we can vest our democratic hopes in something other than an unchecked market, and especially if we can acknowledge that the market does not substitute for legal regulation. Markets might provide the metaphors for democracy and political debate, but they are not inherently democratic. The role I see for law goes beyond the creation and protection of property rights. The role of law is to maintain and, when necessary, create the infrastructures required for citizens to participate in decisions as citizens, not just as consumers of services, or according to rules they had no part in making. I argue that the demands of democracy are not satisfied by one-time legislative initiatives or executive decisions in favor of markets over law. If democracy actually exists, it is in the day-to-day operations of both public and private institutions. To reach this point, the first step is to recognize that the private sector is not the antithesis of the public sector; today it often functions as a privatized public sector. This new domain is my main concern in this book, since acknowledging the public interest in the privatized public sector opens up a new space for citizen participation and public accountability—in effect, a new dialogue on democratic responsibility. When it comes to constitutional law, an interactive, vibrant federalism is necessary and is best achieved if the Supreme Court avoids unduly narrow approaches to such issues. Some law reform will be necessary to realize that exciting potential, but important resources are at hand in administrative law and with a healthy judicial regard for politics, as I shall explain in detail later.

When we appeal to law as a mode of reform, we usually are asking law to correct injustices. Traditionally, when we speak of law reform, law is usually understood from a rights or remedial perspective. Administrative law represents a crucial additional resource for such discussions, since administrative law exists primarily to mediate between individuals and the government. An important role for administrative law has been to provide procedural protections for individuals before the government, while advancing public goals, usually in the form of an administrative agency.

Administrative law processes not only protect individuals from inappropriate governmental action but, more relevant for our purposes, they also allow for input by citizens regarding policy under review.

Indeed, a primary role of domestic law (particularly domestic administrative law) is to provide the infrastructure necessary for the exercise of participatory rights by citizens. Sometimes this takes the form of new spaces for administrative hearings and citizen input. Other times, it takes the form of judicial restraint in the face of state or federal attempts politically to resolve a variety of societal issues, from the setting of living wages to the importation of prescription drugs. The rights of citizens go beyond rights against the state. They include the right to help shape the structures that control both the allocation and the application of power, including power exercised by nonstate actors, whether domestically or transnationally.

To fulfill this role, law must provide citizens with access to the kind of information necessary for them to make informed judgments—whether that information is held by a public or a private entity. It must create the forums necessary for citizens to enter into meaningful political debate and to decide whether, for example, they wish to opt for market approaches to policy, and if so, the kinds of markets they wish to foster and the mix of market and nonmarket values any given decision-making regime should encompass. These political spaces and opportunities for participation must go well beyond traditional conceptions of representative democracy and public law principles based on bright-line distinctions between public and private or state and federal actors. They must also include the creation of citizen forums in the private sector, domestically as well as in international organizations such as the WTO, advancing approaches that privilege participation, not just market outcomes. For this to occur, however, it is necessary to reassess the relationship of markets to politics and law. Processes of globalization have fundamentally changed the relationship of markets to states both internationally and domestically. Focusing on the domestic face of globalization illuminates untapped resources for democracy at home, as well as clarifying where and how the lines between public and private, state and federal, and domestic and global are blurred by their extension into international and transnational spheres.

1

Three Eras of Administrative Law and Agency Regulation

Before we can pursue an alternative vision of globalization for the sake of addressing at least some of the more critical aspects of the democracy deficit, we must examine how, why, and where it was and is that the present global era is so widely imagined (and institutionalized) as involving an inevitable tradeoff between law and markets as forms of power. The net result of the last twenty-five years of globalization has been a vast expansion of the tendency to conceptualize government functions in terms of the values placed on efficiency and individual economic rights. As already noted, individualism, economic interests, competition, and effective market behavior are widely held to be natural instincts, a sort of modern neo-Darwinian survival of the fittest. At the same time, deregulation, market-oriented regulatory approaches, and the shift of public functions to the private sector have produced a significant concentration of power in the executive branch and, in particular, in the president. This is because of, among other factors, the frequent use of broad-based executive orders and executive treaties, particularly since the 1980s, that have increased judicial deference to issues conceived of as international in nature, as well as deference to executive agency decisions, and increasingly comprehensive and aggressive executive oversight of agency rule making.[1] It is ironic that a political theory dedicated to promoting the democratic functions of the market should have so contributed to disabling Congress in favor of executive power, nowadays relatively unchecked, especially in certain economic areas formerly under active congressional oversight. These trends have only escalated with regard to security and privacy issues, as the role of the executive branch has increased in response to the "war on terrorism." How this came to be is a historical question that takes us back to the early days of the New Deal and the modern development of administrative law. An overview of that history suggests that in vivid contrast to the assumption that markets are, in effect, natural democracies, the democratization of the market was itself produced by and through legal regulation, particularly by Congress and then, eventually, by the Supreme Court's innovative response to the exigencies of the Great Depression, which set the stage for subsequent legislative developments.

In modern times, American administrative law has developed over the course of three main periods, roughly, the 1930s through the mid-1960s, the late 1960s through the late 1970s, and the 1980s to the present. I call these the New Deal era, the environmental era, and the global era.[2] Understanding the main features of these different periods—the effects of which were cumulative—helps explain why the tensions between law and markets, or among the different branches of government, are easily seen in a zero-sum relation, and yet are not inevitably rival forms of power and governance. Rather, such tensions as are now built into the system are outcomes of a particular institutional history that remains open to a range of possible futures.

The New Deal Era

For our purposes, the story begins during the 1930s, the period of the Great Depression and the administration of Franklin Delano Roosevelt. The Depression yielded a major transformation in the relationship of the courts to Congress and, accordingly, of the federal government to the states. At the time, Congress was actively engaged in passing the new president's program for economic recovery. While our discussion is inevitably somewhat technical, it is in those very technicalities that the law-market dichotomy was constructed, as the Supreme Court ultimately gave Congress its head, making Congress the body that would be politically accountable for the new programs.

In 1933, Professor—but soon to be Justice—Felix Frankfurter commented on the special significance of the Great Depression in the United States:[3]

> In this the fourth winter of our discontent it is no longer temerarious or ignorant to believe that this depression has a significance very different from prior economic stresses in our national history. The more things

change the more they remain the same is an epigram of comfortable cynicism. There are new periods in history, and we are in the midst of one of them.

Frankfurter, along with most New Dealers, believed that those extraordinary times required extraordinary solutions, involving both experimentation and innovation. Much of this reform was to come in the form of national legislation. Frankfurter thus advocated the need for judicial restraint in the face of such legislative attempts to lift America out of the depths of the Great Depression. He criticized the Supreme Court as being too activist, far too willing to substitute its economic judgments for those of duly elected legislators. He had good reason to be critical. The Supreme Court had been very tough, indeed, on previous legislative experiments that arguably interfered with the Court's conception of "liberty." The Court's substantive due process approach, evident in *Lochner v. N.Y.*,[4] gave it, in Holmes's dissenting view, the right to read Herbert Spencer into the Constitution.[5] More importantly, the Court's view of states' rights would also make national legislation vulnerable to constitutional attack. Up to the Great Depression and beyond, its decisions reflected a very narrow interpretation of the commerce and the contracts clauses of the Constitution. This view resulted in a number of judicial decisions declaring a variety of federal statutes void on constitutional grounds.[6] Congress's early attempts at delegating legislative power to federal administrative agencies also conflicted with the Court's demand that these delegations be accompanied by clear legislative standards. Thus, in A.L.A. *Schecter Poultry Corp. v. United States*[7] and *Panama Refining Co. v. Ryan*,[8] the Court voided federal legislation for failure to meet the standards established by its nondelegation doctrine.

Eventually, the Court began to adopt the restrained approaches to judicial review of the constitutionality of federal statutes advocated by Justice Frankfurter and other New Dealers. In *West Coast Hotel Co. v. Parrish*,[9] the Court sustained a state minimum wage law for women, taking an approach that reflected a significant change in the Court's approach to a wide range of economic regulatory legislation. This period reflected the end for the doctrine of substantive due process. This more deferential judicial approach to legislation was deepened and extended by such new Roosevelt appointees to the Court as Justices Black, Murphy, Douglas, and, of course, Frankfurter himself. The doctrine of substantive due process was eventually buried, at least in economic cases;[10] the commerce clause was read more and more broadly;[11] the Tenth Amendment became a mere truism;[12] and the contracts clause dropped out of sight.[13] The nondelegation doctrine used to strike down federal legislation in *Schecter and Panama Oil Refining* seemed to have peaked in 1935, only to resurface in the odd dissent from then on.[14]

Importantly, the Court's readjustment involved its acknowledgment of the vital role of political institutions in a pluralistic society. In the words of Justice Oliver Wendell Holmes, the Constitution

> is made for people of fundamentally differing views, and the accident of our finding certain opinions natural and familiar or novel and even shocking ought not to conclude our judgment upon the question whether statutes embodying them conflict with the Constitution of the United States.[15]

Yet Frankfurter did not see judicial restraint as reflecting a desire to have the Supreme Court play a weaker role than the other branches of government. Rather, he wrote,

> [t]he Justices of the Supreme Court are arbiters of social policy because their duties make them so. For the words of the Constitution which invoke the legal judgment are usually so unrestrained by their intrinsic meaning or by their history or by prior decisions that they leave the individual Justice free, if indeed they do not compel him, to gather meaning not from reading the Constitution but from reading life.[16]

Crucially, for our purposes, "reading life" did not mean leaving the market to work in an unfettered way—since the markets had dramatically failed. Rather, the new judicial restraint effectively constituted Congress—the political branch—as the dominant institution in relation to leading the nation out of economic crisis. Justice Harlan F. Stone's famous opinion in *United States v. Carolene Products Co.*[17] epitomized the Supreme Court's recognition of the primacy of legislative solutions for economic problems, and the appropriateness of a restrained judicial role when reviewing such legislation. In that case, the Court rejected a substantive due process challenge to a federal statute that prohibited the shipment in interstate commerce of "filled milk" (a mixture of skimmed milk and nonmilk fats). In so doing, it set forth guidelines defining essentially a rational-basis test for judging the constitutional validity of this

kind of economic legislation.[18] The Court made explicit its presumption
of congressional responsibility:

> [T]he existence of facts supporting the legislative judgment is to be pre-
> sumed, for regulatory legislation affecting ordinary commercial transac-
> tions is not to be pronounced unconstitutional unless in the light of the
> facts made known or generally assumed it is of such a character as to
> preclude the assumption that it rests upon some rational basis within the
> knowledge and experience of the legislators.[19]

In a footnote to *Carolene Products,* though, the Court recognized that
not all legislation should be treated in the same way. It established what
amounts to a two-tiered approach to judicial review—relatively deferent
with respect to economic legislation, but less so in other contexts.[20] The
more stringent standard of judicial review was appropriate "when legislation appears on its face to be within a specific prohibition of the Constitution, such as those of the first ten Amendments. . . ."[21] In retrospect,
it might seem that a two-tiered review privileged judicial activism in matters of civil rights (as requiring closer judicial scrutiny); however, it would
be wrong to assume that economic rights were not important to the
Court.

In the context of the Great Depression, the Court was privileging the
political process by relinquishing its own power to set limits on economic
legislation. The economic crisis was the most pressing issue of the day,
and the Court took the view that a collective problem of such severity
called for collective solutions available only through the political arena.
The Court's priority was not on individuals, but on the American population as a whole—on the nation, not individual states. In short, judicial
restraint was an acknowledgment of the role courts can play when it
comes to widening political debate and focusing that debate on economic
legislation to address the crisis produced by the failure of the market—a
failure that left one-third of the nation "ill-housed, ill-clad, ill-nour-
ished."[22]

Underlying this constitutional approach was a pluralistic conception
of the political marketplace. Though the economic market may have been
moribund, the political market was still vital. For similar conceptual reasons the courts refused to formulate issues in terms of individual economic rights, insisting instead on collective group rights—a right to economic prosperity for all.[23] The doctrine of judicial restraint that emerged

in this period was, in a sense, a form of judicial activism—of revising legal doctrine to widen the scope for legislative experimentation specifically for the sake of ending the economic crisis. But the spirit of an age has a way of working its way into all the cases with which a court deals. Thus, the liberal, expansive interpretation the New Deal Court began to give the commerce clause, as well as the legislative power it authorized, was reflected in its approach to other constitutional issues and clauses of the Constitution.

Economic legislation occupied a central place in the New Deal.[24] In some cases, legislation supported market innovation. For example, Congress passed statutes to help infant industries such as airlines and communications. In other cases, legislation was designed to democratize markets. For example, new law was passed to address problems caused by monopolies such as the one in natural gas pipelines, to ensure fairness in securities markets, and to equal bargaining power in labor markets. New Deal economic legislation was aimed at creating a market economy that worked.[25] The new statutes and the reforms they embodied were fundamentally capitalist in their objective, orientation, and design.[26] The New Deal Congress did not seek to nationalize industries nor, as was evident in *Schecter Poultry Corp.*, did the Court permit a voluntary corporatist approach to regulation.[27] Rather, Congress and the Court sought to forge a partnership between government and business on a middle regulatory ground. The crucial point for our purposes is that the association of markets with democratic values is not a "natural" attribute of markets. In the New Deal, it was deliberately produced out of an intensive effort involving all three branches of government in the project of stabilizing markets by legislation aimed at democratizing them and subjecting them to ongoing scrutiny and accountability through the political and administrative processes.

Administrative agencies were to play a prominent role in achieving such stabilization and democratization of markets. In this context, it would be a mistake to underestimate the importance of the relationship of agency independence and expertise to the underlying conceptions of legislative representation and democratic theory. New Deal regulatory agencies are sometimes seen in a way that casts their independence as political authority and their expertise as political judgments.[28] Yet underlying the willingness of the Court to view employees of agencies as independent experts is their view that they are also the agents of elected representatives. According to one theory of democracy, elected representatives themselves can be viewed as experts.[29] Accordingly, the presumption of legislative expertise is extended to these representatives' agents.

Judicial development of the doctrine of legislative primacy was thus sympathetic to a view that emphasized the legislature's need to designate its own independent agents. The emphasis on the expertise and independence of agency personnel was but an extension of a larger conception of representation. In short, the New Deal Court's deference to Congress and its agencies to regulate economic affairs was based on its understandings of representation and agency as issues of democratic theory. The legal discourse of the New Deal era relied on broad notions of congressional intent in terms that were particularly familiar to the common-law-minded judges who wrote these opinions.[30] Each incremental step taken by agencies to solve a particular problem often led to an expansion of their powers; and most of these expansions were affirmed by reviewing courts.[31]

The overall thrust of the legislation and regulation of the New Deal era was not consumer oriented, as we understand that concept today. This is not to say that protecting consumers from monopolistic pricing (for example) was not important, but rather that the tone and orientation of New Deal regulatory statutes had a distinct producer orientation. The regulatory initiatives of the New Deal conceived of industry less as potential perpetrators of harm than as potential victims of chaotic market forces—and it was those market forces that legislation was aimed at controlling. Ensuring the continued viability of industries was the primary regulatory goal. If the market could be made to work, if unnecessary labor strife could be eliminated, if rates truly approximated what they would be in a smoothly functioning market, then producers, consumers, and society itself would be better off. This view generated a body of administrative law that made administrative agencies the primary sites for the protection of individuals from the excesses of the market.

The Administrative Procedures Act (hereafter APA),[32] passed in 1946, provided the primary statutory basis for most judicial review of federal agency action well into the 1960s. In interpreting the APA, particularly the provisions governing the scope of judicial review, courts usually read it in a way that resonated with the deferential judicial approaches they developed in constitutional contexts during the New Deal. The hands-off approach of the judiciary to the issues of constitutional delegation and statutory jurisdiction, coupled with the relatively deferential approach the APA required when reviewing agency fact finding and policy decisions, facilitated agency change and the evolutionary growth of the administrative state—though this is clearer in retrospect than it could have been at the time.

The basis for this judicial deference is best understood in the larger political, regulatory, and constitutional context in which the courts were operating at that time. Key to that context was a political consensus in favor of an administrative state. This supportive political climate was strengthened by at least four additional and interrelated factors: the constitutional doctrines of judicial restraint that had developed during and after the Roosevelt administration, doctrines that emphasized the primacy of the legislature and the need for judicial restraint; the perceived independence and expertise of the regulators involved and the relationship of that independence and expertise to the concept of representation that typified this era; the development of a regulatory discourse that was particularly conducive to agency expansion and judicial approval; and the essentially economic nature of the regulation in question.

Inherent in the approach New Deal courts ultimately took to the Constitution was great tolerance for the substantive results reached by legislative processes. Congress was permitted to delegate legislative responsibilities relatively freely to administrative agencies. The Court treated the regulatory tasks of a modern, activist government pragmatically, and this meant acknowledging the powers of the three branches of government as essentially overlapping in nature. The Court's practical approach to such questions was most concerned with the overall effects of the legislation on the respective ability of the branches of government to function effectively.[33]

This relatively deferential judicial approach to the structure and function of agencies within the constitutional system contributed to the subsequent growth of the administrative state.[34] The federal government's extensive new role dating from the New Deal already differed significantly from its relatively minimalist role at the beginning of the nation's history.[35] Now it expanded and became more internally flexible—not only with the blessing of the courts, but due to the nature of judicial review. Indeed, to the extent that separation-of-powers principles came to be viewed procedurally rather than substantively, they were made more consistent with a flexible, legislatively defined concept of individual liberty. But those principles were not themselves viewed as a source of substantive constitutional protection. As Philip Kurland noted, "the doctrine of separation of powers was not a rule of decision."[36] Protection of individual liberty ultimately had to be found in other, more specific provisions of the Constitution, particularly in the Bill of Rights.[37] So far as the economic legislation of the New Deal was concerned, individual liberty protections were largely procedural, and the legislative branch was allowed to work its will through the political process.

The Court's more tolerant approach to separation-of-powers issues for the sake of broadening government's political accountability left Congress to implement its legislative program. New Deal judicial interpretations of the Constitution offered relatively little resistance to such legislative efforts. The New Deal courts' approach constitutionalized broad congressional discretion to act, but in so doing, the Court also underscored the ongoing nature of legislative and political change. The New Deal's emphasis on the relative autonomy of the legislature and, ultimately, its agents (i.e., the agencies) enabled the New Deal vision of progress to be statutorily institutionalized. Importantly, however, since Congress and not the Court was the agent of change, that vision as such was not constitutionalized. The Court constitutionalized a political process, but not its outcomes. Congress retained wide powers to pass, amend, and repeal its own laws.[38]

In the concluding chapter, we shall revisit administrative agencies as potential arenas for addressing at least some of the externalities of globalization, most importantly, some aspects of the democracy deficit. For now, let us simply note that the democratization of markets (such as there was) was the product of a sustained political and legal effort over the course of the New Deal era. It was an innovative Court that institutionalized economic affairs as political affairs appropriate to the federal government—specifically, to Congress—and established the legal platform for the expanded, more flexible government that resulted from that change. Much has changed since that time, but it remains the case that law and markets are not antithetical, but inextricably and mutually embedded through politics and law.

The Environmental Era

Just as judicial deference to agency decision making was the hallmark of the New Deal era, more overt judicial activism characterized the environmental era that followed. If Congress's powers had been stretched to the constitutional breaking point by the broad delegation clauses that characterized New Deal legislation, the power used by federal courts to ensure that the various agencies conformed to environmental values raised new institutional concerns. Judicial review of agency environmental decisions in the 1970s highlighted the differences between the absolutist legal requirements of environmental legislation and the costs of economic growth. Indeed, the environmental constraints on economic growth moved to the center of legislative and judicial attention during the environmental era. The definition of progress had changed. Growth now had to accord with an emerging set of environmental values and a more collective approach to risk and risk assessment. As one court put it, "[s]everal recently enacted statutes attest to the commitment of the Government to control, at long last, the destructive engine of material 'progress.'"[39]

The statutes of the environmental era were a new type of regulatory legislation. More detailed than New Deal statutes and applicable to a wider range of industries, they sought to regulate polluters, increase safety on the road and in the workplace, and lower the risk of diseases such as cancer—among other objectives. They often sought to force technological breakthroughs. Their regulatory discourse spoke more in terms of science, probabilities, and risk assessments. Their relationship to the market was, for the most part, indirect, and they established a number of executive agencies that relied heavily on their rule-making capabilities to create new law.

The new environmental statutes often took an absolutist approach to such problems as air and water pollution. These statutes also applied across industry lines and dealt with issues of great scientific complexity.[40] Moreover, these issues were interdisciplinary in character and raised a variety of related legal, social, economic, and ethical questions. Proposed solutions to such questions, more often than not, demanded interdisciplinary and often intergovernmental approaches. The substantive problems that characterized the environmental era spilled over state and national boundaries. The "common-pool" aspects of the market failure that underlie the need for environmental regulation encouraged a concept of the relation of the individual to society that I will refer to as "interdependent individualism." An interdependent concept of individuals recognized more fully that society's overall interest in clean air or clean water cannot be equated with the aggregate of individuals pursuing their own atomistic self-interests. Indeed, it was an atomistic conception of individual freedom that had created many environmental problems in the first place. An interdependent concept of individualism resonated with and was reinforced by the interdependent and interdisciplinary conceptions of both the problems and the solutions that characterize the environmental era. Accordingly, a new understanding of progress was needed to deal with such new levels of interconnectedness.

The new environmental legislation also reflected a distinct consumer perspective.[41] The statutes interjected environmental values into the relationships between the regulated and the regulators. More often than not, producers of goods were now seen in a new light "as producers of harm."[42] Those who sought to benefit from these environmental statutes had an even more compelling interest in the outcome than in the economic benefits of a properly functioning market. They were likely to be the personal victims of pollution or toxic substances. Economic conflicts of interest among the regulated gave way to more fundamental conflicts of value that did not translate as easily into a common economic discourse. Unlike a determination of the cost of capital in a natural gas or electric rate proceeding, economic approaches to the calculation of the value of a human life met not only with technical concerns but also with concerns based on radically different value systems. It was, thus, not at all obvious how a legislature or an agency could calculate the cost of a human life or of irrevocable damage to the environment. The administrative process thus became more complex and contentious as it sought to accommodate a number of new, broadly defined, and often conflicting environmental interests, values, and groups.[43]

Given the interdependent perspectives involved in the nature of the regulatory problems presented and in the congressional and administrative solutions suggested, agency rationalizations for policy change inevitably became more complicated.[44] Because environmental, health, and safety questions now cut across industry lines, single-mission and single-industry commissions waned, as did regulatory issues with reasonably specific economic answers. Setting rates was relatively easy compared with assessing the overall health, safety, and environmental effects of various manufacturing processes. The scientific uncertainty that accompanied these assessments often triggered a more holistic judicial conception of the regulatory problems involved. This is not to say that courts abandoned New Deal deference in all environmental cases. But the nature of these issues did require more explanation of more interrelated factors, even when courts took a deferential, rational-basis approach.[45] Furthermore, the life-and-death nature of the issues at stake often encouraged courts to supervise agency policy making much more closely than did the economic questions involved in the New Deal era. More important, statutes such as the National Environmental Policy Act, as well as the more complicated hybrid-rule-making procedures set forth in most of the health, safety, and environmental statutes passed during this era, provided the legal basis for more exacting judicial scrutiny of agency explanations of whether and how they chose to incorporate environmental values into their decision making. Judicial control grew. Initially, at least, some courts played this role most willingly. Judge J. Skelly Wright wrote in his opinion in *Calvert Cliffs' Coordinating Comm. v. Atomic Energy Comm'n*: "[I]t remains to be seen whether the promise of this legislation will become a reality. Therein lies the judicial role."[46]

The courts had much new legislative and agency material with which to work. Between 1966 and 1981, the administrative bureaucracy grew considerably, in terms of both the number of new laws and agencies involved[47] and the amount of new regulation these agencies produced.[48] Both aspects of this growth created a need for greater supervision of the bureaucracy. The constitutional context in which this new regulation was being created, its nature as well as the kinds of market failures with which it dealt, the value issues it raised, and the more interdependent conceptualization of the individual's relationship to the state and to other individuals that it encouraged, all combined to create a new, value-laden regulatory discourse. Within this context, the courts developed more activist doctrines of administrative law for purpose of reviewing substantive agency action. These innovations in the doctrine of administrative law tended to have distinct constitutional overtones.

The primacy of the legislature and the rational-basis test of the New Deal era helped shape the constitutional context within which the doctrines of deference to proregulatory administrative law developed. The civil rights cases following *Brown v. Board of Education*[49] helped create the climate 'of judicial activism that encouraged courts to scrutinize agency decisions closely in the environmental era. When governmental action was taken that conflicted with fundamental constitutional rights of individuals or significantly and adversely affected a discrete and insular minority, such as a racial minority, the courts now required compelling reasons to justify such action.[50] In short, the constitutional law that developed and flourished during the environmental era had courts playing a major role as the guardians of individual rights. Rather than economic legislation, the more stringent standards of judicial review referred to in

Justice Stone's footnote to *United States v. Carolene Products Co.* became the focus of constitutional law.[51]

This constitutional hard-look approach was reflected in the doctrines of administrative law developing in this period. It is ironic that in a regulatory era characterized largely by its interdependence and complexity, an approach akin to constitutional individual-rights litigation would emerge in administrative law. The most significant aspect of the relationship between administrative and constitutional law during this period was the increasing parallel between administrative law's approach to the supervision of agency rationality and the judicial strict scrutiny prevalent in constitutional contexts. Perhaps the key to this parallel was between certain constitutional rights and the legislature's and courts' concept of environmental, health, and safety issues. Or it may be that the courts tended to look more closely at certain environmental decisions, compelling them to seek judicial justifications that emphasized these similarities.

As noted above, many of the new administrative statutes and agencies that came into being in the early 1970s treated health, safety, and environmental issues in absolutist terms.[52] Air was clean or dirty, water clean or polluted. Questions of degree were not entertained. Evil had been identified, and Congress quickly passed statutes to eradicate it.[53] This approach may have been necessary to generate the political support required to mobilize Congress, but absolutism often resulted in legislation that ignored the importance of economics in general and the cost of regulation in particular.[54] Even statutes that mandated the regulation of only "unreasonable risks" often generated an agency approach that was far more rigorous than a cost-benefit calculation might suggest.[55] As in cases in which constitutional rights were at stake,[56] cost was not viewed as a serious factor mitigating the duty of polluters to conform to the environmental goals outlined in the statutes. Nor was cost seen as a serious factor in limiting the promulgation of agency rules designed to carry out Congress's goals.[57]

This absolutism translated into a demand for quick solutions to the complicated social and economic problems spawned by an industrialized society. Statutes such as the Clean Water Act,[58] for example, were designed to eliminate pollution quickly. Unlike the Supreme Court's approach to eliminating racial discrimination with all "due deliberate speed,"[59] this statute, in particular, set definite, unrealistic dates for the complete elimination of pollution.[60]

The absolutist nature of such statutes also reduced agency discretion and transformed the regulatory discourse. The burden of proof that certain environmental values had, in fact, been adequately considered was on the agency.[61] The deference the courts had shown Congress and its agents during the New Deal era was revoked. The courts would usually not presume environmental rationality on the part of the agencies involved.

The approach most common in environmental litigation[62] treated burden-of-proof questions in a manner similar to constitutional litigation. It put the burden on the party seeking to disrupt the environment, whether that party was the government or a private firm.[63] Constitutional rights such as free speech guaranteed by the First Amendment, for example, could be curtailed or prohibited only if there were a compelling reason for taking such action and only if there were no realistic alternative to the action proposed. This heavy burden of proof rested on the person seeking to prohibit or curtail speech.[64] In a variety of environmental cases, courts similarly put a heavy burden on the party seeking to disrupt the environment.[65]

Environmental statutes combined this absolutist character with an essentially consumer-oriented perspective. The acts reflected new desires associated with the advanced consumer economy that came into being after World War II. Some of these services pertained to outdoor recreation and the allocation of air, land, and water to natural environment management and use; others pertained to new objectives concerning health and well-being and to the adverse effects of pollution on both biological and human life; still others dealt with matters such as "least cost" technologies in energy, smaller-scale production, and population-resource balance.[66]

These quality-of-life concerns generated certain environmental values that Congress sought to impose on decision-making processes. These values were those of individual consumers. Indeed, the statutes themselves sought to eliminate specific harms by preventing specific producers from inflicting these harms on the environment in general and individuals in particular. Unlike the New Deal's more abstract concern with an adequately functioning market from which all might benefit, the environmental era sought the direct benefit of individual consumers. Though a conception of individuals as interdependent may underlie the basic need for environmental regulation, a conception of the rights of individuals energized the enforcement of these statutes.

Environmental, health, and safety problems were also marked by their complexity and by the collective nature of many of the risks they presented. In an increasingly complex and technocratic society, the information needed to act rationally was difficult to acquire and to understand. Sensible risk assessment of potential environmental harm required collective information gathering. Questions such as whether to utilize nuclear power or where and how to build a safe nuclear plant did not lend themselves to individual risk calculations. Nuclear accidents could have ramifications and effects reaching far beyond the people living near the plant. Many early "environmental" agencies were actually very development oriented.[67] The Army Corps of Engineers, the Bureau of Reclamation, and the Federal Power Commission, for example, often found that environmental values were antithetical to their basic missions.[68] Governmental agencies charged with applying environmental values often disregarded them in favor of their own statutory duties and goals. In such cases, courts sometimes acted as if they were superagencies, ultimate guardians of the true public interest. In so doing, courts often reversed agency action by taking a hard look (as opposed to deferring) at the reasons agencies gave for their actions, sometimes finding those reasons inadequate.[69] In short, while the New Deal courts gave Congress the lead, environmental era courts took a role that made federal courts arbiters of agencies that had become substantially autonomous over the course of their existence. The courts recognized that government agencies could be just as indifferent to the public interest as private industry. This was particularly the case when the primary mission or goal of the agency involved conflicted with the environmental values mandated by Congress.

Thus, the courts took it upon themselves to ensure that the government itself live up to the mandates of the National Environmental Policy Act. They chose to play the role of protector of the values and goals expressed by Congress, a role arguably akin to the executive's constitutional duty "to take care that the laws be faithfully executed." In practice, the intensity of courts' scrutiny of the performance of government agencies blurred the constitutionally mandated differences among judicial review, legislative amendments to statutes, and executive administration and coordination of agency policy.[70]

This is not to argue that New Deal deference was obsolete or that the hard-look approach and the environmental era had supplanted the New Deal. Rather, a new mode of legal discourse was added to the law that already existed, and with that discourse, new structural relationships among courts, Congress and agencies, and the executive developed. New interpretive possibilities, especially for courts, were created by hard-look approaches to judicial review, and these coincided with a new set of wide-reaching statutes. The New Deal had established administrative agencies as the literal agents of Congress's reform agenda aimed at legislation to support the operation of the market in the interests of national economic recovery. In the course of the postwar decades of the 1950s and 1960s, these specialized agencies evolved into highly independent and highly judicialized rule-making bodies and, as we have seen, courts were inclined to defer to their technical expertise in terms that paralleled constitutional discourse.

The environmental era, while brief, represented a significant turning point in the development of the contemporary regulatory landscape. On the one hand, the environmental period was a continuation of the New Deal commitment to political institutions as the appropriate site for addressing challenges to national well-being and prosperity. On the other hand, courts were increasingly attentive to the fact that Congress had, to some extent, relinquished its control over administrative agencies, and that it was now the agencies themselves that functioned as political institutions, often more responsive to political shifts of new presidential administrations than to specific directives of Congress. The very nature of environmental issues, inherently ambiguous, potentially transborder, and not always clearly subject to the analysis of experts, made them elusive, often putting courts in the position of judging among competing experts. These developments, in effect, made regulation seem to be a rather elite judicial enterprise of an executive character. The global context was now also changing. During this same period new players in the world economy, notably OPEC and Japan, suddenly called American economic supremacy into question.

The Global Era

The start of the global era was not marked by any specific domestic legislative program. There was no "Global Deal" akin to the New Deal. If it can be said to have an identifiable beginning, it was in a series of deregulatory efforts undertaken for the most part by administrative agencies. If the New Deal era was marked by judicial deference to congressional judgments and the environmental era was marked by a more vigorous form of judicial activism, the onset of the global era was marked by judicial deference to executive power over the administrative process,[71] particularly as administrative agencies sought to deregulate themselves and incorporate various economically based approaches to regulation. Increased executive control over agency policy making in the 1970s and 1980s occurred largely at the expense of congressional control. To some extent, Congress itself participated in this shift, both affirmatively and passively. Congress affirmatively created many agencies that were more executive in character than the independent agencies of the New Deal. Executive control over those agencies was not limited to coordination. The executive introduced substantive changes as well, particularly in the form of deregulation. Many of the substantive, deregulatory policies of the executive have been implemented by agencies, bypassing Congress—which has neither affirmed these new directions nor disapproved of them.[72] With the exception of congressional deregulation of the Civil Aeronautics Board and, later, the Interstate Commerce Commission, and a few other deregulatory statutes, deregulation was—and is—essentially a program carried out by the executive branch through executive orders,[73] appointments of like-minded individuals, vigorous executive control over decisions regarding (non)enforcement of certain existing rules and regulations,[74] as well as rescission of certain rules in favor of their replacement by more cost-conscious or market-oriented substitutes, [75] and a major monitoring role played by the Office of Management and Budget.

The New Deal and environmental eras we have examined were marked by the passage of specific congressional programs, inspired or at least backed by the president. In vivid contrast, the most distinctive feature of the global era is a politics of efficiency—rhetorically fused to the national interest—but involving no specific legislative program. Congress's primary contribution to deregulation has been indirect, in the form of budgetary legislation and tax reductions.[76] These statutes have pressured agencies to scale down their programs, goals, and statutory mandates. But such statutes differ markedly from those of the New Deal and environmental eras. Their impact on substantive law is indirect. They do not provide the legal guidance to courts that statutory interpretation usually requires; they read more like presidential speeches, hortatory rather than prescriptive. In this respect, they reflect the mood of the times—a mood that agencies have occasionally forced into their own statutory mandates.[77]

It is thus no surprise that the rhetoric and politics of efficiency go well beyond attempting to achieve public goals in a cost-effective manner. At times, they take on a distinct negative-rights tone—as if legislators and agency administrators were seeking to protect their constituents from themselves and government in general. Indeed, the political process often seems designed not only to limit the role of law but to deligitimize it. At a theoretical level, regulation is the tool of special interests or it is now, in fact, a producer of harms—cost, red tape, and bureaucracy. Such an approach, almost de facto, leaves the achievement of social justice goals to the market. As law is removed as a viable option and as political discourses focus primarily—often exclusively—on cost, noneconomic values, and the forums in which to discuss them, are increasingly removed from day-to-day life.

The principal hallmark of regulation in the global era has thus been the shift from state-centered, command-control regulation to deregulation, privatization, and market forms of regulation.[78] This trend goes well beyond the use of market incentives in rules issued by administrative agencies.[79] Importantly, it extends to partial (and sometimes wholesale) delegation of public functions and responsibilities to the private sector,[80] particularly when these involve social services for sectors of the population with marginal status. The Honorable Patricia M. Wald has observed,

> State and local governments have contracted with private operations to take care of the most vulnerable, dependent, and disempowered members of society—children, the unemployed, the physically and mentally disabled—whose servicing for most of the twentieth century has been considered quintessentially a "public" responsibility.[81]

Delegation of social services to the private sector represents an important aspect of the ways in which global processes encourage and accelerate what has been called "third party government,"[82] in which "crucial elements of public authority are shared with a host of non-governmental or other governmental actors."[83]

This shift from states to markets began in the late 1970s, with the Carter administration's deregulation of airlines.[84] For the Carter administration, domestic airline deregulation combined the hallmarks of both the New Deal and environmental eras; it was both politically pragmatic (key for the New Deal court) and, from a microeconomic point of view, scientifically correct (expertise being key to the environmental era). The economic rationale underlying deregulation of this industry was not initially presented as necessarily antigovernment nor antistate. The assumption was that this was a continuation of the New Deal approach—the state should intervene in case of market failure, but not otherwise, especially if the market could be reasonably expected to reach results more favorable to consumers than those achieved by regulation. Importantly, "the market" did not mean a general category or ideological value, but a specific economic sector. In this case, regulators found that there was no market failure when it came to the airline industry. An airplane was, in the words of Alfred Kahn, then chairman of the Civil Aeronautics Board, simply a "marginal cost with wings."[85]

The politics of airline deregulation was also decidedly pragmatic from a domestic political point of view. Deregulation promised to lower consumer fares and increase customer service.[86] Airline regulation had nurtured a fledgling industry, but now critics claimed that industry regulation had produced a cartel, regulated by an agency captured by the very industry it was designed to regulate.[87]

Safety regulation was excluded from this calculus. Safety continued to be handled, independently, by the Federal Aviation Administration (FAA). The assumption was that economic competition would not affect safety and that, in any event, the FAA would continue its regulation of these matters. Another key assumption was that real competition would emerge in the airline industry because the antitrust laws in effect would be vigorously enforced.[88] All of this was strongly backed by most Democrats, led by Senator Edward Kennedy.[89] Invoking a return to the market as serving the public interest, Congress abolished the Civil Aeronautics Board with the Deregulation Act of 1978.[90]

In many ways, Democrats were more successful at deregulatory legislative reform than Republicans during the so-called Reagan Revolution.[91] During the Reagan presidential campaign in 1980, and throughout the Reagan-Bush years, deregulation took hold as a political rallying cry, and the political rationales for deregulation became increasingly ideological and shrill. "Getting government off the backs of people" was the slogan of the day. Gone were the New Deal–type arguments for pragmatism; rather, the Reagan-era deregulation came from an antiregulatory ethos advocated by critics of regulation who now argued against most regulation on the grounds that it interfered with fundamental political liberty. Some advocates of deregulation in the Reagan administration saw potential market successes everywhere, and accordingly saw regulation only as an impediment. The market, for them, was a general category and a materialization of philosophical values.

There was a significant global backdrop to the deregulatory initiatives of the 1970s and especially the 1980s that gave added impetus to the political viability of antiregulatory ideology and deregulatory reform. This is particularly apparent when we look beyond domestic airlines to manufacturing industries in general. Intense global competition in a number of key industries had been increasing ever since the countries most devastated by World War II, Germany and Japan, were able to rebuild and reenter the world economy.[92] Meanwhile, less-developed countries began successfully to enter the economic fray.[93] Industries long thought of as mainstays in the United States—automobiles, steel, and electronics, to name just a few—began to decline. Companies in these industries were being defeated by global competitors that could produce similar or even better products at less cost.[94]

Global competition became another compelling rallying cry for domestic deregulatory reform. The domestic refrain of "We're No. 1" masked the reality of the new global context, which was that the United States, while still perhaps the largest economy in the world, no longer controlled the world economy as it once did. More importantly for purposes of understanding the convergence of global forces and domestic rhetoric, that loss of total dominance could easily and plausibly be represented by domestic politicians as a predictable consequence of excessive regulation, especially federal regulation. Such representations were self-fulfilling. The Reagan-Bush regulatory discourse used this new global context to reinforce an ideological preference for private ordering, which in turn rested on a rhetorical construction of globalization as an antagonistic field in which the United States was pitted against foreign competitors. Lower taxes meant less money to fund governmental agencies, regulatory programs, and initiatives, and, in response to the growing deficit that resulted, it required more governmental austerity. In effect, this put substantial pressure on the federal government to downsize, not unlike most of corporate America.

In this sense, global competition places the costs of domestic regulation in stark relief. This was particularly true when some of the new global competitors involved manufactured their products in countries that imposed few or no regulatory costs on domestic industries. This not only favored such industries; it attracted new ones as well. Though a variety of manufacturing costs may account for the decision of some industries to shift the production phase of their operations abroad, a significant cost component for many of them includes regulatory costs, including labor costs.[95] Environmental and worker safety costs, for example, had a significant effect on the copper, silver, and automobile industries in particular.[96] Regulatory costs such as these were exacerbated by the global competitive dimension that now exists in many industries. Perhaps more importantly, the mere perception of this kind of competition can have important political repercussions, easily fueling an antiregulatory rhetoric.

Regulatory cost-consciousness highlighted by global competition has created and intensified a new kind of regulatory politics—a politics of efficiency. This politics is also fueled in the United States by numerous other factors such as the budgetary deficits, growing political sensitivity to governmental expenditure, and the imposition of governmental costs of all kinds (including taxes). Broad regulatory goals must now be translated into monetary terms.[97] Cost consciousness thus pervades the implementation of most regulatory programs today, particularly as administered by the executive branch and subject to Office of Management and Budget review.[98]

The perception of global competition with foreign corporations that do business in countries with few or no environmental, health, and safety rules at all creates increased pressure for domestic regulatory cost cutting. In such circumstances, legislative mandates based on reasonably acceptable notions of market failure arguably may be undermined by the market values and goals of a deregulatory regime.[99] When deregulatory policies, such as those advocated under the Clean Air Act,[100] are superimposed by the executive onto existing legislative and regulatory schemes devised under very different legal assumptions, the Article II powers of the president may begin to take on a new meaning. In extreme cases, the "take care" clause of Article II risks being converted into an independent and unconstitutional source of executive legislation.[101] Thus, particularly in the context of deregulation, judicial deference to executive policy making should be carefully analyzed.

Courts do not always review agency deregulatory actions deferentially. In some cases, especially those dealing with health and safety issues, they often have applied a hard-look approach.[102] Though generalization is difficult, the deregulatory efforts of agencies involved in economic regulation pursuant to the broad delegation clauses that typify New Deal statutes have fared better than the deregulatory efforts of agencies engaged in health, safety, and environmental regulation.[103] Courts are more willing to defer when an agency can convincingly show that it is using the market as a regulatory tool, not as an ideological means of frustrating the goals of the statutes involved. Health, safety, and environmental issues usually involve the kinds of value conflicts that make it difficult, if not impossible, for an agency to contend that adherence to market approaches fully accords with the goals and values of the act involved. Moreover, the nature of the statutes involved, their use of the substantial evidence standard in policy-making proceedings, and the usually more detailed delegation clauses in the statute itself give courts more to deal with when reviewing agency deregulation in these areas.

Of course, deregulation and nonregulation are achieved in a variety of ways, not simply through the rescission of existing rules. Many such deregulatory actions are essentially unreviewable. Agencies have enormous discretion when it comes to deciding which rules to enforce.[104] Moreover, they have a great deal of discretion in deciding whether to regulate new areas or, simply, to leave these new areas to market forces. Courts have usually deferred to this kind of agency deregulation or nonregulation on the grounds that the president is politically accountable.[105]

Judicial deference to the executive also has wider rationales. Deregulatory agency policies coincided with a perceived need for a more active presidential role in controlling and directing agency discretion. Indeed, the explosion of regulatory law and agencies in the 1970s gave rise to what some commentators have called the "Administrative Presidency."[106] This also coincided with the development of constitutional theories that sought to justify greater and greater executive control over the administrative process.[107]

The sheer growth and the complexity of the regulation in the 1970s resulted in a great need for coordination and control across disparate agencies. Given the tendency of agencies to view the world only from their own vantage point, executive coordination helped further a broader, perhaps more realistic, view of the public interest. Increased executive supervisory power also was due to the fact that many of the regulatory structures Congress created in the 1970s departed from the independent-commission model that typified the New Deal. The Environmental Protection Agency, for example, is headed by a single administrator appointed by the president, with the advice and consent of the Senate. Moreover, Congress delegated much of the substantive regulation dealing with health and safety issues to executive cabinet officials such as the Secretary of Labor.[108] Such governmental bodies are naturally more accountable to the president and more easily influenced by presidential views regarding policy. In addition, the executive branch itself has tried to institutionalize its influence and control through greater use of executive orders[109] and a strengthening of its own office of Management and Budget.[110] The Supreme Court in *Chevron v. NRDC*[111] helped transform New Deal deference (to agency expertise) to global era deference to the executive (i.e., gives the political accountability to executive-controlled agencies) noting,

> While agencies are not directly accountable to the people, the Chief Executive is, and it is entirely appropriate for this political branch of the Government to . . . resolv[e] the competing interests which Congress itself either inadvertently did not resolve, or intentionally left to be resolved by the agency charged with the administration of the statute in light of everyday realities.[112]

All of these forces add up to a regulatory process that measures costs only in monetary terms and prefers market forces over command-control regulations. It is also one that tolerates more abrupt change, driven by the president and the executive branch rather than by Congress or the courts. The global era now more easily rationalizes change in terms of executive electoral accountability rather than agency expertise, and partisan political power over reasoned, deliberative, and incremental change.

The rise of the administrative presidency also coincided with the reemergence of constitutional issues that had been largely moribund since the early days of the New Deal.[113] Once again, the constitutionality of independent agencies was in contention;[114] the nondelegation doctrine was showing signs of life. As doctrines of administrative and constitutional law have evolved in the transition from a regulatory era dominated by a national perspective to a deregulatory era typified by more global concerns, the fundamental nature of the change in regulatory perspective that triggered agency deregulation also put constitutional issues in a new light. Judicial attempts to resolve separation-of-powers issues often favored the expansion of executive power and discretion. In general, courts tended once again to become relatively formalistic in their overall constitutional approach and tone, as compared to the earlier periods we have been discussing.[115]

In the 1980s, for example, at the start of the global era, *INS v. Chadha*[116] and *Bowsher v. Synar*[117] exemplified a highly formalistic constitutional approach to separation-of-power issues arising from the administrative process. The decisions in both these cases made it easier to expand the executive's role in controlling the administrative process; however, they did so with a rhetoric that, if carried to its logical extreme, places the constitutional status of administrative agencies—particularly New Deal agencies—in jeopardy.

INS v. Chadha sets forth an approach to constitutional issues and uses a rhetoric that encourages active judicial review of structural constitutional issues. In that case, the Supreme Court struck down a unicameral legislative veto provision as unconstitutional and as a violation of fundamental separation-of-powers principles.[118] The statute in question was the Immigration and Nationality Act. It authorized one house of Congress, by resolution, to invalidate the decision of an immigration judge to allow *Chadha,* a deportable alien, to remain in the United States. The Court's sweeping opinion made very clear that the Court was not at all interested in reviewing the various forms of legislative vetoes already in place.[119] This is consistent with the kind of all-or-nothing rhetoric that usually typifies a formalistic separation-of-powers approach. The rhetoric itself does not easily countenance ambiguity or gradations in the legislative, judicial, or executive effects of governmental action.[120] Thus, despite the Court's recognition that governmental functions are not hermetically sealed,[121] the Court's analysis treated all legislative vetoes as legislative in nature and, by implication, strongly suggested that meaningful lines existed between various governmental functions. Writing for the majority, Chief Justice Warren Burger thus assumed that all legislative vetoes, in effect, constituted amendments to the enabling statutes involved and were essentially new pieces of legislation.[122] As such they could not short-circuit the full legislative process. For these vetoes to have legal effect, they not only had to pass both houses of Congress, but they had to be presented to the president for his approval or veto. Failure to provide for presentment would require even bicameral vetoes to be struck down as unconstitutional.[123]

The formalistic rhetoric the Court used in reaching this result conflicts with the New Deal's overall tolerance for what Professor Landis called "intelligent realism."[124] The Court in *Chadha* focused, not on the democratic nature of the overall structure of government, but on the application of a rather crude litmus test to the complicated and delicate power relationships Congress sought to balance.[125] Was the action in question taken by the legislative branch? If so, it was, almost by definition, legislative. By choosing such a test, the Court substituted a hard-look approach for a more pragmatic deferential approach. The New Deal's James Landis had looked to industry for his model of government, but Chief Justice Burger looked to the Founding Fathers: "In purely practical terms, it is obviously easier for action to be taken by one House without submission to the President; but it is crystal clear from the records of the Convention, contemporaneous writings and debates, that the Framers ranked other values higher than efficiency."[126]

In *Bowsher v. Synar,* the Court took a similarly formalistic approach to the Balanced Budget and Emergency Deficit Control Act of 1985.[127] The purpose of this act was to eliminate the federal budget deficit by requiring, under certain circumstances, automatic across-the-board cuts in federal spending. The Office of Management and Budget (OMB) and the Congressional Budget Office (CBO) were to calculate the budget reductions necessary to meet the maximum deficit allowed. They were to report their estimates to the comptroller general, who would resolve any differences that might result in their approaches and report his conclusions to the president. In reviewing the constitutionality of this act, the Court attempted to ensure an appropriate role for the executive in the supervision of the budgetary process. Enabling the executive branch to infuse current political sentiments into regulatory processes may be an important goal, but doing so in a way that risks constitutionalizing a substantive, deregulatory approach to the legislative issues dealt with by Congress is quite another matter. The logic of formalism and the radical separation-of-powers model implicit in it leans very far in this direction. Whether the Court sees the separation of powers as substantive rules for decisions in individual cases or as a procedural guide to the manner in which power should be allocated among the branches will greatly influence the extent to which the logic of this doctrine is applied. The more the Court chooses to use the doctrine of the separation of powers as a means of protecting individual rights in individual cases, the more it risks judicial activism bordering on a kind of substantive due process.[128] Given the complexity of modern government, formalistic analyses that ignore the wider perspective of the overall power relationships among the branches of government inevitably render much regulatory legislation constitutionally suspect. But short of this possible substantive result, the formalistic perspective implies a very different conception of government in general (and the administrative process in particular).

This conception appears with particular clarity in the lower court's opinion in *Bowsher,* widely reported to have been written by then Judge Antonin Scalia. In striking down the act in a per curiam opinion, the lower court focused on a pillar of the New Deal era, *Humphrey's Executor v. United States,*[129] taking aim at what it called "the political science preconceptions characteristic of its era and not of the present day."[130] The court noted,

> It is not as obvious today as it seemed in the 1930s that there can be such things as genuinely "independent" regulatory agencies, bodies of impartial experts whose independence from the President does not entail correspondingly greater dependence upon the committees of Congress to which they are then immediately accountable; or, indeed, that the decisions of such agencies so clearly involve scientific judgment rather than political choice that it is even theoretically desirable to insulate them from the democratic process.[131]

Along with its substantial doubts about the policy justifications for independent agencies, the district court also expressed serious concern about the overall constitutionality of the so-called headless fourth branch of government: "It has . . . always been difficult to reconcile *Humphrey's Executor's* 'headless fourth branch' with a constitutional text and tradition establishing three branches of government. . . ."[132] The lower court emphasized that changes had occurred since *Humphrey's Executor* had been decided. Specifically, the court focused on *INS v. Chadha* and noted that, at a minimum,

> some of the language of the majority opinion in *Chadha* does not lie comfortably beside the central revelation of *Humphrey's Executor* that an officer such as a Federal Trade Commissioner "occupies no place in the executive department," and that an agency which exercises only "quasi-legislative or quasi-judicial powers" is "an agency of the legislative or judicial departments of the government[.]"[133]

The district court, however, ultimately chose a narrower ground for its decision, noting that "[t]he Supreme Court's signals are not sufficiently clear . . . to justify our disregarding the rationale of *Humphrey's Execu-*

tor. . . ."[134] Relying on *Humphrey's Executor,* rather than overruling it, the court found the Balanced Budget Act unconstitutional. According to the court, the comptroller general was neither a "purely executive officer" nor an officer like the one involved in *Humphrey's Executor.* Though he or she exercised some powers that were unquestionably legislative, the official's powers under the automatic deficit-reduction provisions of the act were neither exclusively legislative nor exclusively judicial.[135] The lower court thus found the comptroller general to be "in the no-man's land described by *Humphrey's Executor.*"[136]

The lower court also suggested that this case could be decided on broader grounds:

> We think it at least questionable whether the power would be approved even with respect to officers of the United States who exercise only "quasi-legislative" powers in the *Humphrey's Executor* sense—since it would dramatically reduce the value of the right to appoint such officers which the Constitution has assured to the Executive or to the Courts of Law, a right that the Supreme Court has regarded as an important element of the balance of powers, prompted by the founders' often expressed fear "that the Legislative Branch of the National Government will aggrandize itself at the expense of the other two branches."[137]

The Supreme Court majority did not take this bait, and affirmed on narrower grounds.[138] The Court reasoned that if the comptroller general exercised executive powers and only Congress could remove him, it would be tantamount to a congressional veto and thus in violation of the principles set forth in *Chadha.* Equating congressional removal with a legislative veto, the Court reasoned further that "Congress could simply remove, or threaten to remove, an officer for executing the laws in any fashion found to be unsatisfactory to Congress."[139] This, the Court said, was precisely what *Chadha* disallowed. In so holding, the Court took a formalistic separation-of-powers approach.[140] It examined the activities of the comptroller general, determined whether they could be labeled executive, legislative, or judicial, and then examined the place of the comptroller general in the administrative structure to determine whether that official was under the control of the appropriate branch of government. The majority found the act to be unconstitutional on those grounds, but sidestepped the more fundamental issue raised by then Judge Scalia: the constitutionality of the "headless fourth branch."[141]

With Judge Scalia now sitting as a justice of the Supreme Court, this issue was very much alive once again in *Morrison v. Olson*,[142] a case involving the constitutionality of the Ethics in Government Act, also known as the Independent Counsel Act. Congress sought to make the independent counsel as independent from executive control as possible, since his or her primary function was to investigate and possibly prosecute high-ranking executive officials suspected of criminal conduct. Congress assumed that a conflict of interest would be built into any such investigation if it were carried out by the Justice Department. Congress thus required the attorney general to request the appointment of an independent counsel, but that person could only be named by a "special court" and the person so named could be removed only for cause. As Justice Scalia argued in dissent, Article II vests *all* executive power in the president and the power to prosecute is nothing if not executive.[143] Yet in this case the Court not only resisted the opportunity to declare a degree of independence from the executive unconstitutional; it also rejected the formalistic rhetoric used by the Burger Court. The Rehnquist Court, at least in this case, opted for the pragmatic rhetoric of functional balancing and chose to defer to the bargains stuck by Congress and the executive. In so doing, the Court pulled back, and refused to constitutionalize its conception of the administrative process; but its overall approach was not necessarily inconsistent with a more political conception of the administrative process.

In effect, the majority in *Morrison*, like Justice Scalia, believed that this case was about power,[144] but it focused on the power of the political process to pass legislation and resolve political problems. The majority thus took a procedural approach to the question of the proper allocation of power in order to ensure the overall functioning of the political process, not necessarily the vindication of individual rights in individual cases. Implicitly, at least, individual-rights questions were matters best left to the interpretation and application of more specific constitutional provisions. For the majority, only a dramatic shift in power among the branches of government would trigger the judicial activism typified by the hard-look approach of formalism. Anything short of such a dramatic shift would involve the Court in political value choices for which there were no judicially principled bases for decision.

The *Morrison* balancing approach is, thus, consistent with the judiciary's increasingly political view of the administrative process and with the overall trend toward greater executive influence over the administrative process. The flexibility of functionalism can favor executive as well as legislative power, while the logic of formalism is potentially very restrictive of both. In a practical sense, *Morrison* may, in the long run, provide for even greater executive flexibility in supervising administrative discretion because it can more easily allow great tolerance for the executive use of legislative power. It also seems to have put to rest some persistent attempts to repeal parts of the New Deal through the courts rather than through Congress. The majority at least implied that if certain administrative agencies had outlived their usefulness, Congress, not the courts, would have to act. As we will see in chapter 2, however, the formalism used in these cases now seems to appear in the form of federalism and a new judicial hard look at congressional processes more generally.

There were, of course, more direct and, theoretically at least, easier ways to accomplish the deregulatory reforms proposed by Reagan-Bush reformers. Congress could have amended or repealed the laws that had created and empowered existing federal agencies, especially the New Deal agencies; however, especially during the years when the Democrats controlled Congress (through most of the 1980s) and, throughout this time, the House of Representatives, Congress was not about to deregulate so completely or in an across-the-board manner. The forces of globalism that Reagan-Bush so effectively translated into an ideological call for domestic reform were, ultimately, constrained by Congress and, to some extent, by the courts.

As noted above, the Reagan-Bush deregulatory strategy eventually sought to bypass the Congress by using the courts and the agencies themselves to achieve its deregulatory goals. But deregulating pursuant to statutes that had created the very regulatory structures these administrations sought to remove required some deft maneuvering. The Reagan-Bush reformers infused these regulatory regimes with market approaches since courts were generally willing to approve of agency attempts to rescind rules if they could plausibly argue that market forces were in the public interest. This is well illustrated by the federal court cases that arose out of the deregulation of both the Federal Communications Commission (FCC) and the Interstate Commerce Commission (ICC). The judicial reaction to deregulation of the FCC was generally favorable, given the nature of the congressional mandate and the changed perception for the need to regulate the broadcast industry.[145]

The courts were not inclined, however, to allow market forces to substitute for regulatory approaches where Congress, particularly in various health and safety statutes, had rejected the market.[146] Nor were the courts willing to adopt constitutional separation-of-powers arguments that would, in effect, declare certain New Deal agencies unconstitutional because they unduly interfered with executive power.[147] Quite apart from the ideological fervor with which deregulation was proposed, the result was that national politics and national institutions, especially the courts, constrained the Reagan and Bush administrations in this regard. Most New Deal agencies remained in place, though they were much less active and effective.[148] The deregulation and market approaches upheld by the courts were viewed as public-interest governmental responses to regulatory problems.[149]

The Bush-Quayle Administration

The Bush-Quayle administration largely continued the thrust of the domestic deregulatory program begun during the Carter years, pursuing it, however, in a more ideologically forceful (if less legislatively successful) way than had either the Carter or Reagan administrations.[150] The ideological component proved to have far-reaching substantive and structural consequences for the unfolding of globalization, domestically and abroad.

The Bush-Quayle administration hitched its domestic deregulatory reforms directly to the issue of global competition.[151] For example, a Council on Competitiveness, headed by Vice President Dan Quayle, had as its primary task the rejection of proposed and existing regulations that it found to be undermining U.S. global competitiveness. The administration committed itself to an aggressively deregulatory antigovernment campaign.[152] At the same time, deregulation itself represented a powerful muscle flexing on the part of the administration.

A deregulatory approach grounded in individual freedom easily accommodated a vision of the state as relatively independent, sovereign, and distinct in relation to the international community of states. Deregulation under Bush-Quayle responded to globalization by recasting it as a foreign threat challenging domestic institutions. This rhetoric securely tied the globalization of markets, politics, and law to the very immediate concerns of local politics, but in a way that left the political sphere in a largely reactive position. More to the point, for these administrations, big government was the problem. Private enterprise, large and small, was the answer.

In some ways, the circle back to the pre–New Deal now seemed to be complete. The laissez-faire philosophy and the domestic political rhetoric often reminiscent of the 1920s coincided perfectly with the domestic political needs of the conservative administrations of the 1980s. Ironically, deregulation could thus be seen as a strong, state-centered approach to a global challenge, as if dismantling the administrative state was but one of many open, free choices available to a sovereign state. At the same time, but less obviously, it was a concession of weakness, in that the impact of global economic forces beyond U.S. control had made some version of this domestic legal and political response inevitable, at least in the administrative context that was the legacy of earlier eras. Characterizing deregulation as a victory for the forces of individual freedom had a certain domestic political effect, but the reality was that the global economy eluded American control, and business now sought to participate in an (in effect) unregulated world economy without state interference.

The Clinton-Gore Administration

How different was the Clinton-Gore approach from that of Reagan-Bush and Bush-Quayle? And how different were the Reagan-Bush proposals once they were tempered by Congress and the courts? Rather than reject government outright, as the Reagan-Bush and Bush-Quayle administrations unsuccessfully sought to do in many cases, and certainly as the Gingrich-led revolution in the House of Representatives also sought to do in 1994,[153] the Clinton administration sought to reinvent government largely in the image of a lean and cost-effective government corporation. The regulatory politics in the 1990s had a distinct corporate rhetoric that continued the privatizing trend, but in a manner that kept the federal government involved and a collective sense of a national public interest relevant. Rhetorically and ideologically, government was not rejected, but it was essentially converted to the forms, approaches, and goals of the private sector. When it came to translating their proposals into law, however, most of the Clinton-Gore regulatory proposals were very much steeped in the market and of a piece with the general direction of regulatory reform for the preceding twenty years.

Congress and the courts filtered and limited the more stridently ideological aspects of the Reagan-Bush and Bush-Quayle administrations'
deregulatory attempts. In the 1990s, it was an awareness of the globalization of markets, capital, and economic problems that limited the way
in which regulatory reform was now conceptualized, even by those who
were not philosophically opposed to an activist national government. The
National Performance Review (NPR), a report written largely under the
direction of Vice President Gore,[154] must be read against a global backdrop of increasing global competition for markets and investment, de-
clining nation-state sovereignty and power, and a view of the nation-state
that sees as one of its primary roles the attraction and retention of jobs
and a high level of economic prosperity within its borders. Viewed in this
light, the language of public law and the regulatory policy it created continued to rely heavily upon market approaches, rhetoric, and goals. But
unlike the Council on Competitiveness headed by Vice President
Quayle,[155] the Gore Commission viewed the national government in an
essentially positive light. It did not make government and the market into
adversaries but, rather, put the government in a position to coopt the
market.

The NPR, in short, treated government like a business—since government bought and sold goods in the process of carrying out its functions.
In addition, like a business, government was expected to deliver its services, regulatory and otherwise, as efficiently as possible. When government acts as a buyer or, in effect, a consumer, it needs to do so efficiently.
Still, government is so unusually large a customer that it cannot ignore its
potential impact on the creation, modification, or destruction of markets.
When it acts as a seller of services, citizens are its customers. Throughout,
the Report thus emphasized that the government, in its roles as both producer and consumer, was like any good business or smart consumer. It
must be flexible, responsive, and efficient. These market values resulted in
legal approaches to regulation that were not significantly different in content or direction from those previously advocated by the Reagan-Bush
and Bush-Quayle administrations.

These trends have continued and, if anything, have become even more
ideological in the Bush-Cheney administration. The market is seen as separate and distinct from government, and the private sector is growing, in
the sense that it is being invoked more and more as a distinct alternative
to government, not just a tool of governance.[156] The privatization of social security has become a serious proposal and the diminishment of en-

vironmental protection in favor of energy production, a reality.[157] The pace of privatization and deregulation is increasing, and the federal funds necessary to provide governmental alternatives or supplemental governmental approaches to markets are diminishing, as deficits increase. At the same time, federalism and the power of the states are making a comeback, both in the courts and as a primary mode of federal policy making.[158] Issues once dealt with federally may now be devolved to states, but the federal funds to deal with them seldom are forthcoming.[159] Thus, as we shall see below, this constitutionalized change has its own deregulating effects. State and local politicians must raise the taxes necessary to provide these services and, as we shall see, the current global competition for jobs and investments, along with an increasingly ideological rejection of government, results in significant political constraints when it comes to taking such action. More importantly, the turn to markets as distinct and separate from states has profound effects on democracy as well.

The Democracy Deficit and the Concept of Unbundling

The logic of deregulation in many economic contexts is the logic of unbundling, i.e., an accounting of the various cost components of a particular service and the assignment of those costs to the contributing parties according to their share in each component. Subsidies of all sorts are to be avoided. Costs are to be allocated with great precision among the users of a service.

The unbundling approach is particularly apparent in energy law, especially in rate making at the federal and state levels. Prices for electricity or natural gas, for example, invariably combined energy, demand, and capital costs in a single rate. Consumers pay for the cost of the coal or gas necessary to produce the energy they use, with different rates based on times of day when the energy is demanded. At peak times, for example, electric energy is more expensive than energy demanded at off-peak times. The costs of the overall energy infrastructure and delivery systems necessary to provide this service (so-called demands costs), are also allocated among users. Unbundled rates assign energy and demand costs more precisely and fairly to those consumers whose needs generate them. They also allocate joint costs, that is, costs incurred by the system that are necessary for all consumers to enjoy the service provided. The allocation of joint costs is inevitably a political decision. Indeed, putting a precise dollar figure on these and the other cost components requires the application of a good deal of judgment to a mixture of economic, financial, engineering, and political judgments. These decisions are not susceptible solely to formalistic rationales. Yet, particularly in the global era, a decision to cut or to assign costs in this way is so common that it is, perhaps, too easy to forget that these are political decisions that should be transparent, subject to public input, and accountable to the public. Failure to recognize this is yet another manifestation of the democracy deficit.

The unbundling approach, however, goes far beyond the technicalities of rate making. A decision to privatize a service is in many ways a decision to unbundle the costs of those services and to use private entrepreneurs to do this. Markets themselves can decide what is worth paying for and who is willing to pay to undertake responsibility for which costs. Since costs can be assigned more fairly and precisely in this way, there is a kind of economic justice to such an approach. But just as deregulation and privatization can unbundle costs, they can also unbundle citizenship. This is because of the political nature of the costs involved. It is one thing to differentiate among rate payers who share and must pay for electricity on the basis of allocated costs, but quite another when the services involved almost exclusively go to economically disadvantaged recipients or involve noneconomic values incapable of the kind of relatively precise cost-allocation approaches that typifies electricity pricing. There are other, even more profound segmentations of the political market for certain kinds of social services, as we shall see in chapter 3, that encourage citizens to treat them primarily in economic terms, separate and apart from issues involving a broad, collective sense of social responsibility. There are many forms of the democracy deficit, but those that derive from the unbundling of citizenship may be the most pernicious.

It would be a mistake, however, to credit all of these deregulatory policies and trends to a domestic politics that is, for now, conservative and economically motivated. As already discussed, the embedded nature of globalization at the domestic level has fundamentally changed the way states, markets, and other elements of the public sphere interrelate. Globalization yields intended and unintended effects on institutions and democratic participation within nation states, resulting in a number of externalities, including the democracy deficit. This historical review shows something of where, why, and how the democracy problem arises from the disjunction between global socioeconomic and political processes on the one hand (whether as the Great Depression, environment, or global competition) and local domestic processes on the other. From this stand-point, the local and the global are not two spheres, but one. Globaliza-tion is embedded in domestic institutions by the ways those institutions define their operating logics and, accordingly, involve themselves (whether as engagement or withdrawal) in meeting globalization's chal-lenges or rising to its opportunities.

This embedding is not a matter of mere rhetoric. Institutional practices and, more fundamentally, the relationship between the three branches of the federal government, between federal and state governments, and be-tween state and nonstate entities are profoundly shaped by whatever un-derstandings prevail at any given time. Indeed, to an important degree, those institutional dynamics of change are the domestic face of global-ization. The story I have told in this chapter shows the development of broad federal powers vested in Congress during the New Deal, powers mandated by the courts and Congress in the environmental era, and, gradually (still through the process of judicial review), a concentration of those powers in the executive branch during the global era. This history is now culminating in an unprecedentedly powerful presidential role, and a corresponding reduction in the political sphere, i.e., the sphere of de-mocratic debate.

The new deregulatory context places a great deal of legislative power in the executive. Congressional programs defined the New Deal and en-vironmental eras; the president and Congress worked together. Much of the deregulatory reform that has occurred in recent years, however, has taken place through the executive's aggressive reading of the "take care" clause of Article II of the Constitution. Thus, an intense contradiction ex-ists between the democratic tone of the constitutional and administrative rhetoric of the deregulatory era and the lack of congressional participa-tion in the actual changes that have occurred. The global era continues to evolve. The economic discourse of global competition and world trade is now intensifying in the new security context of the so-called war against terrorism. Domestic problems tend to be seen in light of their relationship to global forces predefined as those over which local legislators and reg-ulators should have little direct control.

The prevalence of the individual-liberty discourse makes the history of law-market relations, not to speak of alternative futures, counterintu-itive. Yet these are the essential contours of the contextual and structural transformations that have put presidential power at the fulcrum between markets and law, to the extent that these are imagined as rival forms of power. They are not, in fact, antithetical, except insofar as an antiregulatory ideology has increasingly focused (as some would argue) on liberating markets from government oversight. More fundamentally, the perception of zero-sum tensions between law and markets points toward the shifting lines of tension between increasingly conservative presidential administrations in the last third of the twentieth century (and relatively more liberal Congresses), as well as political divisions within the country at large. That was the context in which elements of New Deal pragmatism and environmental era technocracy were combined to maximize presidential power. This was the result, though perhaps not the motive, of a judiciary that approached the new demands of the 1980s and 1990s with, initially at least, a more formalized approach to separation-of-powers questions, and then, as we shall see in chapter 2, to a more formalized approach to federalism, as if to encourage a return to a pre–New Deal era of state and federal power. Globalization, then, is integral to the structure, function, and operation of national and local institutions of government and the ways they interact. It is for these reasons that it is productive to examine globalization from its domestic side.

2

Federalisms Old and New
The Vertical Dimensions of Globalization

Domestic federalism and internationalization should be seen as different aspects of denationalization. Devolving power to the states quite literally denationalizes federal policy; delegating power upwards to international organizations also places the policy focus elsewhere, shifting it from the national to the international level. There is also a third kind of delegation at work as well, often de facto in nature; that is, there are a number of issues the federal government chooses to leave to the market and the private sector, either because the government concludes that market outcomes are the best we can achieve or, as is the case with transnational issues such as child-labor or slave-labor working conditions abroad, it may be difficult or impossible to regulate the practice in question without undertaking a multinational effort. I will examine explicit delegations to private actors and, to some extent, de facto delegations as well in chapter 3. For now, my focus is on two delegations most often conceived as a vertical legal system, as if it had only two layers, domestic and international. My example of the international is the WTO. I shall look at the delegations of federal power upward to the WTO and then examine devolutions of power downward, to the individual states. In both instances, I shall analyze those two forms of federalism with reference to their impact on democracy and the democracy deficit. Later I will challenge the vertical image of these delegations up and down, but for the moment, let us explore the parallels between these two institutional layers as they have been constructed in recent years, beginning with some of the core assumptions underlying those constructions.

The prevailing analysis of globalization is statecentric in nature. This may be because the legal responses to global problems are usually the responses of states, often in the form of multilateral treaties such as the Montreal Protocol on Ozone Depletion or the creation of international organizations such as the WTO. But in such contexts, by virtue of the ways in which the individual sovereignties of states are, in effect, pooled, the output of these treaty regimes and international organizations is also partly denationalized. The very nature of the compromises necessary on the part individual states that engage in such multilateral forms of governance means that they are not likely to be able to pursue their national interest in exclusive terms.

From a democracy or legitimacy point of view, a statecentric approach to globalization can yield a range of approaches to regulation, from a narrow national self-interest to a broad global public interest. One's position on this spectrum affects how one views what might be necessary to legitimize, for example, the outcomes of the WTO. To illustrate the limitations of a statecentric approach from another sphere altogether, I turn to the music of Charles Ives, a major twentieth-century composer who (while maintaining a successful insurance business) experimented throughout his musical career with the limits of harmony and polyphony. His biographers, Henry and Sidney Cowell, ascribe his fascination with the far side of harmony to a formative childhood experience:[1]

> [H]is father invited a neighboring band to parade with its team at a baseball game in Danbury, while at the same time the local band made its appearance in support of the Danbury team. The parade was arranged to pass along the main street as usual, but the two bands started at opposite ends of town and were assigned pieces in different meters and different keys. As they approached each other the dissonances were acute, and each man played louder and louder so that his rivals would not put him off. A few players wavered, but both bands held together and got past each other successfully, the sounds of their cheerful discord fading out in the distance.

The statecentric approach treats as inevitable the directionality and dissonance in this episode, that is, between the global economy and international institutions such as the WTO coming from one direction and domestic law regimes from another. As the jurisprudence of the WTO illustrates, broad trade agreements, increasing standardization of rules in the areas covered by those agreements, and adjudicatory enforcement processes that privilege trade above all else, combine to result in significant and frequent clashes between domestic law and the rulings (and demands) of the WTO. Harmonization at the WTO involves the adoption of international standards that adjust the regulatory standards of two or more countries until they are the same. Given the WTO's influence, under certain circumstances, on domestic law,[2] is it possible to achieve an appropriate or acceptable level of harmonization without, in effect, always playing the same tune, especially when the name of the tune is likely to be the market? Is there room for counterpoint between domestic law regimes and the WTO? Can these bands share the street? Yes, if we can rethink their points of articulation in a broader context that allows them to communicate and coordinate effectively. Yes, too, between the WTO and domestic law, if along with economic integration there is procedural integration as well. In this way, democratic legitimacy can expand simultaneously at both the domestic and international levels. Accordingly, my focus in this book is necessarily two-sided: I consider transnational adjudicatory and rule-making processes within the WTO and also the ways that domestic lawmakers might anticipate and even influence those processes.

The more statecentric one is, the more comfortable one is likely to be with an equation of state representation (e.g., at the membership level of the WTO) with democracy. We can sketch three main positions along this spectrum. First, for some, the statecentric nature of an international organization means that very little is required in the way of legitimizing process because the organizations involved are treated as extensions of the member states, lacking any independent power. Since they reflect the member states themselves (those who hold this view might continue), those states' participation in these organizations is all that democracy requires. A second, even stronger statecentric view might deny the validity of any claim to democracy at the transnational level. Democracy requires a demos, they might say, that can exist only in territorial states, with a national culture and a concept of citizenship with rights enforceable in court. A third statecentric analysis does not deny the legitimacy of these organizations but views through a public-choice lens any attempt to legitimize them through democratic devices such as participation, transparency, and accountability. That is to say, these are all opportunities for interest groups to engage in rent-seeking behavior. Transparency reforms, narrowly defined, may be acceptable, but the more open the regulatory process and proceedings are to nonstate actors, the more likely it is they will be captured by the very interests they seek to regulate. Such analyses seek to translate economically based approaches from the domestic level to the international level, as if this were the next step of an essentially New Deal regulatory progression.

Denationalization and the Decentered State

But globalization also means that states partner with nonstate actors, not just states. The externalities of globalization must be identified, and this often occurs at the international level. The remedies involved, however, are almost always local. The democracy question—that is, the question of the relevance of domestic democracy to international law making—looms large in both contexts. Within the WTO, as many critics have argued, there are questions of legitimacy derived from principles of accountability, transparency, and, especially, participation by nongovernmental organizations.[3] Within the individual states, as commentators have also argued, the impact of WTO rulings might seem to sweep away domestic legislative and administrative processes, as domestic laws become subject to repeal or amendment in accordance with procedures effectively well beyond the reach of elected legislators or administrators held to the values of the APA (to continue the U.S. example).[4] As already discussed in chapter 1, the phrase "democracy deficit" is a common way of referring to this kind of problem. Unlike a budget deficit, which can be stated in arithmetic dollar terms, the democracy deficit arises from an asymmetry within democracy itself. Specifically, when the democratic requirements for legislation or regulation are not matched by those affecting deregulation, a democracy deficit arises. For example, amendments to federal statutes require passage by both houses of Congress and the signature of the president. The repeal of rules under the APA follows processes similar to the promulgation of new rules; there is always room for real deliberation and debate.

Global competition creates strong pressures on state and nonstate actors alike to carry out their responsibilities as efficiently as possible—indeed, given the history outlined in chapter 1, efficiency in terms of costs and shareholder value is rhetorically fused to the national interest. Be that as it may, many businesses respond to global forces and processes by organizing themselves in ways that both influence and adapt to the political and legal economy of which they are a part. During the New Deal (when a state-centered approach to law was dominant), corporations were more local in their organization, more national in their orientation, and more hierarchical in their dealings within and outside the corporation.[5]

Today, many global companies no longer do business this way. New technology industries, including computers and those companies whose operations are transformed by new technologies, such as banking, are now global in scope and operation.[6] They are "weblike" in the ways in which they use technologies to link up with suppliers, fabricators, and the manufacturers of some (or all) of the parts necessary for the product involved.[7] Sometimes it is hard to know where the center of a particular company is, as it is, in many ways, made up of a series of independent contractors around the world, each performing a particular task in the most cost-effective way.[8]

Just as the state is decentered, so too are the many industries that now organize themselves and operate globally. Flexibility, networks, and contractual approaches to manufacturing and other phases of business parallel changes states are undergoing. They also represent the kinds of challenges states face if they are to exercise influence over global businesses. That law both influences and is influenced by the dominant corporate organizational forms of the day is no surprise. The corporation of the twenty-first century is more flexible, multicentered, weblike, and global in its reach than its twentieth-century ancestors.

Given the current trend toward a merged private-public sphere, the processes of globalization that have encouraged decentralization among businesses also encourage decentralization of government at the national level, leading to devolution policies in the Congress and, coincidentally, a revival of federalism doctrines in the Supreme Court. The revival of federalism seemingly reverses long-standing trends toward greater centralization of power at the national level. Federalism denationalizes the federal state by devolving power back to the states in a variety of ways. Such devolutions involve a wide range of issues, especially safety-net issues like welfare, Head Start programs for children, health care, and housing for the poor.[9] Delegating power to international organizations such as the WTO also yields denationalizing effects. Let us consider these delegation issues in greater depth.

Globalization and Federalism

Since the founding of the republic, power in the United States has flowed from the states to the national government.[10] As local economies became more integrated with a growing national economy, the logic of Supreme Court decisions, particularly those after 1937, almost always resolved disputes between federal and state levels of government in favor of national power.[11] After the New Deal, the outcomes in cases involving the scope of the commerce clause of the Constitution seemingly had become such a foregone conclusion that it prompted then Justice Rehnquist's pointed concurrence in judgment in *Hodel v. Virginia Surface Mining and Reclamation Assoc.*:[12] "Although it is clear that the people, through the States, *delegated* authority to Congress to 'regulate Commerce . . . among the several States,' one could easily get the sense from this Court's opinions that the federal system exists only at the sufferance of Congress."[13] Indeed, he viewed the proposition that Congress, in our system of government, exercises only power delegated to it as "one of the greatest 'fictions' of our federal system. . . ."[14]

Chief Justice Rehnquist now speaks for a majority on a Court that approaches federalism issues in a way far more open to state autonomy and quite willing to reject expansive readings of the commerce clause. The legacy of the Rehnquist Court may very well be that in the end its constitutional approach to federalism ultimately prevailed. The Court has taken issue with attempts by the federal government to "commandeer" state bureaucracies to carry out federal mandates.[15] It has breathed new meaning into the Tenth Amendment, arguing, for example, that federal regulation of guns near schools is too local an issue to be supported by the commerce clause of the Constitution.[16] The reasoning in these cases suggests a shift in the Court's methodology and philosophy of federal-state issues. This shift in emphasis from federal power to autonomous state power coincides with economic and political shifts in the global economy that also encourage the decentralization of power. Further, the Court's approach to federal-state relations diminishes the flexibility of federal and state policymakers to experiment with new regulatory approaches, running the risk of substantially undermining the range of policy alternatives and administrative structures necessary for the global state to be effective.[17]

Consider, for instance, the Court's invalidation of the Violence against Women Act (VAWA) in *United States v. Morrison*.[18] Over the dissent of

Justice Souter, the Court held that Congress does not have the power to pass VAWA. Justice Souter was joined by three other justices. In support of his argument that VAWA is a constitutional exercise of Congress's power, Souter cites "the state support for the Act based upon the States' acknowledged failure to deal adequately with gender-based violence in state courts, and the belief of their own law enforcement agencies that national action is essential."[19] Justice Breyer, in a separate dissent in which three justices joined, emphasizes the procedures Congress engaged in for the purpose of protecting federalism values:

> It provided adequate notice to the States of its intent to legislate in an are[a] of traditional state regulation. And in response, attorneys general in the overwhelming majority of States (38) supported congressional legislation, telling Congress that "[o]ur experience as Attorneys General strengthens our belief that the problem of violence against women is a national one, requiring federal attention, federal leadership, and federal funds."[20]

The states' support for the VAWA was further illustrated by the fact that when the act was challenged in court, "[t]hirty-six of them . . . have filed an *amicus* brief in support of [the United States], and only one State has taken the respondents' side."[21] Breyer concluded from the procedures adopted by Congress and the overwhelming support of the states that "the law before us seems to represent an instance, not of state/federal conflict, but of state/federal efforts to cooperate in order to help solve a mutually acknowledged national problem."[22]

A Global Perspective on Federalism

The Court's constitutionalized shift in the power relationships between the nation and the states, its underlying rationale for this change, and a trend towards devolution in Congress itself are all likely to encourage more competitive models of the state, at the expense of developing more cooperative-based understandings of issues at both the national and the international levels of government. The emphasis on the individuality of states increases the transaction costs of reaching cooperative agreements that could apply to all states. In a sense, an extreme view of federalism would make national legislation as difficult as negotiating multilateral treaties. This is not to argue that a race to the bottom is always inevitable in such a situation,[23] but it does mean that creative, cooperative approaches to issues may be constitutionally excluded when they should be subject to political debate. Indeed, the pre–New Deal era was one characterized by many issues now prevalent at the global level, from child labor to monopolistic private power. The principles of federalism, carried too far, can exacerbate the most significant externalities of globalization: democracy deficits and poverty.

The strong-state assumptions currently used by the Supreme Court in its analysis of federalism opinions, coupled with its emphasis on dual citizenship, cost, and accountability, no longer sufficiently capture the heterogeneous quality of states as actors in today's global economy, nor the multicentric complexities of the relationships that now typify the transnational actors that states seek both to attract and to control or, at least, influence. Nor does it capture the more cosmopolitan nature of citizenship today. A citizen of a particular state is also a citizen of the United States and a global citizen as well. Individuals carry all of these identities with them on a daily basis.[24] The Court's emphasis on democracy and accountability at the state level overestimates the degree of choice states have when working by themselves, especially when the problems involved simultaneously include state, federal, and international components. It also underestimates the cosmopolitan nature of citizens today, and the fact that individuals are able to differentiate among various levels of power with which they are involved and with which they identify. Our political processes need to reflect such complexity, not compress it. The power relationships now involved due to globalization are multidimensional, not simply federal or state, national or international, public or private.

Paradoxically, perhaps, globalization exerts a downward pull when it comes to the exercise of both federal and state power, providing incentives for more state autonomy and power and more local authority within states.[25] At the same time, globalization also creates pressures from outside the nation state to take actions that allow international solutions to problems such as ozone depletion or global warming.[26] In addition, there are horizontal competitive forces at work as well, brought about by transnational corporations, with economic power sometimes approximating the power of a small state and with the capability of locating their operations anywhere in the world. Indeed, a multicentric world, consisting of nonsovereign power centers pursuing their own private interests, adds another important power dimension to federalism issues. As a consequence, issues involving sovereignty and democracy arise that go beyond the traditional discourse of federalism, as it has developed so far. This is true of citizenship issues as well, as citizens in a global world regularly function on multiple levels of political awareness and in multiple arenas of participation.

The Downward Pull of Globalization

Globalization encourages increasingly intense international competition among nations, states, and cities to attract and keep industries that they believe can create economic growth in their jurisdictions. Though the location of a plant or manufacturing operation turns on numerous, primarily cost-related factors, low taxes, as well as the imposition of minimal regulatory costs on industries located in these jurisdictions, usually constitute important elements of a jurisdiction's strategy to attract industry and jobs to a particular locale.[27] The tax and regulatory policies devised on the local level to attract industries to a certain locale are often the result of decision-making processes that are more akin to local corporatism than more traditional forms of democracy. Indeed, one commentator has noted, on the basis of a study of Japanese investment in the Midwest, that a kind of embedded corporatism best describes the process by which new investment is sought.[28] This involves, among other things, "an activist local state working with the business class to attract foreign investment and thereby stimulate the local economy."[29] As a result of agreements among business, government, and labor, substantial tax relief and various other economic and cultural incentives are commonly offered as forms of currency in this global competition for business.[30]

Individual states and municipalities within the United States, eager to attract such new investment and to retain its current industries, have a great interest in gaining control of as many factors as possible that affect firms' decisions to locate to or remain in the jurisdiction. They can create currency for global competition when it comes to providing services (such as welfare) more efficiently than neighboring states,[31] thereby lowering taxes or entering into incentive-based arrangements with companies they wish to attract to their locale.[32] But this need not always lead to fewer or poorly funded services for the poor if those investments can pay off in the jurisdiction involved. For example, if a state depends on low-wage labor to attract certain kinds of industry, it may offer labor laws (or the lack thereof) and low-income housing to attract the labor force it needs.[33] The key point is that economic competition drives social policy. A sense of decency or what is best for society in the long term are rationales that are not nearly as persuasive as the ability to be maximally competitive in the global economy.

Closely related to global incentives for regulatory cost cutting and the imposition of lower taxes at the federal, state, and local levels is the increased desire of each particular jurisdiction seeking increases in economic investment to control its own costs. Relocating federal regulatory responsibility for costly regulatory programs in the individual states arguably gives states the opportunity to create more global currency by maximizing the efficiency with which they provide such services, allowing them to reallocate scarce funds in more globally effective and competitive ways.

There may, of course, be some forms of global competitive currency individual states should not be allowed to create.[34] And, there may be national interests that should take precedence over state concerns. Level playing fields, however, are not necessarily sought by states when the primary motivation involved is competition with other states. Moreover, a level playing field within the United States would not solve the competitive problems of states arising from their competition with other countries, other regions, and other partnerships around the world. The multicentric aspects of the global economy stem from the fact that there are multiple state and nonstate power centers capable of affecting where investments may or may not occur. All of these pressures militate in favor of decentralized and denationalized decision making.

The Pull from the Top—National and International Pressures

Increasing a state's power to control the costs imposed on its inhabitants and potential investors through devolution is, however, only one aspect of current federalism trends. There are also forces operating simultaneously to reinforce federal powers. National standards and approaches may be necessary to prevent the creation of illegitimate global currency,[35] stemming, for example, from the denial of constitutional rights. They also are necessary to achieve certain levels of regulatory uniformity if businesses are to avoid an unnecessarily complex patchwork quilt of state rules and regulations.[36] More important, there also are issues such as the environment, in which it is in the interest of nation states to play an active regulatory role at the global level. Effective national participation at the global level requires a national "presence" in certain domestic areas affected by these global concerns. And indeed, international agreements and multilateral approaches have been increasing at a rapid rate.[37] For example, if there were no effective national control over air pollution, it would be very difficult for the national government to speak for all fifty states and enter into serious negotiations at the global level.

The ability of the national government to participate effectively in global issues at the international level also can help mitigate the extremes of global competition. Along with the trend toward devolution of federal power to the states, there is also at least the beginning of an evolutionary trend involving the national government more directly sharing in the responsibilities of international governance.[38] At the national level, this trend toward multinational decision making and problem solving often expresses itself negatively in debates over the undue restriction of national sovereignty,[39] but international cooperation and multinational agreements are nonetheless increasing.[40] Yet it would be a mistake to assume that recourse to an international approach always means national legislation or national regulation. Indeed, as we shall see below, delegating authority upward to an international organization such as the WTO can also result in the imposition of a market-oriented, deregulated approach domestically, reinforcing decisions by either the Congress or the Court in favor of devolving power to the states. Such an approach to international delegation can also increase competition at both the global and domestic levels. Nevertheless, international cooperation and regulation highlight the importance of the national government's ability to play an active role at the domestic level even in the context of—and even because of—such supranational governance. To the extent that federal power is limited in this regard, enforceable international regulatory regimes are more difficult to create than when only one major decision maker is involved.[41]

Horizontal Forces and the Transnational Corporation

Federalism is traditionally seen in vertical terms,[42] involving a flow of power between state and federal centers of authority. Viewed in these terms, a global perspective introduces not only an additional vertical level of power (the international "level") but additional horizontal dimensions as well.[43] A global perspective emphasizes the fact that states outside the United States now play an increasingly important role when it comes to global competition, and it also highlights the significant role nonstate actors, such as transnational corporations, now play in influencing local legal regimes and policies. Their ability to render a sense of place relatively irrelevant when it comes to deciding where to locate a plant, for example, substantially threatens the ability of individual governments, state or federal, to regulate the activities of such entities effectively. The fact that capital moves relatively freely from state to state also means that investment can sometimes leave as quickly as it may have come.[44] The jurisdictional difficulties faced by states trying to influence such actors cannot be dealt with as they were during the New Deal, when federal regulatory regimes leveled the playing field nationwide, and that usually was good enough. There are now many other countries involved, and international approaches are necessary if state intervention and a more cooperative approach to international governance is the goal.[45] If a strong-state laissez-faire response is the goal, then maximum decentralization of power would further that kind of global economy. As I shall argue below, however, this should be a political decision, not one subject to constitutional dictates by the Supreme Court. It should be one subject to change by the government of the day.

In short, the transnational or horizontal character of these entities involves significant independent power relationships that substantially undercut the power of states to influence multinational corporations according to what states may perceive as their individual interests. The economic power of some transnational organizations and their constraining effects on states makes them somewhat akin to states, at least in their social and structural effects.[46] Such private-power centers cannot easily be regulated by uniform rules, even at the national level.

A global perspective on power-allocation issues between federal and state governments thus provides us with additional criteria with which to evaluate the Court's federalism decisions. It also creates additional concerns when it comes to global governance and the role of individual states in that process. As we begin to analyze concepts of federalism from a global perspective, democracy and public participation questions loom large. Traditional federalism responses and calls for a return to pre–New Deal days do not necessarily solve these problems, given the global dispersion of power that now exists. Just as it is impossible to recreate the sense of the private that existed in an earlier historic era, it is impossible to view states as independent units of power, unaffected by actors and problems that do not correlate with geographic boundaries. It may be that there needs to be more local control over certain issues, but there may also need to be new forms of governance and participation at the global level. Judicial approaches that unnecessarily limit these new possibilities may do more harm than good by, in effect, playing a role somewhat akin to the role the Court played as this country began to come to grips politically with the legal and economic implications of a national economy.[47]

Sovereignty, Federalism, and the Court

The Court's recent opinions declaring certain federal acts in violation of the commerce clause or the Tenth Amendment imply a rights conception of state sovereignty.[48] Such strong-state assumptions are at odds with the fluid and multilevel mix of governmental and private partnerships characteristic of globalization within the United States.[49] The Court's notion of state sovereignty is steeped in nineteenth-century precedents, entailing a view of state power that regards member states as separate and distinct in relation to each other and relative to the federal government. Individual member states, like nation states, are integral to the global economy.[50] Indeed, while the prevailing metaphor of federalism is the vertical dimension, it is important to recognize these lateral relationships, particularly as private-public partnerships multiply and disperse power centers—an issue to which we return in chapter 3.

The Court's opinions also reflect an aspect of public-choice theory by emphasizing accountability and cost as important bases for its decisions, especially in situations where the federal government attempts to use the apparatus of states to implement its policies. In so doing, however, the Court emphasizes the importance of differentiating clearly between the levels of government responsible for these additional costs. The Court holds that democracy, freedom, and liberty require that those who make decisions should be accountable to the electorate who must pay the costs of those decisions.[51] Unfunded mandates, in this sense, violate the spirit of democracy and undermine accountability for those who are responsible for its costs.[52] While these precepts may be correct in some cases, it does not follow that funding never follows; politics may change so as to favor or demand a commitment of funds. These decisions stop such political processes before they even begin, constitutionalizing this limitation on the political process.

The Court's conception of state sovereignty as self-contained in nineteenth-century terms is most apparent in *Gregory v. Ashcroft*.[53] At issue in *Ashcroft* was Missouri's mandatory retirement law for state judges. That law had been challenged as a violation of the Age Discrimination in Employment Act (ADEA) and the Equal Protection Clause of the Fourteenth Amendment. In rejecting these arguments, Justice O'Connor, writing for the majority, found that the ADEA was not applicable to the case at bar, using a "plain statement" statutory interpretive approach to reach that result, one infused with federalistic values and constitutional assumptions. In so doing, Justice O'Connor emphasized the sovereignty of states in a fashion that suggested a zero-sum game approach to the allocation of federal and state power. She writes,[54]

> As every schoolchild learns, our Constitution establishes a system of dual sovereignty between the States and the Federal Government. This Court has recognized this fundamental principle. In *Tafflin v. Levitt* "[W]e beg[a]n with the axiom that, under our federal system, the states possess sovereignty concurrent with that of the Federal Government, subject only to the limitations imposed by the Supremacy Clause."

Justice O'Connor then goes on to quote from an 1869 case that describes the constitutional scheme of dual sovereigns in greater detail:[55]

> "[T]he people of each State compose a State, having its own government, and endowed with all the functions essential to separate and independent existence. . . . '[W]ithout the States in union, there could be no such political body as the United States.' Not only, therefore, can there be no loss of separate and independent autonomy to the States, through their union under the Constitution, but it may be not unreasonably said that the preservation of the States, and the maintenance of their governments, are as much within the design and care of the Constitution as the preservation of the Union and the maintenance of the National government. The Constitution, in all its provisions, looks to an indestructible Union, composed of indestructible States." *Texas v. White*, 7 Wall. 700, 725 (1869), quoting *Lane County v. Oregon*, 7 Wall. 71, 76 (1869).

The idea of sovereignty propounded by Justice O'Connor implies a bright line between the powers of states and the national government. Her sense of that line seems strongly anchored in a sense of place typical of approaches to state prevalent in the nineteenth century.[56] Such approaches minimize the zone of overlap that can (and often should) exist between two sovereigns. Once again, this concept of sovereignty is not an end in itself, but a way of securing for "the citizens the liberties that derive from the diffusion of sovereign power."[57] Indeed, it is like the doctrine of separation of powers: "The Constitutional authority of Congress cannot be expanded by the 'consent' of the government unit whose domain is thereby narrowed, whether that unit is the Executive Branch or the States."[58] The Court believes that sovereignty, so conceived, is essential to the infrastructure of policy making. Not unlike the doctrine of separation of powers aimed at preventing the aggregation of power by any one branch of government, federalism and state sovereignty also reflect commitment to distributed power as a basis for civil liberty. As Justice O'-Connor notes,[59]

> This federalist structure of joint sovereigns preserves to the people numerous advantages. It assures a decentralized government that will be more sensitive to the diverse needs of a heterogeneous society; it increases opportunity for citizen involvement in democratic processes; it allows for more innovation and experimentation in government; and it makes government more responsive by putting the States in competition for a mobile citizenry.

Indeed, in the majority's view, the constitutional scheme requires such clear lines demarcating the powers exercised by the states. "Just as the separation and independence of the coordinate branches of the Federal Government serve to prevent the accumulation of excessive power in any one branch, a healthy balance of power between the States and the Federal Government will reduce the risk of tyranny and abuse from either front."[60]

The notion of sovereignty on which the Court's rationales are based fails to take account of the fact that many private actors within states have power on the level of states themselves.[61] Justice Breyer, speaking for the four justices who often dissent together in recent federalism cases, emphasizes the potential negative ramifications of the Court's decisions on the effectiveness of government in his dissent in *Federal Maritime*

Commission v. South Carolina Ports Authority.[62] In this case the Court held that state sovereign immunity prevented Congress from compelling a state to answer the complaints of private parties before the administrative tribunal of an agency.[63] Breyer argues that federal administrative agencies are not covered by the Eleventh Amendment since they do not exercise the judicial power of the United States.[64] He adds that the practical consequences of the opinion are negative:[65]

> The decision, while permitting an agency to bring enforcement actions against States, forbids it to use agency adjudication in order to help decide whether to do so. Consequently the agency must rely more heavily upon its own informal staff investigations in order to decide whether a citizen's complaint has merit. The natural result is less agency flexibility, a larger federal bureaucracy, less fair procedure, and potentially less effective law enforcement. . . . At least one of these consequences, the forced growth of the unnecessary federal bureaucracy, undermines the very constitutional objectives the Court's decision claims to serve.

When viewed from a global context, these policy goals (heterogeneity, democracy, innovation, and a mobile citizenry) look different than when they are seen as a function of federal and state power operating jointly, but alone. Global competition and the incentives for states to attract and retain private foreign investment encourage integration rather than difference. Moreover, most states seek to minimize public costs so as to maximize their appeal to private investment. Thus, while democracy may very well be furthered by keeping certain issues local, globalization creates important pressures toward transnationalism at the local level, where minority interests may have even fewer procedural protections than at the federal level. Thus, federalist privileging of the local may be at the expense of a more vibrant national democracy, one that allows citizens an opportunity not only to vote and express themselves, but also, crucially, to form coalitions across state boundaries, giving minority groups a greater chance to aggregate their power and to speak in a more audible voice. Indeed, the kind of segmented citizenship that the Court espouses does not accord with the complex realities and multiple citizenship identities that the global economy produces.[66] Federalism denationalizes issues, and it unbundles the concept of citizenship, fragmenting our political responses and further disaggregating the public.

More important, public innovation, too, is likely to be homogenized and only take the form of minimal taxes and lower regulatory costs, though this, in turn, may encourage more private experimentation. Yet, the more activities move from the public realm to the private sector, the greater the risk that global currency coined at the local level will be at the expense of the weakest members of society.[67] The intense competitiveness that this model encourages may, indeed, encourage more mobility among citizens in their quest to find a modicum of financial stability. More likely, though, such mobility will occur at the higher end of the income spectrum, rather than the lower.[68] Freedom in the sense of making national action more difficult to achieve may be enhanced, but at the expense of developing a more cooperative model of global capitalism at the international and national levels. Greater decentralization may also lead to a race to the bottom in some areas,[69] but more importantly, it raises the transaction costs involved in achieving more cooperative approaches to coping with the problems of global capitalism and the externalities of globalization.[70]

The idea of a state's integrity is at the basis of the majority's opinion in *New York v. United States.*[71] Once again the Court is more concerned with the forms of power than with structures that make it easy to exercise power in a flexible way. In this case, the Court dealt with the constitutionality of the Low-Level Radioactive Waste Policy Amendments Act of 1985. The act in question was the result of various state efforts to devise a federal structure for the regulation of low-level waste that avoided federal preemption and retained a role for states to play. In many ways, the legislative process was akin to the negotiation and the enactment of a treaty, whereby the individual states involved retained considerable flexibility when it came to meeting their regulatory obligations. The act was the result of a cooperative approach to federalism that allows states to maintain flexibility and the primary regulatory role in their traditional realm of protecting public health and safety.[72] The federal government set the basic standards, but rather than preempting state law, the act allowed states to design policies their lawmakers believed best achieved the federal standards.[73] As one commentator noted, "In theory, the system allows states to experiment and innovate, but not to sacrifice public health and welfare in a bidding war to attract industry."[74]

Specifically, Congress sought to achieve its federal goals by crediting certain incentives to ensure that states provide for the disposal of radioactive waste generated within their borders. States were authorized to impose a surcharge on radioactive waste received from other states, a portion of which would be collected by the Secretary of Energy and placed in a trust account for those states that achieve a series of milestones in developing waste disposal sites.[75] States were also authorized to increase the costs of access to sites to those states that did not meet federal guidelines, eventually denying them access altogether.

Neither of these "incentives" violated the Court's sense of state sovereignty. A further incentive, however, provided that a state that fails to provide for the disposal of all internally generated waste by a particular date must, in most cases, take title to and possession of the waste and become liable for all resulting damages suffered by the waste's generator or owner.[76] For the Court this provision created constitutional problems.[77] In rejecting Congress's attempt to force certain states to take title to and possession of low-level waste, the Court emphasized that Congress could not force the states to regulate in ways that made them direct agents of the federal government. Congress could regulate individuals, but not states, because states were sovereign:[78]

> In providing for a stronger central government, therefore, the Framers explicitly chose a Constitution that confers upon Congress the power to regulate individuals, not States. As we have seen, the Court has consistently respected this choice. We have always understood that even where Congress has the authority under the Constitution to pass laws requiring or prohibiting certain acts, it lacks the power directly to compel the States to require or prohibit those acts. The allocation of power contained in the Commerce Clause, for example, authorizes Congress to regulate interstate commerce directly; it does not authorize Congress to regulate state governments' regulation of interstate commerce.

In the majority's view,[79]

> The take title provision offers state governments a "choice" of either accepting ownership of waste or regulating according to the instructions of Congress. Either type of federal action would "commandeer" state governments into the service of federal regulatory purposes, and would for this reason be inconsistent with the Constitution's division of authority between federal and state governments.

In short, the Court's concept of state sovereignty precludes states from entering into agreements to take certain kinds of actions to carry out their promises in the federal legislative process—unlike countries that enter into a treaty and agree to enact certain enabling legislation to realize its goals.

The Court's more recent federalism decisions take the principles of democracy, accountability, and cost a step further. In *Printz v. United States*,[80] for example, the Court struck down the Brady Handgun Violence Prevention Act on grounds that the federal government was, in effect, commandeering the state's enforcement apparatus to carry out a federal policy. There was little doubt that Congress had the power to regulate in this area, but it could not force states to carry out its mandates. Writing for the majority, Justice Scalia emphasized the structural rather than the textual nature of this decision.[81] He also emphasized democracy and accountability:[82]

> We held in *New York* that Congress cannot compel the States to enact or enforce a federal regulatory program. Today we hold that Congress cannot circumvent that prohibition by conscripting the State's officers directly. The Federal Government may neither issue directives requiring the States to address particular problems, nor command the States' officers, or those of their political subdivisions, to administer or enforce a federal regulatory program. It matters not whether policymaking is involved, and no case-by-case weighing of the burdens or benefits is necessary; such commands are fundamentally incompatible with our constitutional system of dual sovereignty.

As Justice Stevens emphasized in dissent,[83] the result in this case had no textual basis in the Constitution. More important for our purposes, it relied once again on a concept of sovereignty with little bearing on global realities. Only Justice Breyer chose to see this case in comparative—if not global—terms, noting that no other federal system in the world today would prevent the use of state enforcement powers in this way.[84]

Viewed from a global perspective, the "all or nothing" quality of the Court's approach both overstates and understates what is at stake. It overstates the potential restructuring effects of power flowing from one body to another, as power has flowed from the states to the federal government for over two hundred years. In a global economy, multigovernmental approaches may often be necessary and power arrangements should be more fluid. Constitutionalizing these decisions removes a good deal of this flexibility. At the same time, the Court's approach to power levels also understates what is at stake to the extent that it overlooks entirely the fact that nonstate actors, especially transnational corporations, are now major power centers in many ways comparable to states. Thus, a concept of federalism that does not take into account how global power is allocated today runs the serious risk of undermining the very goals it seeks to further—democracy and liberty. Perhaps moving some decisions to the national level might more easily neutralize inappropriate uses of private power. Be that as it may, constitutionalizing outcomes in this way removes an important political option.

The Commerce Power

Apart from issues involving the use of a state's own enforcement apparatus, the ability of Congress to regulate at the national level has also been limited by the Court's view of the commerce power. In *U.S. v. Lopez*,[85] the constitutionality of the Gun-Free School Zone Act of 1990 was at issue. This act "made it a federal offense 'for any individual knowingly to possess a firearm at a place that the individual knows, or has reasonable cause to believe, is a school zone.'"[86] For the majority, this was "a criminal statute that by its terms has nothing to do with commerce or any sort of economic enterprise, however broadly one might define those terms."[87] Moreover, according to the majority, the argument that guns in a school zone may result in violent crime that substantially affects interstate commerce proves too much. "Thus, if we were to accept the Government's arguments, we are hard pressed to posit any activity by an individual that Congress is without power to regulate."[88] Indeed, the majority feared that a decision holding this act to be within Congress's commerce clause power would convert congressional authority under that clause to a general police power of the sort retained by states. The Court thus concluded that the commerce power was not infinitely expandable, and that there are limitations "inherent in the very language of the commerce clause."[89]

Justices Kennedy and O'Connor concurred, emphasizing the policy benefits of a governmental structure that divides power between federal and state authorities:[90] "the theory that two governments accord more liberty than one requires for its realization two distinct and discernable lines of political accountability: one between the citizens and the Federal Government; the second between the citizens and the States."

This kind of separation was crucial for true accountability to occur:[91]

> If, as Madison expected, the federal and state governments are to . . . hold each other in check by competing for the affections of the people, those citizens must have some means of knowing which of the two governments to hold accountable for failure to perform a given function. Were the Federal Government to take over the regulation of entire areas of traditional state concern, areas having nothing to do with the regulation of commercial activities, the boundaries between the spheres of federal and state authority would blur and political responsibility would become illusory.

These policy justifications for the textual interpretation given by the majority are very much based on a conception of the state as a unitary entity, where citizens clearly differentiate among those who exercise power. Of course, citizens of the states also have a vote at the federal level, and the idea that they are easily fooled by the federal level of government at the expense of the states may not give sufficient credit to the discerning nature of the voters involved. But quite apart from the policy arguments, there is the broader claim that guns, violence, and the global economy are all interrelated, especially when education is involved.

In his dissenting opinion in *Lopez*,[92] Justice Breyer takes a very different perspective on this case, focusing more on the school children involved and on the interrelationships between education and the national economy and beyond. Indeed, he emphasizes that education and business are directly related: "technological changes and innovations in management techniques have altered the nature of the workplace so that more jobs now demand greater educational skills."[93] Three justices joined in dissent, but only Justice Breyer made the link between the national economy and global competition:

> Global competition also has made primary and secondary education economically more important. The portion of the American economy attributable to international trade nearly tripled between 1950 and 1980, and more than seventy percent of American-made goods now compete with imports. Yet lagging worker productivity has contributed to negative trade balances and to real hourly compensation that has fallen

below wages in ten other industrialized nations. At least some significant part of this serious productivity problem is attributable to students who emerge from classrooms without the reading or mathematical skills necessary to compete with their European or Asian counterparts.[94]

Justice Breyer seems to have a clear concept of global competition. His premise is that every school child will eventually compete for jobs against other school children all over the globe. Local jobs and prosperity will turn on the outcome of this competition. He notes, "there is evidence that, today more than ever, many firms base their location decisions upon the presence, or absence, of a work force with a basic education."[95] For Justice Breyer, guns, education, and business are interrelated: "The economic links I have just sketched seem fairly obvious."[96] He questions, "Why then is it not equally obvious, in light of those links, that a widespread, serious, and substantial physical threat to teaching and learning *also* substantially threatens the commerce to which that teaching and learning is inextricably tied?"[97]

For Justice Breyer, the links among local violence, education, and success in the global economy are sufficiently direct to justify federal involvement. Though he takes a global perspective on the issues before him, his judicial approach to the commerce clause is reminiscent of *Wickard v. Filburn*.[98] Though Justice Breyer is quick to add that his approach does not "'obliterate' the 'distinction between what is national and what is local,'"[99] his willingness to define the national interest by looking beyond national borders to an interdependent global economy represents an approach that ultimately would vest most regulatory decisions at the federal level, should the national government decide to act.[100] In short, globalization does not necessarily render concepts of state sovereignty based on territory irrelevant, but a national government intent on maximizing competitiveness in a global economy is at cross-purposes with itself when it opts to constitutionalize such issues rather than seek a national, political consensus (even if that consensus is to decentralize certain issues).

Perhaps the Court should not be faulted for analyzing federalism issues in a framework that is dominated by nineteenth-century concepts of federalism, embodied in nineteenth-century precedents. Courts usually look at the past as they move forward. Yet, in the Court's effort to reestablish what often appears to be a pre–New Deal position vis-à-vis national power, it is overlooking an aspect of New Deal judicial processes that remains highly relevant for the global state. As just noted, courts should avoid constitutionalizing issues when it is not necessary to do so. Though the Court may have been concerned with federal costs unnecessarily imposed on states, such matters are best dealt with legislatively. Diluted federal power need not be the inevitable outcome of the global state, and courts need not be drawn into taking the lead in sculpting the state of the future. It is ironic that at the edge of the twenty-first century, the Court would opt for constitutional approaches that unduly limit legislative flexibility. The New Deal Court constitutionalized a political approach to issues. The Rehnquist Court is constitutionalizing outcomes that unbundled the use of federal power and, in the process, citizenship as well.

In suggesting that the Court's approach to federalism is insufficiently attuned to the current fluidity and multicenteredness of federal/state/private power, I do not wish to be misread as advocating that the Court lend its authoritative weight to globalization. Rather, I am suggesting that its construction of federalism as entailing (or requiring) a preference for discrete powers of member states is unlikely to achieve its stated goal of widening the political process. Quite the contrary, local jurisdictions may be far more exposed to market constraints than the country at large, with the result that citizens' roles in democratic deliberation are likely to be less substantial as a counterweight to globalization, for example, than at the federal level. In other words, a strict approach to federalism may, in many contexts, increase the democracy deficit.

In globalization, federalism is no less a form of denationalization than are the international public sphere and the transnationalized private sector, both of which are more often associated with this concept. These denationalizing effects of federalism privilege competition between and among states as well as markets and market outcomes, underscoring the extent to which our current national policy looks to the market as an arena of delegation and to market incentives as a substitute for traditional regulation. The politics that produces these results in Congress has been emphatically reinforced in the Court's opinions in terms of the rhetoric of its federalism decisions and in a way far more rigid than a purely political decision to place responsibility at the state instead of the federal level of government. As we have just seen, this is particularly apparent in Supreme Court decisions over the last decade or so.

The relationship between federalism and the democracy deficit may seem counterintuitive. Indeed, throughout the federalism cases discussed above, the Court's persistent rationale is that it intends to increase democracy by ensuring that in matters involving state issues, power will be exercised by officials closer to the people directly affected. This may further democracy in some contexts, but the multicentric nature of globalization means that this assumption does not hold categorically. The idea that democracy is enhanced if power is exercised geographically closer to those affected tends to overstate territory and distance as general criteria for democracy. More to the point, it ignores the "divide and conquer" effect that the denationalization of decision making can have, particularly with regard to issues involving new challenges on behalf of marginal constituents. Delegating power down or, in effect, devolving power to the states, fragments minority and marginal constituencies, sometimes to the point that these groups are effectively excluded. Sending Head Start programs or other programs for the poor back to the state without specific federal funding and guidelines makes such funding vulnerable to the needs and politics of those states that may have neither the resources necessary nor the political will for such programs. Though the theory of devolution is that it increases democracy by bringing decisions closer to stakeholders, it can have the opposite effect when those stakeholders are weak politically and widely dispersed.

The likelihood of control by powerful local groups often increases with decentralization of political authority. As Professors Crenson and Ginsberg have pointed out,

> Madisonian logic suggests that small constituencies are more likely than large ones to fall under the domination of a single interest. Its hegemony may discourage opposing interests from mobilizing, or it may use its political privilege to structure local institutions so that other interests find it difficult to organize. Organization . . . is the mobilization of bias; some interests can be organized into politics while others are organized out.[101]

Quite apart from the intrusive role that courts now play in these contexts, there are strong political and economic incentives at the state level that argue persuasively for the devolution of regulatory and safety-net issues. Given the increasing competition that exists now at all levels of government for the attraction and retention of economic investment to their respective territories, devolving welfare responsibility or housing for the poor to the state level, for example, means that individual states will vary in their approaches to such issues and in the priority they give to them. The financial capabilities of the states vary. Moreover, as states compete for investment and the retention of taxpayers, they have distinct incentives to minimize the costs of redistributive programs such as welfare, Medicaid, or poverty programs in general. Some states will reduce payments for these programs more than others because of lack of funds; other states will reduce them for ideological reasons. Yet, programs directed toward the poor were precisely the kinds of programs that Congress tried to (and to a large extent did) send back to the states in the 1990s. The agenda was, if not their elimination, at least their minimization in terms of importance and costs at the federal level. These payments were to be no longer of national concern, but rather a matter of local choice and subject to competition for investment. Differences in state wealth and a politics of choice in such contexts tend to make poor constituencies far more vulnerable than when these interests are aggregated at the national level.[102] Political decisions such as these, however, can always be reversed. Moreover, as we shall see in chapter 4, even when Congress or state legislatures seek to preempt state and local experiments dealing with the importation of prescription drugs or local minimum-wage legislation (to take just two examples), the politics generated by such actions keeps such issues alive and part of the political discourse. But when courts constitutionalize such issues, they lock in these outcomes for generations to come, in effect taking them out of national politics and in reality taking them out of local politics as well.

As noted above, denationalization is more often associated with the international and transnational spheres. Delegating power up to what some have referred to as the international branch of government also has negative impacts on democracy at the domestic level. The WTO, for example, implements the policies of GATT agreements, and those agreements govern approximately 90 percent of global trade.[103] A federalist analogy is often used to describe the role of international organizations such as the WTO or the UN, as if they constituted a sort of suprafederal government—an extension of the New Deal, gone global. It should be noted that in such contexts, domestic law is subject to external control largely through domestic executive power, given the strong built-in pressures to defer to the executive branch in international matters generally, and international trade in particular.[104]

Appreciating the extent to which globalization involves important elements of denationalization informs a shift of emphasis from a federalist analogy based on hierarchy (with respect to the relationship of international organizations to domestic law) to a more pragmatic, pluralist, and flexible conception of such arrangements both at home and abroad. As I will suggest in the next section, the hierarchical analogy to federalism is flawed. Advocates of the federalist analogy in a WTO context usually restrict their attention to applications of compliance with trade law provisions, subsuming issues of democratic participation within the constraints of sovereignty defined as representation by member states at the WTO.[105] Anticipating what follows, this is the same conception of democracy that is evoked to justify great deference to the executive branch in trade and other matters as well, as we have seen in chapter 1. Such deference, however, is often to the exclusion of timely and significant domestic participation throughout the regulatory process, from treaty making to the harmonization and application of rules. The democracy deficits that result are those that come not from the preemption of domestic legislative and administrative processes by international and transnational processes, but rather from the fait accompli nature of the invocation of supranational processes and their use by the executive branch.

For example, WTO decisions and treaties derive their legitimacy from a formal conception of democracy, claiming legitimacy from the fact that only member states participate and, therefore, the WTO's actions are representative of the people of the member states. As a result, the executive branch of government decides what national trade policy should be in various contexts, and moreover increasingly justifies its decisions without the participation of the legislative branch, the states, or nonstate actors.[106] The electoral accountability of the president and the international character of the issues involved are presumed to satisfy the legitimacy demand for representation. But inherent in this approach is another kind of analogy to federalism as a vertical axis, with federal power that extends "upward" to the international level rather than devolving "downward" to the states. In other words, the same principles are in play through the federalism analogy among these various levels of government within the United States. The sharing of power, whether national or international, is treated largely as a zero-sum game. The international/national distinction parallels the rigid state/federal distinction utilized by the Court in the federalism cases discussed above and is subject to the same criticisms regarding its underlying analysis and its unintended effects.

Both the courts and the executive play an important role in these federalist contexts by furthering the economic and political effects of globalization. Both types of federalism (domestic and the international analogy) tend to privilege the market in its own right. The market outcomes encouraged by the denationalization of domestic federalism often are reinforced by market-based trade policies mandated by the WTO. As we shall see, the concepts of democracy that animate federalism theory and approaches to law at both the domestic and international levels are far too limiting on the range of political solutions to problems that might be possible if we view these issues through a global lens. They fail to appreciate the multidimensional aspects of global issues such as the environment at the WTO level or unconscionably low wages at the domestic level; they in effect compress the noneconomic values associated with such issues with a market-oriented statecentric approach to decision making.

Traditional distinctions between federal and state as well as national and international should be at least theoretically open to revision. Distinctions such as public and private, state and federal, national and international, domestic and foreign, or local and global no longer accurately capture the power relationships as they actually exist. There remains a strong tendency on the part of courts and policymakers to treat changes in the allocation of what is public or private (or federal or state or international or national) as if these were either/or questions about power. However, globalization does more than reallocate power among preexisting categories; it changes the categories themselves, as well as the actors involved.

What roles courts and legislatures might play in the process of acknowledging these new realities is a crucial question. Courts would necessarily allow the kind of experimentation New Deal Courts permitted to enable a concept of a global public interest to emerge. As yet, there is no "Global Deal" readily discernible, but if the democracy deficit is to be narrowed, our own political processes must become more creative and interactive with various levels of government, governance, and the market at home and abroad. Federalism doctrines now threaten political creativity in ways reminiscent of the pre–New Deal Courts.[107] As a recent debate between Justice Breyer and Justice Scalia shows, at least two very different attitudes towards these issues currently are in play in the Supreme Court and throughout our politics in general. For Breyer,

> Modern commerce and the technology upon which it rests need large markets and seek government large enough to secure trading rules that

permit industry to compete in the global marketplace, to prevent pollution that crosses borders, and to assure adequate protection of health and safety by discouraging a regulatory "race to the bottom."[108]

As a matter of constitutional law, he argues for an approach to federalism that permits "flexible context-specific legislative responses that are not constitutionalized by an historic view" of sovereignty. "That is why the modern substantive federalist problem demands a flexible, context-specific legislative response (and it does not help to constitutionalize an ahistoric view of sovereign immunity that, by freezing its remedial limitations, tends to place the State beyond the reach of law)." For Justice Scalia, however, "[l]egislative flexibility on the part of Congress will be the touchstone of federalism when the capacity to support combustion becomes the acid test of a fire extinguisher."[109]

A decentralized approach to governmental power may very well be of a piece with a global era in which the competition for investments at the state level is ever increasing; however, constitutionalizing these issues is quite another matter. The democracy deficit to which these approaches contribute becomes even clearer when one takes a global perspective on these matters, illuminating the similarities between vertical concepts of power at the international and domestic level. In the international sphere, they reinforce deferential approaches to executive power, privileging market approaches at the expense of democracy. Since this dynamic is especially clear in the context of the WTO, let us turn to that context now, as an extended case in point. The WTO shows not only the flaws in the federalist analogy but also the way that analogy sharpens the democracy deficit within the United States.

Globalization, Democracy, and the WTO

The WTO has an increasingly prominent law-making role. With respect to domestic law and law-making processes, that role is often presented by critics as involving an inevitable friction (as already noted), as if there were an inevitable zero-sum competition between the authority of the WTO and the sovereignty and democracy of individual member states. Many commentators who are concerned with such a trade-off address it through the lens of sovereignty.[110] Accordingly, some recommend that we focus on the WTO itself,[111] making it more democratic (and thus legitimate) by reforming the conditions of WTO decision making with respect to individual states, for example, with proposals regarding accountability, transparency, and participation, as well as more substantive proposals to overhaul the WTO itself. Others seek to maintain the status quo or, if anything, reintroduce some of the diplomatic informality that characterized the earlier GATT adjudicatory regimes.[112] In short, almost everyone who focuses on the WTO alone sees it either as the bane of our democratic existence, an intrusion into our sovereignty, or a reasonably effective way of achieving deep economic integration around the world with relatively little interference from rent-seeking interest groups.[113]

There is no gainsaying the room for improvement in the legitimacy of WTO processes and outcomes, but the debates over potential reforms can be productively broadened. The current debates, including proposals to maintain the status quo, usually assume the nature of the trade-offs between sovereignty and democracy on the one hand and the exercise of WTO decision-making power on the other. I focus on three aspects of this assumption, each of them problematic.

First, the assumption that there is a trade-off between sovereignty and democracy conflates sovereignty and democracy as if any one state's democratic needs are to be addressed as an issue of representation and participation at the WTO.

Second, it conflates democracy with market-based outcomes. That is to say, legitimacy flows from the successful application of and compliance with the free trade aspects of the treaties applied by the WTO, quite apart from the processes used to reach them.

Third, the prevailing assumptions about trade-offs restrict debate to the universe of WTO decisions and their aftermath, taking, essentially, a compliance perspective on these issues, whether in relation to the adjudicatory panel decisions of the WTO or in relation to administrative agency attempts to harmonize domestic rules to WTO decisions.

These problems are my main concern in this section. We shall examine specific reforms in chapter 4. My main points are that (1) sovereignty and democracy involve crucially different issues with respect to the possibilities for integrating international and domestic rule making; (2) democracy involves process requirements that are not equivalent to the processes that yield market outcomes; and (3) the opportunities for meaningful democracy are greater at the domestic level in anticipation of WTO action than afterwards, in the compliance context.

A trade-off between WTO decision making and democratic sovereign states is not inevitable, no matter how real the tensions may be in specific cases. Rather, a conceptual emphasis on sovereignty (as if sovereignty were synonymous with democracy) paradoxically exacerbates the democracy deficit in globalization. I propose turning the equation the other way: democracy in global governing institutions, broadly construed, produces sovereignty. The WTO and domestic lawmaking can mutually reinforce the other's democratic procedures without requiring us to consign ourselves to a formal view of democracy satisfied simply by the representation of individual states in an international body. American lawmaking can preserve and expand its democratic robustness through the political and administrative process, while also increasing participation and transparency at the WTO and other arenas of international and transnational governance.

The WTO is a traditional, state-centered organization. It is an intergovernmental institution whose membership is made up of 140 states, a fact that arguably makes it global; however, this fact makes it an international institution, not a global one. The distinction is important, in that internationalization is by definition statecentric.

In the relationship established by treaty between the WTO and U.S. domestic law, there appears to be relatively little discretion allowed at the domestic level once the WTO finds a U.S. statute or rule in violation of a trade agreement. In theory, the United States need not follow a WTO ruling, as our domestic law makes clear.[114] But in reality, it would not be practical to be a member and fail to adhere to the treaty. In this context, it is easy to see why a democracy deficit might arise under such circumstances. The processes involved at the domestic level often can have a distinct rubber-stamp quality to them. Compliance proceedings at the WTO level are quite limited in terms of who may participate and how transparent the process actually is. When these WTO decisions are considered at the domestic level, there is often little choice but to comply, though this may be done in various ways. Harmonization and equivalency proceedings seek to adapt domestic rules to international standards, but by the time these rules are available for comment at the domestic level, there is seldom much chance to change them in any significant way.[115]

Indeed, the processes involved for conforming the domestic laws of the United States to the mandates of the WTO do not match the full range of debate and deliberation that produced them. I agree with the critics who focus their reform efforts on the WTO to the extent that the procedures used by the WTO are essential to its legitimacy and effectiveness.[116] However, the democracy-deficit problem cannot be cured within the WTO alone unless democracy in purely representative terms is defined very narrowly.[117] The requirements of U.S. sovereignty can perhaps be satisfied by this formal condition, but the rubber-stamp quality to the domestic law produced in response to the WTO would remain no matter how full and fair the processes at the WTO may have been. Thus, addressing the democracy deficit means attending to the aspects of democracy that are "not covered" at the domestic level by the fact of state representation or even an improved competitive market outcome.

It is at this juncture that the limitations of state-centered approaches, especially those that privilege the market, become clear. The requirements of sovereignty are perhaps satisfied by reliance on the executive branch to represent our interests at the WTO and in the negotiation of the treaty beforehand in the harmonized rules that follow, but the requirements of democracy are broader. Democracy is not the same as sovereignty, nor is it the same as the market. Improved process at the WTO level and maximal compliance at the local level cannot satisfy the demands of democracy nor provide legitimacy for the substantial impact of WTO rulings. A greater degree of domestic administrative democracy is also necessary.

The Relationship of the WTO to Domestic Law

Democratization of compliance and harmonization are more likely to be accomplished if we consider the interaction of WTO requirements and domestic law not as two distinct and separate legal systems in a strict hierarchical relationship to each other (as if it were simply a projection of the federal arrangement) but as a single ongoing process in which many institutions with diverse constituencies and powers are in an ongoing dialogue. One model for such a process is the administrative agency. WTO rules and rulings are the logical outcomes of a delegation of law-making authority by treaty to what one commentator has called "the international branch"—the international branch of government.[118] Importantly, as I suggested earlier, that branch need not be imagined as replicating the federal structure of the United States as a whole. Rather, it could be understood as an extension of the administrative agencies—intersecting arenas of specialists whose deliberations are subject to basic democratic requirements. In this sense, effective global governance does not imply a suspension of national sovereignty or a universal "demos" but rather a vigorous *national* demos that is maximally engaged internally and externally.

The process of fixing a relevant baseline for democracy can start from the premise that the law-making process does not end with the passage of a domestic law. It continues at the international level—for purposes pursuant to U.S. treaty agreements. But what does this make of the WTO? Given the fact that 140 states are involved and there are in effect 140 principles governing this agent, the WTO is clearly likely to be an agency with more than the usual amounts of independence and autonomy (at least in the global era). Is it a distinct administrative entity in and of itself? This is an important question for purposes of determining the kinds of processes that may be necessary to legitimate its actions from a domestic democracy standpoint.

Domestic and international regimes are interdependent in ways that require an understanding of how the levels of multilayered global governance can work. Organizations such as the WTO are not mere extensions of the states that have created them—agents, if you will, that are legitimate solely by virtue of their statecentric beginnings and the participation of national representatives. Nor are they wholly separate governmental entities unto themselves, carrying out their functions without regard to the interconnected and interdependent regimes of which they are a part. Instead, they are part of an intricate layering of governance networks that now include states, nonstate actors, and various inter- and supranational entities, as well as the member states that constitute their primary governing bodies. At their best they serve as a bridge between and among not only the member states involved but also the growing number of transnational nonstate actors with a stake in the outcome and important nonstate perspectives to contribute to the issues involved. They enable the process of governing to broaden to one of governance.

The shift from government to governance encourages a pluralistic conception of the role of the WTO, one that implies a concept of globalization that goes beyond the traditional statecentric models that often dominate analysis of such entities. It also requires an approach to democracy that allows for the possibility of transnational democracy and forms of legitimacy that go beyond voting to include forms of transparency and opportunities for multiple actors and the networks they represent to participate in the decision-making processes of the WTO. In short, the statecentric nature of the WTO, with its membership consisting only of states, ought not to limit the way we think about the relationship of its rulings to global processes and domestic law, not to speak of the various networks with which it intersects. To explain why this is so, it is necessary in the next section to focus on globalization as a form of denationalization.

Globalization as Denationalization

As I indicated at the outset, most observers see globalization as essentially an international field comprised of states acting together. Seeing globalization instead as intersecting fields of transnational actors, both inside and outside the state sphere, yields a richer account of democratic possibilities. Commentary on the WTO, both for and against, emerges from all the various points along this spectrum: each position corresponding to a different diagnosis and prescription for improving the legitimacy of the WTO or curing the democracy deficit. Considering globalization as denationalization, i.e., as intersecting transnational fields of state and nonstate actors, facilitates understanding WTO processes as inherently pluralistic. Multiple actors are involved (state and nonstate), representing various national and transnational networks in a set of relationships. These relationships amount to governance more than government.

Viewed as denationalization, globalization draws attention to processes that are essentially deterritorialized and even largely independent of states. This is especially true of economic, social, and cultural processes, but it also includes various law- and norm-creating processes that are mainly outside the political structures of nation states and international organizations. These are dynamic processes that take place within an integrated whole without regard to geographical boundaries. Conflating the global and the international neglects important differences between them and important resources for simultaneously strengthening both the effectiveness of the WTO and the relevance of democracy among its member states. States thus remain highly relevant to our analysis. This is particularly true given the intergovernmental nature of the WTO; however, the essence of globalization as denationalization is the recognition that along with states, nonstate actors (as well as international and supranational bodies) are all significant players.

Such a view of globalization necessitates a concept of governance, namely, one that includes more than just states as actors, decision makers, and implementers of the policies agreed upon. States alone cannot solve global problems or fully take advantage of global market opportunities. As Philippe Schmitter notes,

> Governance is a method/mechanism for dealing with a broad range of problems/conflicts in which actors regularly arrive at mutually satisfactory and binding decisions by negotiating and deliberating with each other and cooperating in the implementation of these decisions. Its core rests on horizontal forms of interaction among actors sufficiently independent of each other so that none can impose a solution on the other— and yet sufficiently interdependent so that each would lose if no solution were found.[119]

The essence of such a conception of cooperation and the successful exercise of power is that it depends less on hierarchy and more on the inclusion of the relevant networks of actors involved. The statecentric nature of the WTO's structure and the legal power it can wield are not at all inconsistent with a denationalized perspective on globalization. The breadth and impact of its decisions, which are truly global in a denationalized way, create, foster, and encourage stakeholders other than territorially bounded actors such as states. This is especially true when the decisions involve nontariff barriers to trade such as environmental laws. Indeed, a denationalized perspective makes broad-based participation and a transparent decision-making process a natural part of any institution that is global in its impact. The cross-cutting nature of the issues and the players involved requires a process at least as broad as the impact of its outcomes.

A denationalized perspective on globalization highlights the need to emphasize networks and multiple decision sites and, if you will, a kind of global pluralism when it comes to understanding how the global economy evolves and, in a sense, regulates itself. Pluralism does not mean relativism in this context, but rather a decentralized system of deliberative decision making that is interconnected by at least some common values and practices of legitimation. A pluralist system is open to processes and actors that conceptualize problems and opportunities in ways that are not bound by jurisdictional boundaries. Problems of pollution, for example, are not bounded by territory, and even economic opportunities such as free trade involve the conception of markets that are not—in theory, at least—limited by state jurisdictional lines.

Governance involves the resolution of transnational problems such as these, as well as implementation of the policies necessary to carry out the agreed-upon solutions. Indeed, the inclusion of affected actors with a stake in the outcome is an integral part of the legitimacy of the process, not only because of process reasons but also because of the practical concerns that flow from implementation of the policies involved. An important aspect of legitimacy is the fact that agreed-upon solutions are implemented. Nonstate actors play an important role in this process. But to make the legitimation that flows from such a process work at the international stage, it also needs to be a part of the domestic process as well. The two systems are not separate. Legitimacy flows from the way decisions are made in both arenas.

A denationalized approach to globalization naturally yields a conception of democracy that is pluralistic in nature and extends well beyond national states. Along with a shift from government to governance and from hierarchy to network, appreciating the extent to which globalization involves important elements of denationalization informs a shift of emphasis away from a federalist analogy to the relationship of international organizations to domestic law toward the more pragmatic, pluralist, and flexible arrangements by which national and international legitimacy and democracy might be strengthened simultaneously. Indeed, advocates of the federalist analogy restrict their attention to applications and compliance, subsuming issues of democratic participation within the constraints of sovereignty as representation by states. The more pluralist approach, in which the WTO is not a suprafederal structure but an agency among states, obviates questions of a single or unified "world demos" in favor of a plural demos for whom democracy is not just a structural question (of state representation) but also a basis for inclusion in substantive and procedural terms.

As implied earlier, such inclusion should not be limited to states. Indeed (paradoxically, perhaps), it is precisely the inclusion of entities and groups that define themselves without regard to borders that would create the conditions for developing the kind of demos necessary for improving the legitimacy of outcomes reached for states.

In chapter 4, I will return to some specific arguments for increasing the legitimacy of the WTO and for privileging our own domestic processes (at least at the harmonization stage). Beginning with the proposition that globalization is a form of denationalization, and considering the implications of this formulation for reform, we can better understand a number of things: why legitimacy requires broader decision-making processes at the international level so as to include a wide range of nonstate actors; why it is necessary to rely on our own domestic law-making processes as the best way of ensuring a public voice and a flourishing political arena for contesting international rulings that should not be rubber stamped; and why (and where) there is untapped space in the emerging global legal order and more room for dissonance than more statecentric concepts of globalization might seem to allow.

3

Privatization and Deregulation

The Horizontal Dimensions
of Globalization

Chapter 2 focused on the vertical dimensions of the impact of globalization on state actors, considering federalism as a suprastate arrangement, as well as on the supranational institutions of the international sphere and their relationships to the United States as a single member state. This chapter turns to the horizontal dimensions of globalization, by which I mean primarily privatization and some types of deregulation. The main examples involve the privatization of prisons and social services. These examples highlight the ways the global era's formula of deregulation through (and to) the private sector contract public discourse around economic terms alone. Later we shall turn to the question of how wider values—beyond profitability and efficiency—might be reintroduced to the administrative state by means of widening public participation as well as transparency. In this chapter, though, we focus on planned and de facto delegations of power to the private sector. Outsourcing public functions to the private sector are planned delegations to the market. The democracy issues raised by privatization and globalization, however, are especially apparent in de facto contexts such as the implicit authorization of child labor or slave wages, but they are inherent in any context where public functions are delegated to the private sector. This is not to say that the public could or should be directly involved in all such delegations, but for our purposes, understanding the pervasiveness of the democracy deficit as a structural matter must come before any discussion of criteria and means for widening public involvement and government accountability.

In contrast to European countries, government ownership of industries such as electric utility companies, communications companies, or airlines has been rare in the United States.[1] The U.S. approach to fulfilling the public interest in such services has been to regulate the private enterprises that provide them. As a consequence, as we have seen in chapter 1, much of the global era has been dominated by privatization and deregulation, rather than through the sale of governmentally owned enterprises.

Both privatization and deregulation take many forms. Some forms of deregulation, such as those accomplished by legislation, result in the outright repeal of regulatory structures and agency enabling acts.[2] Others, instituted by administrative agencies themselves, result in the repeal of some rules and/or their replacement with rules that use markets and market approaches as regulatory tools, thereby replacing command-control regulatory approaches with incentive-based regulation.[3] It is important to remember the often-neglected point that such uses of the market and market-based approaches are, in this sense, a means to an end, not ends in themselves. At the federal agency level, such forms of deregulation are usually subject to the Administrative Procedures Act (APA).[4] The APA treats an agency's repeal or change of an existing rule,[5] for example, the same way procedurally as it treats the promulgation of a new rule. In other words, for purposes of the APA, deregulation is a form of regulation. Accordingly, as we noticed in chapter 1, substitution of market approaches for more direct regulation has usually been upheld by reviewing courts, particularly when economic regulation has been involved.[6] We reviewed the New Deal origins of this particular form of judicial deference in chapter 1.

There are many forms and degrees of congressional and agency deregulation. Similarly, privatization can also take many forms, each representing a different "degree of separation" between the public body delegating its responsibilities and the private actors to whom that delegation is addressed. As Professor Lester Salamon has noted, privatization in the United States has meant the development of new forms of governance.[7] He uses the term "the new governance" for the variety of tools that government at all levels now employs in carrying out its public functions, including contracting out (also known as outsourcing), grants, tax expenditures, vouchers, direct loans, government corporations, and franchises.[8]

Like deregulation, some forms of privatization result from legislative action—aimed at providing a market in place of a regulatory regime. The legislature may, for example, sell off a governmentally owned entity to private parties, as was common in Europe in the 1980s.[9] Like the deregulation that results from the wholesale statutory repeal of a regulatory regime,[10] the market in these instances is intended to replace the government completely when government-owned assets are sold to private buyers.

Perhaps the most common form of privatization in the United States (and the primary focus of this chapter) is the use of the private sector to deliver what once were governmentally provided social services. The primary governance tool in these cases is the contract. The management of prisons, for example, has been increasingly outsourced to the private sector at both the federal and state levels.[11] Garbage and snow removal also are now commonly handled by private providers,[12] and various aspects of welfare administration,[13] such as eligibility determinations, are carried out by private entities as well. Contracting out for such purposes is akin to agency deregulation in that government agencies remain involved but now use the private sector to carry out their statutorily mandated goals. In the outsourcing contexts, the governmental agency is still responsible for the services provided, but opts for a private means to achieve public ends. A major difference between this kind of privatization and deregulation, however, is the fact that privatization involves the government's delegation of responsibility for services to private actors, whereas supervision of even the deregulated activity remains within the governmental agency involved. When federal governmental agencies employ market incentives or market-based rules to carry out their goals, their outcomes constitute regulatory action by state actors.[14] As federal agencies, they are subject to American public law, including the requirements of the due process clause, the Administrative Procedures Act, and the Freedom of Information Act. When agencies contract out for social services, however, the resulting public/private partnerships implicate administrative law in ways that are more complex than when an administrative agency remains directly involved in the regulatory process.[15] It is possible that some private providers might be considered, under some circumstances, to be state actors for purposes of the due process clause, but even if that is the case, neither the APA nor the Freedom of Information Act would apply. Moreover, our process requirements, as imposed by federal courts, are now less extensive and predictable as the so-called due process explosion has largely contracted under the Rehnquist Court rulings.[16]

My main argument in this chapter is that the privatization in the public sector should be understood as a principle effect of globalization in the United States. We have seen how the history of administrative law since the New Deal opened the way to this effect, and how the new federalism continues to reproduce its structural elements. Thus, privatization is not merely one means among others for making government more efficient or for expanding the private sector. Nor is it just an expression of current political trends as the regulatory pendulum swings from liberal to conservative. Rather, the increasing reliance on "the new governance" is indicative of a changing relationship between the market and the state itself.

As I explain in the next section, my term for this dynamic relationship is the "globalizing state." The globalizing state is characterized by a fusion of public and private values, rhetorics, and regulatory practices (including deregulation). The fusion is itself integral to the interdependence of global and local economies. Privatization is both the engine and the outcome of that interdependence, increasing the exposure of the state to external economic and political pressures that in turn tend to accelerate globalization, since private actors fully exposed to the global economy are now charged with carrying out delegated state tasks. The global political economy places great pressures on all entities, public and private, to be cost effective.[17] In the United States, this has further encouraged such delegations of power to the private sector. Do the cost savings that result from such public delegations to private entities occur at the expense of democracy, legitimacy, and individual justice? Are these cost savings real or imagined?[18] The answers given by our actions to date suggest "yes" rather than "no."

Given the role that the public/private distinction plays in U.S. administrative law, the globalizing state is one in which privatization tends to correspond to a reduced democratic public sphere. In lieu of public debate within the institutions of government, privatization favors other arrangements less likely to be transparent and accountable to the public, and less exposed to competing noneconomic value regimes. This is an important source of the democracy deficit. The pragmatics of globalization make privatization the critical terrain on which a new administrative law might respond to the democracy deficit by assuring public forums for input and debate, as well as a flow of information that can help create a meaningful politics around the decisions of private actors.

The changes in the global political economy that are known under the rubric of globalization are fundamental and fundamentally structural in nature. They are the result of a new kind of complexity in the interplay of various legal jurisdictions: the broadening of economic and political networks, a technology-driven capacity for rapid change and response to change, and an increasingly large number of powerful nonstate actors—actors who, in large part, derive their power from an ability to operate simultaneously in a number of jurisdictions within and across state and national boundaries. The changing nature of the individuals and entities that make up the state itself also contribute to the globalizing state. The rhetoric of global competition may provide the United States with what appears to be a wholly domestic agenda—without discounting the reality of competition—but it masks fundamental changes in the underlying nature of the state, as well as the new realities of global competition and of the way states respond to this new situation.

The Relationship of Globalization to Domestic Law and Politics: Three Approaches

The global economy encourages a politics of competitiveness that is both real and, at times, excessive. The values of competition resonate with certain fundamental values such as liberty and individualism, and they can give credence to traditional domestic arguments that have long been part of the political debates over the appropriate roles of government vis-à-vis the market, especially the federal government.[19] For analytical purposes, it is helpful to differentiate among three approaches to the nature of the state as a subject and object of domestic law reform and politics, recognizing, of course, that such approaches overlap in many ways. Still, they also represent significantly different visions of the state and thus different starting points for an analysis of the prospects for reform.

One approach involves a conception of a strong state, capable of imposing its will at home and, if necessary, abroad. A common version of this approach seeks to revive laissez-faire capitalism in the context of global capitalism, by linking domestic economic reform with economic approaches that dominate at the global level. To this end, strong-state laissez-faire proponents emphasize the importance of low taxes and minimal regulation.[20] This approach sometimes coincides with libertarian approaches to constitutional issues, such as the takings clause of the Fifth Amendment, or other constitutional interpretive approaches that limit substantially the regulatory powers of government, especially the federal government.[21] Alternatively, other strong-state regulators believe it is possible to maintain and improve upon current regulatory structures and approaches to achieve domestic goals.[22]

A second approach represents the state as the object of "reinvention." The reinvention-of-government movement[23] seeks to streamline government to make it more competitive and efficient. As different as the more market-oriented discourse sounds when it comes to discussing citizens as customers, there is also an implied status quo aspect to this approach to governance. It assumes that producing a government that works better and costs less can result only from structural and procedural changes within the government itself rather than from substantive changes.[24] The market and market forces are but means to ends, and those ends often are intended to be essentially the same as before. Market approaches and market discourses, however, can change more than just the means by which governments act. Not all public-law values are capable of being translated into a cost-benefit discourse.[25] Inevitably, there is something lost in translation when citizens are viewed primarily as customers or consumers rather than active participants in the public policy issues the provision of government services embody. Moreover, at times, the attempt to apply a market discourse to regulatory problems may be a substitute for a kind of procedural laissez-faireism, falling more into the first category above. There are limits to the extent to which the market metaphor can apply effectively to public services or functions without changing outcomes.

The third approach to law reforms is closely akin to the efficient state model I just described. As already noted, we shall call this approach the "globalizing state" because the state is being transformed by the processes of globalization even while it plays an active role in those processes. It is both an agent of globalization and an entity that is itself shaped and changed by these very processes of which it is a part. This approach blends public and private power in ways aimed at maintaining the importance of a public role, even though a market discourse may be prominent. Moreover, the use of the market and market approaches does not necessarily imply a status quo ante approach. Performing governmental tasks more efficiently is not the only goal. Change in the form, structure, and substance of regulatory approaches is also contemplated. Indeed, the globalizing state seeks to maintain a public perspective on transnational issues as well as to recognize that multigovernmental approaches and the involvement of nonstate actors may be increasingly necessary if the state is to be active, even in issues that once were thought to be wholly private and domestic in nature.

Delegating Power to Domestic Private Actors

The public/private distinction once demarcated two relatively separate worlds: government and the private market.[26] Private capital markets tended to be primarily local, and capital had little mobility;[27] however, "private" in this sense has long passed into history. Moreover, deregulation and the various other regulatory reforms we earlier called the efficiency state have merged the public and the private in various ways, utilizing what were previously primarily private-market means of advancing public-interest goals.[28] Given the dynamic aspects of the globalizing state, and the fact that the state is an agent transformed by the processes of globalization, it is important to understand fully the global implications of these various market-oriented reforms at the legislative, administrative-agency, and judicial levels. In this section, I shall examine three contexts in which globalization affects public and private power.

Congressional Delegation to the Market

The globalization of the private sector has profound influences on public, domestic, and international law making. Given the pluralistic nature of our law-making processes, these changes encourage harmonization, if not deregulation or privatization of these very processes. The infusion of market forces is facilitated by the fact that public-oriented, participatory processes already give the private, globalized sector very definite roles to play in law making. This opening to the private sector begins at the legislative stage, when Congress considers new legislation.[29]

The purest kind of deregulation is that which removes governmental regulation altogether.[30] For example, during the Carter administration, when the head of the Civil Aeronautics Board (CAB), Alfred Kahn, declared that airplanes were, in effect, "marginal costs with wings,"[31] his view was based on his belief that that industry was an essentially competitive one and price regulation was not necessary. The administration advocated deregulation of the industry, as well as the abolition of the CAB itself. Congress agreed, and it passed the Airline Deregulation Act of 1978.[32] Similarly, when President Reagan took office in 1981, one of his first official acts, by executive order, was to deregulate completely the price of oil at the wellhead,[33] a process that had begun pursuant to the

Emergency Petroleum Allocation Act.[34] Oil producers were now subject to the discipline of a competitive market, and (it was argued) there was no need for governmental intervention. The same reasoning applied to the trucking industry, leading to its deregulation and ultimately to the Clinton administration's support for Congress's abolition of the Interstate Commerce Commission.[35]

In all of these examples (and more) the deregulation involved was relatively pure—Congress or, in the case of oil pricing, the president removed completely certain aspects of the regulatory structure based on the assumption that a free and fair market existed and that the market itself would protect consumers. The line between the public and the private could thus be seen as a bright one, with deregulation indicating a clear preference for the private ordering of market forces.

Those who adhered to a strong-state laissez-faire philosophy greeted these reforms with enthusiasm. At the same time, advocates of a strong regulatory state could rationalize these decisions as well. The theory of airline deregulation was that it would actually lower prices for consumers and abolish the role of an administrative agency that had, in effect, been captured by the very industry it sought to regulate.[36] The same can be said of trucking deregulation and the abolition of the Interstate Commerce Commission.[37] Oil pricing deregulation also occurred at a point when oil prices were coming down and competition could be trusted to create affordable sources of energy for consumers of average means. In this sense, these deregulatory decisions were very much in accord with the theory of the efficient state, as well. A large, costly bureaucracy was not necessary to yield the lower prices the market could now provide. This was another example where the government could accomplish its end results with less cost to society.

Both the strong and efficient state rationales, however, depend on a state-centered form of analysis. They assume the state can make such decisions largely on its own and that the decision to resort to the market is completely voluntary. They also assume that there is a clear divide between the public and the private. Thus, in the case of price controls on airlines, trucking, or oil, proponents of deregulation argued in terms of their philosophical and practical, political reasons to relinquish a governmental role and return these activities to the rigors of the marketplace.

Viewing these changes through the prism of the globalizing state does not require disagreement with the results reached in these particular examples, but it does require a different analysis entailing different implications for federal power and the political process. First, by eschewing any bright-line distinctions between the public and the private, this concept of the state starts from the premise that what is involved is not a liberation, but a delegation of power by government to the private sector. The deregulatory reforms of the Carter, Reagan, Bush, Clinton, and even Bush II administrations were politically "sold" as if they were a form of consumer legislation. Indeed, whether it was airline prices in the 1970s, oil prices in the 1980s, trucking prices in the 1990s, or prescription drugs for seniors in 2003,[38] the promise of these deregulatory reforms was lower prices for consumers.

The same continues to be true today in the Bush administration. Lower taxes are held out as the primary way the economy might revive, and, in the process, lift all boats on a sea of economic prosperity. Advocates argue that health care as well as social security will also benefit from a heavy dose of privatization and the discipline of markets.[39]

Whether or not one agrees with these reforms, it remains the case that when wholesale market reform is undertaken by legislation, the resulting privatization, initially, at least, avoids the democracy problems otherwise associated with globalization.[40] The fundamental decision to deregulate at the legislative level was the subject of democratic debate, open legislative processes and, ultimately, a vote. The return of these pricing functions to the private sector was accompanied by a legislative understanding not only that there were competitive markets involved but also that the results of those markets would be favorable to consumers. The privatization that resulted did not, therefore, take power away from citizens. There was also a kind of regulatory discipline added, the kind that a well-functioning market can provide.

Quite apart from such substantive deregulatory reforms, other recent deregulatory reforms at the legislative level deal explicitly with the global economy and focus as much on the process of legislative change as on its substance. For example, recent legislative proposals involving fast-track legislation for trade bills seek to enhance the president's autonomy and to limit the legislature's role in the process of considering trade legislation by limiting its power to amend legislation on the floor of the House or Senate.[41] In other words, with certain kinds of trade legislation, there must be an up or down vote. Unlike the democratic approaches to deregulatory legislation described above, such proposals to deregulate the legislative process itself should raise democracy concerns.[42] Perhaps the outer edges of a deregulated legislative process tailored to produce globally influenced legislation is the treaty process itself. The nature of this process is that a treaty can be ratified with a two-thirds vote of the Senate alone. Executive agreements do not require even the Senate's approval.[43]

Just as administrative agencies initially were more successful in deregulating their respective areas of the law than Congress,[44] they are also more likely to be responsive to globalization processes. Agencies are less publicly visible; they often deal with highly technical issues that are not easily politicized, and they can engage in a focused, substantive dialogue through the administrative process with those entities and interests most likely to be affected by them. The fact that administrative agencies would increasingly resort to market tools and market discourse is the result of the kind of synthesis that goes on as agencies seek not just to be responsibly responsive to the interests with which they deal but to be effective as well. These market approaches and outcomes are very much in accord with the direction that pressures from international organizations like the WTO create. Markets and market outcomes are increasingly privileged from multiple directions.

Administrative Agencies and the Market as a Regulatory Tool

Legislative deregulation through privatization can be usefully distinguished from an agency's substitution of markets for command and control regulation. Perhaps the most extensive U.S. example of this approach is the use of market regulation by the Environmental Protection Agency (EPA).[45] Rather than trying to mandate precisely how certain industries might lower their pollution levels, the EPA has sought to provide market incentives to achieve such goals, creating, for example, a market for pollution reduction by selling pollution permits. Those industries capable of lowering their pollution below mandated levels can receive compensation from those companies unable to meet their goal.[46] Using the market in this way is a form of deregulation in that it provides more alternatives to the regulated for achieving certain policy goals and more flexibility for regulated entities in determining how best to achieve them. Such approaches usually are less costly to implement and enforce.

As we have seen above, such approaches mesh very well with concepts of the efficiency state. Despite the market-based nature of these rules and programs, however, such regulatory regimes are the products of Administrative Procedure Act processes and are thus subject to standard public-law procedural requirements notice, public participation, and a clear statement of the basis and purpose of the rules involved, even those that rescind previously existing rules. Yet, it is this very openness to the viewpoints and arguments of global participants that contributes to the globalization of rule making. In other words, it is one way in which domestic processes democratize and, in effect, renationalize various global processes, thereby furthering, albeit indirectly, economic integration and regulatory harmonization. This can occur in a mechanical fashion, with little opportunity to consider alternatives to proposed rules. For example, as we saw in chapter 2 (and will explore further in chapter 4), some of the processes of harmonization that accompany WTO agreements use APA administrative processes but do so in a manner that renders them little more than a rubber stamp for harmonization decisions negotiated by the executive branch.[47] The closed nature of the negotiating process is even worse when standards established by private parties internationally are then introduced into the rule-making process with a presumption of correctness.[48]

For those who see the globe as a potential marketplace, a great deal is at stake in such law-making processes, especially if business is facing competition from firms that play by different and often less exacting rules in other foreign jurisdictions. In pursuit of a competitive edge, the private sector may press government for standardization or harmonization in the regulatory areas that ultimately affect them.[49]

The essence of globalization is that it involves cultural, economic, and social processes that usually have little directly to do with any one particular state. The processes of globalization are, in effect, denationalized processes. This fact does not mean that domestic law will not apply to some aspects of these processes, but rather that the law that does emerge includes and is affected by these denationalizing forces. I am not arguing that globalization is necessarily good for business or that globalization is a natural process. Rather, this discussion is aimed at highlighting two important aspects of this process: (1) how the public sector is fused with the private sector; and (2) how the private sector fuses the global into local transactions.

Thus, for example, when certain private groups propose or support certain types of environmental or safety regulation, they often seek to encourage adoption of approaches that, to a large extent, further their harmonization goals. In an important sense, then, the political, domestic rule-making processes in which such actors participate serve, in effect, as a means of renationalizing a set of rules driven by global as opposed to solely national concerns. The end result may be the provision of a U.S. regulatory stamp to a set of rules that are more global in their outlook and creation than they are local or national. This process furthers a kind of deep integration of the national economy with the global economy. The market-oriented rules that often result need not be exactly like those in other jurisdictions, but they are likely to be reasonably compatible with other legal systems, making it easier for transnational nonstate actors to carry out their operations more efficiently, as well as for states to retain and to compete more effectively for their business.[50] The question that emerges is, when are we nationalizing or rubber stamping law that was made in a denationalized way without broad public input?

This relationship between the ways public law-making processes can incorporate and translate private, global perspectives and interests into binding rules is paralleled, to some extent, by the relationship between such processes of deep integration and democracy. To the extent that integration occurs essentially outside of national or state legal structures with, for example, the development of a global system of rules that facilitates the goals of transnational actors, such rules are less likely to have anything to do with a state's democratic processes. Though global law can develop in the shadow of the state, it is, usually, a private creation, controlled by the needs of the nonstate actors.

If the invocation and use of the market is seen only in statecentric terms, however, the debate over globalization that ensues is likely to be the familiar contest between pro- and antigovernment or pro- and antimarket advocates that has dominated policy and politics to date. As this book argues, however, it is necessary to go beyond conceptions of the market and the state that depend upon bright-line distinctions between the public and the private. It is also necessary that we understand that using one discourse or the other does not necessarily, for legal and constitutional purposes, render some activity either public or private.

In many ways the examples of public/private mixtures of power discussed at length in the next section are emblematic of the global era and our need to understand clearly how much is at stake as we begin to redefine what we mean by public and private. In the process, it is important to maintain the broader values and goals of administrative law, including the ability to foster democratic involvement in a multitude of decision-making forums. In other words, in addition to the perspective of an individual litigant, there are the information and politics that can flow from citizen involvement in the creation of rules and policy and not just in their application and enforcement.

Contracting Out Public Services

So far we have considered two kinds of regulatory reform: the substitution of markets for state control through legislation and the use of markets and market incentives by administrative agencies to achieve their legislatively mandated goals. In this section we take up a third category of regulatory reform that combines aspects of both of those reforms, yet is nonetheless distinct. In this context, the state may not be relieved of the responsibility of accomplishing certain tasks, but it need not do them itself. Contracting out (or outsourcing) tasks once performed by government to the private sector turns such tasks as snow removal, garbage collection, and the management of prisons over to the market. The tasks, though performed by private companies, clearly remain public responsibilities and, as we shall see, the market is often more a metaphor than a reality. On the other hand, using the private sector in this way enables the state to take advantage of such efficiencies of the market as exist.

The performance of these public functions by private entities is not ordinarily supported by any of the traditional administrative procedures involved in formulating the market-oriented rules normally used by administrative agencies. Rather, the language of the market is often substituted for that of administrative law. In this language, citizens are referred to as if they were only consumers of these public services, and not expected to be involved in deciding how services should be provided. Such a paternalistic approach may increase the efficiency of the private company engaged in the service in question, but it is likely to do so at the expense of fundamental public-law values.

Contracts involving public services are more complex than contracts between two individuals participating in a market economy.[51] A distinction must be drawn between customers and consumers.[52] For example, when a city enters into a contract with the provider of a street-cleaning service, the customer is, in effect, the city, but the consumers are those who live on and use city streets. The decision to provide this service is a public one and the price charged (through user fees or taxes) is not necessarily the market price from a consumer-sovereignty point of view.[53] The amount charged may be equal to, above, or below the market price.

This is not, in other words, the kind of market transaction that results when the consumers of a product are also the primary customers.

Thus, opting for the private sector as a politically preferred alternative to government, coupled with a politics that substitutes the results and processes of a private ordering system for those of a public-law approach, may make what is, in fact, a public decision appear to be private. Indeed, one of the most important tasks courts have in resolving disputes that flow from the way these public/private arrangements are perceived is to determine how best to conceptualize these mixtures of public and private power.

The limits of the market metaphor are even more apparent when applied to privatized prisons. Private prisons differ significantly from public-services contracts for street cleaning or snow removal. The customers in the private prison context are, as before, the state or federal agencies that seek to hire private-prison service providers. But who are the consumers? If anything, communities are more akin to third-party beneficiaries of this contract, not its consumers. If it is the inmates who are the consumers, they are not willing buyers of the service provided. And, of course, the demand for the product itself is set by the state's own criminal laws and its ability to enforce them. Thus, this kind of service is not marketable in any usual sense of that term. Counterintuitively, perhaps, the idea of private prisons differs only by degree from other public services, for which some citizens may be willing to pay additional or variable amounts for more of the services provided (such as private security forces or gated communities)[54]—but not all or always, as in the case of good schools or even the flouridation of water.

The kind of rhetoric that contractual approaches to public services might apply in other contexts is, thus, not applicable here. This is not a case of increasing individual autonomy and freedom. In the prison context, outsourcing is primarily an attempt by the state to lower its costs and to operate prisons more efficiently by encouraging competition among prison providers.[55] Indeed, some states, in their search for the lowest-cost providers of the service, have even explored the possibilities of "off-shore prisons." Arizona, for example, has considered using Mexico as a site for the construction and administration of new prison facilities necessary to house some of its prisoners.[56]

It would seem that, under such circumstances, the contract between the state and the private provider involved would mandate an extension of state power into what otherwise would be a state-run facility. Yet, as we shall see, there are reasons to resist either/or thinking in this context, even though the privatized prison would seem to be an obvious extension of the public. More important, the privatization movement vis-à-vis prisons also can be motivated by factors beyond costs. To the extent that the private sector is viewed as tougher, it is also seen by some as more efficient than the state. Efficiency in this context takes into account the rights of prisoners, which are increasingly considered as involving unnecessary "costs" (literally and figuratively) to the taxpayers. We consider these issues in more detail in the next section.

Private Prisons and the Global Economy

Global competition has, as we have seen, focused on the need for individuals, corporate entities, and states to be maximally competitive. This has spawned a rhetoric that, along with the drive for efficiency, can be intensely antistate in its assumptions, as well. Any number of state functions, when compared to the ideal of the market, usually come up short.[57] As noted above,[58] however, it is very difficult to compare public duties with pure market approaches when only outsourcing is involved. Private prisons, in particular, do not fit easily into the private-ordering, contractual model.

Private prisons are not new in the history of the United States.[59] They were particularly common in the nineteenth century,[60] but they have reemerged as an important reform in the last fifteen years or so.[61] At hand there are many reasons for their popularity. As prisons have become overcrowded, privatized prisons offer an arguably lower-cost alternative to the state's building and managing more prisons on its own. The theory is that private-sector providers will compete among themselves for a state's business by providing for efficiently run and, in some instances, more efficiently built prisons than the government can provide.[62] Implicit in this approach is that every few years or so, at contract time, competition will reemerge, ensuring that the present provider is, in fact, the most efficient. This, of course, assumes that if the price of entry is the construction of a new facility, that is not a significant bar to future competition. But if only the management of prisons is involved, such competition theoretically can occur much more easily.[63]

When one compares private prisons to publicly managed facilities, the question arises as to what the bases of this competition might be. Clearly, if the competition is based on providing a secure and humane environment more cheaply than a public bureaucracy can do, private prisons increase the global competitive currency of a state in an acceptable manner. If some of these lower costs, however, derive from the fact that fewer constitutional protections are applied to private inmates than those held in public prisons, legal issues may arise that eventually may (and should) eliminate such forms of competition.[64] If there are no cost savings, then what is the driving force? Some new emerging literature suggests the ideological basis of the private prisons trend.[65]

Nevertheless, apart from the potential savings in cost that a more efficiently managed prison promises, there are other reasons, some of them dubious or even illegitimate, that also can fuel this transfer of functions from the public to the private sector. It is not entirely clear how far courts will go to extend constitutional protections such as due process, for example, to privately run prisons.[66] Were they to be exempt from all or part of these constitutional protections, they would be indicative of the worst of globalization trends—the removal of public rights and dialogues by the simple device of moving what was once public to the private sector. This is perhaps unlikely,[67] given the nature of the relationship between a contracting governmental body and a private prison provider, the states' duty to enforce their laws and house their criminals, and the various ways in which the market cannot apply with full rigor to such responsibilities.

Advocates of private prisons defend them in terms that reinforce some of the more retributive trends in current approaches to criminals and criminal behavior. In the views of some people, prisons exist primarily to punish those who break the law. For them, the impersonal harshness of the market may seem more appropriate for such law breakers, especially if it means that an efficiently run prison will not provide certain legal amenities or services that criminals will be deemed to have forfeited. A "no-nonsense" efficient market environment can be seen politically as being more punitive, thus also increasing the popularity of privatized prisons as a regulatory reform.[68]

How should the courts treat private prisons? The context of global competition requires courts ultimately to assess carefully not "just" what is public or what is private, but what the blend of these two systems should be. To do this, courts should be skeptical of labels and determine at what point the market becomes a metaphor that is inapplicable to the issues at hand. When that occurs, are the policies of the market appropriate for an institution that is privately run, but publicly required? When the market becomes more metaphorical than real, how should a court assess the blend of public and private power that results? To what extent can public input into private-prison decisions be required and how often should this occur? Finally, at what point should a court conclude that the global currency created from certain aspects of privatization should not be allowed? These are some of the key questions presented in *McKnight v. Richardson.*

McKnight v. Richardson

Ronnie Lee McKnight brought suit against two prison guards in a private prison in Tennessee. He alleged that they had violated his constitutional rights by injuring him with extremely tight physical restraints. He brought suit under section 1983 of the U.S. Code, even though he was incarcerated in a private prison. The private prison guards moved to dismiss, claiming the same kind of qualified immunity that would apply if they had been guards in a public prison facility. The U.S. district court, the court of appeals, and the Supreme Court all agreed that qualified immunity did not extend to private, as opposed to public, prison guards. Recognizing that section 1983 can sometimes result in the imposition of liability upon a private individual, all three courts resisted the application of a defense commonly used by public officials doing essentially the same job.

The Supreme Court split 5-4 on this issue. Writing for the majority, Justice Breyer found that there were no historical precedents mandating an extension of qualified immunity to private prison guards.[69] More importantly, Justice Breyer analyzed the market context in which immunity might apply and rejected its extension on policy grounds as well.[70] The dissent disagreed on the counts both of history and of policy. For the dissent, nothing in the past affirmatively prevented the extension of qualified immunity to private prisons. In fact, public and private prisons were functionally the same. For the dissent, the fact that there was no precedent barring the extension of this common-law-based immunity meant it could be applied.[71] For the majority, the fact that there was no precedent authorizing this extension was further evidence that the extension of this immunity was not required.[72]

It is at the policy level where the differences between the majority and the minority are particularly instructive. The mix of private and public

that the majority's decision sanctioned arguably would provide more protections for the prisoners than if qualified immunity were to extend to
them. The majority saw the use of the market more as a means of assuring certain public values than as an end to itself. Its refusal to adopt the
functional approach advocated by the dissent resulted in a complex approach to issues involving both citizen/consumers and prisoners. The majority's conclusion that private guards were not entitled to the qualified
immunity public-prison guards would receive was ironically premised on
public-law values, including the constitutional rights of the prisoners involved and an implicit argument that cost was not the only relevant factor in deciding how best to determine the appropriate public/private
blend in this case. In short, the results in this case are best explained by
seeing the majority's preference for a private approach as best serving the
needs of the prisoners involved, as well as the public's responsibility. The
dissent's more functional approach would have extended the public label
to this context, but primarily for cost considerations.

The Public/Private Mix

The majority analyzed the market approach of a private prison against
a backdrop of public law. In fact, in contrasting private prisons with public prisons, the majority implied that, in this context at least, public prisons seemed to embody the status quo:[73]

> [G]overnment employees typically act within a *different* system. They
> work within a system that is responsible through elected officials to vot-
> ers who, when they vote, rarely consider the performance of individual
> subdepartments or civil servants specifically and in detail. And that sys-
> tem is often characterized by multidepartment civil service rules that,
> while providing employee security, may limit the incentives or the ability
> of individual departments or supervisors flexibly to reward, or to pun-
> ish, individual employees.

Indeed, though the majority sought to describe two different systems or
worlds (the public and the private), it opted for the mixture of the two,
favoring greater reliance on the market when it came to advancing the
primary purpose of the immunity doctrine, namely, encouraging guards
to avoid either timid or overly aggressive behavior.[74] Indeed, in the public-prison context, immunity from suit was justified primarily on the

grounds that public guards should not have to fear that simply by doing their duty, they will be subjected to a lawsuit.[75]

For the majority, private prisons provided ample incentives for guards to behave properly, including more opportunities for market sensitive supervisors either to reward or to discipline them if they were too aggressive or not aggressive enough when dealing with prisoners.[76] In addition, the majority emphasized that in the private sector, it was commonly understood that the providers of the prison would purchase insurance coverage for guards who were held liable for damages resulting from prison lawsuits such as in this case.[77] Moreover, as the majority saw it, there also was more public input into this process when prisoners were, in fact, in private prisons. Since the prison contract expires after three years, its performance is disciplined not only by state review but also by pressure from potentially competing firms who can try to take its place.[78] In a sense, this three year review and the choice of other providers the state may have is a very effective way of ensuring public input that is focused and directed specifically towards the tasks of running a prison.[79] More important, by not extending immunity to the guards themselves, the court recognized but disregarded the significance of any distractions that might result from lawsuits. This was a small price to pay, given a continued and conceded need for determining constitutional violations.[80] Indeed, one could view the resulting jury trials as another form of public/citizen input into this private regime, one that does not normally exist in the public realm. In the context of qualified immunity, the use of market forces may, in fact, not only result in a well-run prison but actually enhance the prison's accountability and the public-input aspects of this regime. In short, the majority opted to treat private prisons as private when it came to the qualified immunity doctrine.

The Limits of the Market Metaphor

It is ironic that the more conservative wing of the Supreme Court, through Justice Scalia, would argue for a result that would extend the public aspect of prisons to this private regime. Justice Scalia, however, was not interested in drawing distinctions between the public and the private in this context. Indeed, opting for a functional approach to public and private prisons and their guards, the dissent could see no difference between the public and the private in the qualified immunity context.[81]

Prison guards performed the same functions no matter whether the prison was privately or publicly run. Not extending immunity in this context made little sense, the dissent argued,[82] and in fact, market incentives might actually encourage cost-cutting behavior that could be harmful to the prisons involved.[83] The insurance private providers regularly purchase could also be obtained by public prisons, and the bureaucratic complexity that made sanctions or rewards in the public sector difficult was not, in the dissent's view, necessarily required. In the final analysis, the dissent concluded that failure to extend immunity protection in this case only added to a private prison's costs;[84] it was, in effect, now a disincentive to privatize in the first instance.

Cost was an important reason underlying the dissent's desire to extend the public umbrella over privatized prisons. But more importantly for purposes of our discussion, also underlying the dissent's opinion was a bright-line approach for determining what was public, and what was private. This was clear in the way the dissent focused on the limits of the applicability of what it considered to be "real market" forces and, by implication, the limits of the market as a metaphor. The majority tested those limits against the policies it thought the approach might generate; the dissent tested those limits against micro-economic theory.

In fact, the dissent refused to use the market as a metaphor, or as a means of blending aspects of the public and the private. There was a clear line between the two, and this justified the "all public" approach it advocated:[85]

> [I]t is fanciful to speak of the consequences of "market pressures" in a regime where public officials are the only purchaser, and other people's money the medium of payment. Ultimately one prison-management firm will be selected to replace another prison-management firm, only if a decision is made by some *political* official not to renew the contract. This is a government decision, not a market choice.

The dissent goes on to discount the significance of public input at this point, and resists comparing that input to anything like a "real market" choice. The dissent does not suggest such input is impossible, but it certainly is unlikely:[86]

> The process can come to resemble a market choice only to the extent that the political actors *will* such resemblance—that is, to the extent

that political actors (1) are willing to pay attention to the issue of prison services, among the many issues vying for their attention, and (2) are willing to place considerations of cost and quality of service ahead of such political considerations as personal friendship, political alliances, in-state ownership of the contractor, etc.

In effect, the dissent refuses to recognize the market as a metaphor, and thus resists blending the public with the private, or the uses of the private, to accomplish public ends. As far as the dissent is concerned, the running of prisons is a public function, and it sees no difference between public prisons and prisons run on behalf of the public by private providers. The dissent's preference for the public is premised on the belief that a bright line exists between these two worlds, and that the real reason for opting for the private sector is price.[87] Since a contractor's profits must depend upon its costs, the end result of the majority's decision was, quite simply, to increase costs.[88] Under such circumstances private prison guards are in as much need of immunity as their public counterparts.[89]

Similarly, the dissent discounts the majority's reasoning regarding the differences privatization of prisons makes as far as insurance coverage is concerned, as well as the relatively easy ways that exist for private employers to discipline private employees.[90] The dissent finds it ironic that outsourcing prisons should result in rules that make them more expensive.[91] For the dissent, public prison guards can also purchase insurance,[92] and there is no reason why they need have so many civil law service restraints.[93]

More important, the dissent sees no difference between public and private prison guards when it comes to the constitutional rights of prisoners:[94]

> One would think that private prison managers whose § 1983 damages come out of their own pockets, as compared with public prison managers, whose § 1983 damages come out of the public purse, would, if anything, be more careful in training their employees to avoid constitutional infractions.

The dissent concluded that it saw no sense in the public/private distinction, nor does it "see what precisely it consists of."[95]

The methodology used by the majority in this case to determine whether a private or public perspective was to prevail resulted in a decision that favored the market approach for essentially public reasons. By resisting a precedent-bound historical approach, the majority was free to entertain a variety of policy arguments that in effect, applied private rationales for public ends. The dissent's more functional approach certainly has the merit of resisting a simple labeling approach based on the nature of the service provider, but it is also indicative of an assertion of a bright line between the public and the private sectors.

Bringing the Courts Back In

Much is at stake when courts review the public/private blend of power that certain forms of privatization produce. There are limits to the extent to which judicial decisions can further global public-law principles without legislative and executive leadership (examples of which are discussed in chapter 4). There also are limits to the extent to which some of the more ideological aspects of global competition can and should determine completely the blend of public and private that such relatively new regulatory reforms reveal.

The basic framework that emerges from the contracting out of public services can help courts address some very important questions. First, where do market approaches end and the market metaphors begin? By this I mean that some privately provided services may genuinely be marketable, i.e., contracted for by the actual consumers of the services and paid for at the market price, such as private security forces.[96] Most outsourced public services are not this pure. Though they may be paid for by taxes or users fees, the amount involved is not the same as the market price.[97] Strongly related to this fact is the identity of the actual customer involved. When a city, state, or federal entity contracts for a service, it is, in fact, the customer and not necessarily the consumer of the services involved.

This raises a second question. Are citizens customers, consumers, or simply interested parties, in the way that all citizens are when governmental policies are involved? Developing answers to these questions advance our understanding of the common stake citizens/consumers have in these services and, moreover, the role they can play in determining how, where, and when they might be provided.

It is at this point in the analysis that important questions of democracy surface, albeit in ways that can conflict with some of the economic goals of the privatized services involved. Democracy and public participation will, in the short run, usually increase the costs of decision making. This may, in turn, cut deeply into the global currency a purely privatized approach may create. Nevertheless, the more decision makers opt for such distinctions as administration and policy making or private and public, the more the global economy can undermine democracy. A fundamental tenet of outsourcing, for example, is that a clear demarcation exists between the policy to delegate certain duties to a private company and the administration of those duties by the company involved. By ensuring that the responsibility for prison administration rests completely with a private provider, the contracting agent is free to assess the provider's performance. In many states, the public input in this process usually is involved only at the renewability stage of the contract. The assumption is that a kind of outcome-based analysis can be used to determine whether these contracts should be renewed or not.[98] The more bottom-line-oriented the review, the greater the incentives on the part of the company to perform efficiently, but the less ongoing public input and involvement there is.[99]

Policy questions and administration can never fully be separated, even in what might seem to be relatively straightforward tasks such as garbage collection or snow removal.[100] Whose garbage or snow is removed first? Who has priority in emergencies? It may be that some of these issues can be resolved in the contracts that are negotiated, with those contracts being a kind of private constitution when it comes to providing these services.[101] How should the public participate in negotiating those contracts in the first instance? What are the prerequisites of democracy in the new private public sector?

Globalization and Democracy

Domestic public law has long struggled with issues of democracy in assessing, for example, the appropriate allocation of power between courts and legislatures and among courts, legislatures, and administrative agencies.[102] The democracy problem inherent in globalization, however, is even more fundamental.

Global economic forces, their interaction with essentially liberal states committed to market economies and the rule of law,[103] and the structural preferences they create for market solutions to various problems pose a very different question: when should the exercise of power by the private sector be viewed as essentially public? Put another way, when is private ordering an expansion of democracy? When does it restrict democracy? The globalizing state involves four very significant, simultaneously ongoing processes.

First, the decentered, globalizing state not only reallocates power between the public and private sectors. It also redefines what is public and what is private, putting these in novel ways.

Second, this fusion of the public and the private is occurring within a dynamic context, one in which the state increasingly is in intense competition with other states for jobs and the investment that creates these positions. This fact places its legal system in competition with other legal regimes around the world. States with overall lower production costs and more supportive legal structures may be more successful in retaining current levels of investment and in attracting new capital as well.

Third, the move from states to markets, however, is due not only to regulatory competition and separate jurisdictions trying to maximize their economic attractiveness vis-à-vis other states. Many of the global actors within each of these states do business in multiple jurisdictions, and they conceptualize their operations as essentially borderless. There is, thus, increasing pressure on states to harmonize regulatory regimes to fit the global realities of the global entities that are affected by these laws.[104] The global pressures felt by domestic lawmakers stem not only from increased regulatory competition between and among separate nation states but also from global actors who simultaneously are located in many of these states and wish to create legal systems that can facilitate their ability to carry out their operations as profitably as possible. As a result, there are increasing pressures for various forms of harmonization or deep integration of national economies into the global economy.[105]

Fourth, along with harmonization and deep economic integration, there is a growing body of global or, in effect, denationalized law, as well as various international standards designed to resolve disputes and structure the legal relationships of entities whose activities cut across jurisdictions.[106] This body of law can also be both in competition with and a force for harmonizing various domestic law regimes, as global actors seek to construct legal regimes suitable to their needs worldwide. Unlike harmonized national or state legal structures, however, global law is often developed with little transparency and even less regard for public participation.[107]

The pressure for deeper economic integration applied by various global actors and the competition individual states experience from other state and global legal regimes usually result in the creation of more economic approaches to regulatory issues and governmental tasks. Such approaches to governance emphasize flexibility, efficiency, and cost, all of which are very much a part of achieving success in the global economy. They are not, however, simply the result of new functional regulatory approaches employed by the same state that brought us the New Deal or nineteenth-century laissez-faire. As the state itself both emulates and coopts the market to achieve its goals, these various transformations change the meanings of "public" and "private" in ways that differ significantly from that earlier time.[108] They also necessitate a broader conceptualization of democracy beyond traditional concepts of political representation and suffrage. Recourse to markets by itself does not guarantee an expression of community will or collective interest.

Global Competition and the State

In his seminal treatise on constitutional law, William Croskey argued for a conception of the commerce clause that applied not just to the movement of goods between states but also within states.[109] In his view, the test was the impact on interstate commerce, not its geography. This broad reading accorded with the powers of the national government as he perceived them in the 1940s and 1950s.[110] In today's world of increasingly integrated global markets, it is logical to think of nation states, too, as territories where global commerce is taking place regardless of whether a particular exchange occurs across a national border. National states undertake to ensure and facilitate this kind of economic activity and—consistent with Croskey's view—for purposes that go beyond the financial well-being of its residents. Safety, health, education, and basic human rights are also functions of the state and these, too, are served by economic prosperity.[111]

National state functions are integral to the global economy today, placing a premium on markets and the organization of economic life; however, these functions do not map neatly onto their territorial boundaries. States are not self-contained units when it comes to the fluidity of capital. Some observers point to what they see as the increasing irrelevance of territory in structuring the global economy.[112] Supporters of strong states navigate around this paradox by advocating the state's role in terms of leading the fight for national prosperity in the global economy. For some, the rhetoric describes the state as a combatant in a new war, a war for markets and jobs.[113] In general, advocates of strong states adopt a statecentric model of law based on global competition. We discussed various statecentric models in chapter 2, and we return to state models in the next section.

As we shall see, the paradox of a strong-state approach is that "strong states" confront global competition with a state response that, at the extremes, is comparable to the laissez-faire capitalism of the nineteenth and early twentieth centuries.[114] Rather than yield to worldwide markets, such states seek to use market forces to maximize their own economic prosperity. In so doing, they further a model of globalization that is focused on individualism, a liberal conception of the economy, a limited conception of the role of the state, self-reliance, and competitiveness.[115]

Market values can, of course, be tempered by government (as they were on the national level from the New Deal on), but the realities of global competition and the decentered aspects of the state described tend to reinforce market values.[116] The end result of the development of this type of global capitalism is one that encourages international competition and confrontation: state against state, and firm against firm in the quest for economic dominance and prosperity.[117] Indeed, this conception of globalization makes dominance both the precondition and the result of prosperity.[118]

This view of globalization yields investment-friendly regulatory and tax policies, and it also creates pressures on states to maximize their own efficiency and effectiveness.[119] More than simple corporate mimicry is involved, though the ability of the government to speak the language of cost containment, downsizing, and re-engineering in today's world undoubtedly adds to any administration's political legitimacy.[120] More importantly (and again, paradoxically), the very policies government makes to lower costs and attract investment necessitate new cost-effective regulatory techniques. Beyond such economic necessities and the cost-based regulatory reforms they inspire, the strong-state model is challenged by changes in the fundamental nature of the state from a social perspective. People may identify more with their employers than with a particular city (or even country), especially if they work for global companies or for businesses that are in global competition.[121] The questions of who makes up the state, what (or whose) interests matter, and how they affect the ability of a state to act purposefully are much more open questions when the "war" involved is neither cold nor hot, but economic.[122]

Has it not always been thus? Yes and no. Yes, in the sense that economic prosperity has always been important, but no in the sense that global competition has never been so fierce or pervasive at every level of the domestic sphere.[123] The Cold War, which gave states and state borders some of their symbolic meaning, no longer exists to the same degree.[124] Yet, this does not mean the state is withering away, nor does it mean that it is simply the sum total of the preferences of its inhabitants at any given time.[125] The extent to which a state's power can be used to further a collectively derived public-interest goal has been a major issue in modern public-law debates.[126] The need to achieve a global conception of the public interest is even more difficult, but this is the challenge of the state and transnational politics. The diffuseness of the issues involved and the difficulty of creating the politics necessary to create a global conception of the public interest makes it all the easier for market approaches to dominate domestic discourses of globalization, virtually by default.

As a result, a more corporatist role for states may be emerging, as states seek to assert their view of the public interest. Such an approach sees the state's role as something more than that of a neutral arbiter of the interest-group politics that predominate in a pluralistic conception of the state. It also differs from more public-choice conceptions of the state, where it is assumed that certain dominant interests will exercise more control over the state than the more neutral, pluralistic conception envisages. Indeed, for public-choice theorists, this scenario confirms the nonexistence of a collective public interest. A corporatist approach is not so democratic as other forms of interest-group behavior, but it does posit the existence of a public interest, one that the state tries to further. In this way the state is, in a sense, "just" another actor. Though obviously a very powerful one, it is not nearly as independent as the pluralists or republicans might imagine, nor so susceptible to capture or manipulation as the public-choice theorists might assume.[127]

Thus far, I have discussed various changes in the national state, ranging from structural economic changes in the way nonstate and state actors now must operate to political changes in the way the role of the state is conceptualized. The end result is enormous competition between, within, and among member states for investment and a regulatory language and approach that, in many ways, itself has become corporatized. Thus, a common representation of government at federal, state, and local levels is as something akin to a corporate entity, providing services to its customer/citizens and attracting jobs and capital to its locale.[128] It is as if the state itself were a TNC locked in competition with others for success in a series of zero-sum political and economic games. When Toyota chooses one country over another for the location of its plant, one state over another, and one locale within that state as opposed to another, there is, in effect, a multiplier effect when it comes to the various competitions that take place to attract prosperity to their territorial space. There are strong pressures on each level of government to assist in this competition that are, in effect, bottom-up in their impact. That is to say, even if federal regulations subject all states to the same federal costs (a level playing field), that does not necessarily mean some states or units within them do not believe that they could become more "efficient" and, thus, more competitive, given the chance to do so.

The welfare reform debate in the United States is a case in point. One of the cost considerations driving welfare reform from a state perspective was the desire on the part of states to control their own costs and make their own determinations of how best to distribute federal and state funds to deal with those who could not compete effectively in the global economy.[129] Their belief in their own management skills and decisions created a corresponding belief in their ability to lower welfare costs in their states, thereby increasing their own productivity.[130] Thus, states in global competition are not content to have a level playing field when it comes to welfare costs, if they believe they can cut those costs, achieve their goals, and thereby out-compete other states in attracting foreign investment. Indeed, all such common expenditures among states become the source of currency with which they can compete against each other.

The pressures from below state governments are even greater. Since municipalities wish to compete effectively for investment, they too want their state to have rules and regulations that are more cost effective than those imposed on nearby communities by neighboring states with whom they are in competition. If a state wishes to be successful, it must help its own local communities attract jobs. Since it is at the local level that the end result of this competition is finally realized and a plant or facility is or is not built, it is not surprising that the competition at the local level might be particularly fierce and a relatively pure corporatist approach to decision making increasingly common.[131]

The competitive philosophy so prevalent among governments at all levels now as they compete for jobs and investment within their own territories is derivative of the heavy competition that occurs among transnational corporations at the global level.[132] Member states have adopted the dominant rhetoric of the private sector as well as many of its structures, goals, and methods.[133] Indeed, governments at all levels increasingly play the game as if they were transnational corporations. Such an approach reinforces a conception of government that is so market driven as to preclude consideration of nonmarket values, such as those embodied in certain provisions of the Bill of Rights in the U.S. Constitution, as well as the limits of the market metaphor when it comes to governmental decision making and the role of individual citizens. As we have seen, if privatization of prisons means the deprivation of constitutional rights of prisoners,[134] or if contracting out snow removal or garbage collection[135] means that politics is viewed as separate and distinct from administration, democracy and constitutional rights will suffer. There are, in effect, limits to the sources of currency available to states for competing effectively in the global economy.

A competitive model of global capitalism may take many forms, some of which are more cooperative than a simple laissez-faire model might predict.[136] Moreover, how a state responds to the rhetoric of global competition is a matter of degree, since not all industries within a state are necessarily in global competition to the same extent and since states are not unified corporate entities. States are not transnational corporations even if the prevailing discourse suggests otherwise. This is because effective global governance requires more than competition among individuals and firms, as indicated in the Lisbon Report on the Limits to Competition:[137]

> [T]he pursuit of competition in search of profit as the single legitimate overarching concern of firms is unjustified as the main motivation for private and public choices in a world of increasingly global processes, problems, and interdependence. Competition among firms alone cannot handle long-term world problems efficiently. The market cannot properly discount the future; it is naturally shortsighted. Putting together thousands of myopic organizations does not enable them, individually or collectively, to see the reality and acquire a sense of direction, or to provide governance, order, and security. The same applies to competition among nations, which, in excess, inevitably leads to a rat-race mentality and global economic wars and hinders the ability of policymakers to address national and global priorities.

The rhetoric of competition and the metaphors of the market can, at times, seem to dictate governmental responses more than they should, sometimes leading to inappropriate results. For example, many policy choices are said to be required by global competition, when, in fact, they are not. The issues are much more complex, as Paul Krugman has argued:[138]

> Most people who use the term "competitiveness" do so without a second thought. It seems obvious to them that the analogy between a country and a corporation is reasonable and that to ask whether the United States is competitive in the world market is no different in principle from asking whether General Motors is competitive in the North American minivan market. In fact, however, trying to define the competitiveness of a nation is much more problematic than defining that of a corporation. The bottom line for a corporation is literally its bottom line: if a corporation cannot afford to pay its workers, suppliers, and bondholders, it will go out of business. So when we say that a corporation is uncompetitive, we mean that its market position is unsustainable. Unless it improves its performance, it will cease to exist. Countries, on the other hand, do not go out of business. They may be happy or unhappy with their economic performance, but they have no well-defined bottom line. As a result, the concept of national competitiveness is elusive.

Moreover, there are obvious limits to other metaphors spawned by global competitiveness, particularly when they are applied to citizens.[139] The role of citizen as customer, for example, is a passive one. It assumes too bright a line between what government does and who the government is.[140] Comparing citizens to owners is often a more appropriate analogy.[141] The citizen/customer metaphor, however, also implies that people have choices when it comes to, for example, municipal services;[142] however, this is not usually the case, at least for the duration of the contract involved. Moreover, the citizen-as-customer metaphor has implications for the way we think about the service performed by private providers.[143] It suggests that there is a bright line between the service provided and policy making, as if all of the policy is made when government decides to contract out a certain service.[144] In reality the public's role or interest in the activities contracted out does not end at the delegation stage, i.e., the point at which the contract is signed. The way a service provider goes about the job involves any number of policy choices into which there often is no public input. When the concept of citizenship is privatized, the implicit assumption of most such market reforms is that citizens will know if they like the service they are getting, but they are not expected to be players in the fundamental policy decisions that determine whether, how, and to whom those services should be dispensed.[145]

As we have seen, one of the major concerns with privatization and globalization is that issues that once were public and subject to democratic decision-making processes are, once privatized, removed from public view. States may choose metaphors such as that of citizens as customers to legitimate their decisions, but this does not alter the fact that those decisions are increasingly taken without appropriate levels of public input and with increasingly narrow market justifications. Moreover, metaphors based on market competition can mask a variety of assumptions concerning the role of the state and the role that public law can play in various regulatory contexts.

Because familiar political debates involving the appropriate role of government vis-à-vis the market can easily be fitted to the rhetoric of global competition, it is easy simply to assume that market approaches are better than regulatory approaches or that, at the very least, the pendulum is simply swinging in the direction of less government. As noted, this kind of rhetoric makes it easy to lose sight of the fact that significant structural changes impinging on states are under way, changes that necessitate new conceptualizations of the roles of law and of politics.

Let us now return to prevailing state models and revisit the globalizing state as an alternative conception and direction of analysis.

Back to the Future: The Strong State

There are at least two polar versions of the strong-state thesis. Both versions involve domestic, political, and legal responses that clearly resonate with long-standing political assumptions and public-law theories, both domestic and international.[146] One looks to strong states as defenders of laissez-faire economic policies. The other looks to strong states for regulation.

The Strong Laissez-Faire State

To advocates of the laissez-faire or minimal state,[147] deregulation, privatization, lower taxes, and smaller and less government involvement in economic affairs are ends in themselves.[148] They reason that a market economy knows no boundaries, and to them, this fact, along with the additional impetus the ideology of competition receives from global competition, mandates a return to the pre–New Deal state. Such an approach coincides with the shift occurring from states to markets outlined above, but the market approaches that result are not simply functions of the difficulties in asserting regulatory control over transnational actors and transnational problems; they represent an affirmative choice on the part of a strong state to re-impose a laissez-faire economy.[149]

This model of a strong state also involves key assumptions about law, particularly the law that governs governmental actions and the boundaries between public and private powers and between state and federal jurisdiction. Perhaps the most significant aspect of a laissez-faire, strong-state conception of global competition is its call for a clear-cut line between public and private powers. For proponents, the purpose of privatization and deregulation is to return decision making "back" to the private sector, where private ordering and a market economy, coupled with clear property rights and effective criminal law enforcement, will presumably supply the structure, order, stability, and rules needed for the economy to prosper—as they (again, presumptively) did before the Great Depression. Their goal is to move as much power as possible from the public to the private sector; their means entail maximizing the role of the private sector and, even in the public sector, maximizing the private-sector values and operating procedures.[150]

Another tenet of the strong laissez-faire state thesis is that if a public response in the form of law is necessary, it should occur at as local a level of government as possible.[151] Thus another structural legal assumption underlying this tenet is that there should be clear lines among national, state, and local governments.[152] This view of the allocation of governmental power is also essentially a pre–New Deal approach to the federalism aspects of the Constitution. It conforms to the idea that national power should be decentralized and minimal and that this is a federal choice. Not unlike the balanced budget amendment,[153] constitutionalizing such basic premises and removing even the temptation of choice often is seen by advocates of this position as a desirable outcome. Of course, the United States (a strong national state) might pass federal laws mandating certain laissez-faire approaches at the state level, if necessary. In general, however, proponents of this model see the federal government's appropriate leadership as limited to maximizing the economic freedom of citizens, leaving market problems to the private sector and, if necessary, individual states.

This model does not play out in a pure form.[154] It is strongly evident in the isolationist approaches of some policymakers to international law, though, as well as in some approaches to free trade and, on the domestic front, certain cost-benefit-analysis approaches to regulation.[155] Adding an explicit cost-benefit dimension to regulatory processes can mean many things, but in the context of strong-state laissez-faire advocates, it can be a means by which procedures are used to achieve substantive ends, i.e., minimal or no governmental action.[156] Indeed, market discourses are used not only to refine governmental choices and decision making but also to limit significantly the substantive role of the state.

The politics generated by advocates of a strong laissez-faire state is remarkably similar to traditional political debates between conservatives and liberals, at least regarding issues within U.S. borders. The market, freedom, and liberty are placed in opposition to command and control regulation, federal bureaucracies, and governmental intervention. The bright lines between the public and the private, government and markets, rights and freedoms, among and between nations (as in the immigration debates), and between nations and internal states all reinforce legal and political debates that appear to continue without regard to the very different economy and world in which we live today. They also reinforce a theory of the state that suggests that, in relation to intervention into the market economy, there is no public interest beyond what the market itself might provide.[157]

The Strong Regulatory State

A second type of strong-state response to the global economy is the strong regulatory state model. Proponents of this view take issue with a purely market approach to state governance. They decry some deregulation and privatization. They are skeptical of international regulation,[158] especially if it dilutes national regulatory attempts. This vision of the state resurrects a certain nostalgia for the past. It assumes that the federal government can return to regulating markets—including global markets—and the rest of the world will follow our lead.[159] The global aspects of today's markets, actors, and technologies need not limit our responses, they say, if we can muster the political will to act.[160] By setting the appropriate regulatory standards at home we can set standards for the rest of the world. If they choose not to follow our lead, that should not inhibit our use and further development of a strong regulatory approach and of a public law based on transparency and participation.[161]

Not unlike the strong-state response of the laissez-faire advocates, those who advocate the regulatory strong-state response also believe in a public/private divide, but inversely. To strong regulatory state advocates, the public sphere, particularly when it comes to the economic and environmental well-being of individuals should be a broad one, and the private sphere relatively narrow.[162] What is private relates more to rights such as individual privacy, or the separation of church and state.[163] Given the need for uniformity and the fear of a race to the bottom when it comes to economic legislation, they advocate strong national regulation and a view of states that limits substantially their freedom from uniform and unifying national regulation.[164]

While debates between these strong-state advocates often somewhat predictably focus on what should be public and private, or federal as opposed to state, the debate can sometimes be less predictable when it comes to the role that free trade and treaties such as NAFTA or legislation such as fast track should play in our economy.[165] The strong-state free traders are usually eager to expand markets in whatever ways they can, especially if more wage and job competition results in the United States.[166] The strong-state regulators fear that domestic legal institutions will be undermined, and private power will be greatly enhanced at the expense of public control and public-law values.[167] At the extremes of the regulatory view are those who advocate direct forms of economic protectionism as a response to global competition.[168] Less extreme is a view that would not remove free trade agreements such as NAFTA in the absence of clear regulatory solutions to environmental, wage, and labor issues.[169] In summary, one response to the global economy is to assert the strong will of the state either in a manner that seeks to maximize competition at home and abroad, or in a manner that seeks to soften, if not minimize it at home. Both views, however, assume a theory of the state in which states are the primary actors in the international system and have substantial control over their own national economy.[170] However, this view of the state and the public law and policy that flow from it are no longer in accord with the realities of the global economy today. Holding to this view means ignoring the domestic impact of a pure laissez-faire economy on those who are unable to compete effectively, or alternatively, claiming rising costs of doing business as a defensive strategy.[171]

Reinventing Government: The Efficient State

The second major approach to the state mandates its core function as efficiency. As already noted, "efficient state" advocates see the state as a unit made up of individuals and groups, whose preferences matter—and whose preferences are formed increasingly beyond national borders.[172] Quite apart from whether the state is strong or weak in relationship to global markets, the reinventing-government movement tries to maintain active state involvement, but in different terms than in the past. It need not withdraw state power completely in favor of the power of markets. The goal of governmental efficiency is asserted in place of the ideological debate against regulation. Indeed, at the heart of the reinvention-of-government approach is its belief that procedural and structural legal reforms make it possible to have a government that works better and costs less.[173] Market rhetoric and the reliance on market approaches enable advocates of efficient state reforms to resonate with the contemporary global-competition discourse. The reinvention approach also results in government that looks like (or at least sounds like) the private entities it tries to influence.[174]

The reinvention approach to the state borrows heavily from the corporate sector, including its emphasis on downsizing, decentralizing, and, generally, re-engineering its own bureaucratic structures and procedures to maximize its global competitiveness.[175] Turning to the private sector for ideas is not unusual. Governments, especially activist governments, have usually borrowed their regulatory forms and structures from the very entities they seek to influence and control. In the New Deal, for example, government borrowed heavily from the more fluid organizational conceptions of corporations when it came to designing the internal structures of independent regulatory agencies.[176] Strict separation-of-power approaches were eschewed in favor of a more practical governmental model, not at all dissimilar from the way large corporations internally shared responsibility and power.[177]

Today, the increase in direct global competition from other corporate entities, coupled with potential opportunities to expand in worldwide markets, drives many companies to lower their costs and maximize their flexibility. In this regard, the Weblike nature of transnational corporations is, perhaps, the ultimate form of this drive for efficiency.[178] Sometimes, processes are farmed out to subsidiaries in other countries;[179] at other times less lengthy or formal relationships are involved as various tasks are contracted out to a variety of independent contractors to ensure that the lowest-cost providers can be found.[180]

Applying these approaches to governments has its limits, but one way the regulation-versus-no-regulation debate has changed is by the interjection into that debate of market concepts of efficiency that are intended to apply to the government.[181] More often than not, the focus on governmental efficiency is an attempt to recognize some of the state's shortcomings in the past, and to try to make amends by achieving its goals in less costly and less intrusive ways. At the heart of such a response, however, is a fundamentally status-quo-ante strategy. A government that seeks to be more productive and less costly by making primarily procedural and structural changes is not necessarily one that is fundamentally changing the substantive politics of what it is trying to accomplish; rather, it is only changing the means to achieve those ends.[182] Nor is it necessarily intended to be representative of a state that differs in any significant way from the conception of the nation state that has dominated our legal imaginations since the New Deal.

At the same time, from the perspective of those who advocate either a return to a more laissez-faire economy or a more traditional regulatory state, the very change of the language of regulation, from one steeped in demands and requirements to one that emphasizes costs and benefits, provides a discourse that can have a very definite substantive effect. When public-law values involving long-term judgments regarding the value of life, the beauty of the environment, and other noneconomic issues are translated into cost-benefit economic terms, the shift of discourse involves not simply an alternative translation but, as with any translation, introduces nuances and substantive changes as well.[183] Economic language in itself can have a deregulatory effect, depending upon one's definition of costs and benefits.[184] Moreover, whether from the point of view of strong-state laissez-faire advocates, or regulators and efficiency-minded governance advocates, the metaphor of citizen as customer also has serious limitations. As I have noted above,[185] the idea of citizen as customer can often encourage a passive view of the electorate.

The public law that the theory of the efficient state encourages is similar to what some commentators call the new public law.[186] New public law assumes a state with choices, if not always a strong state. It also assumes the existence of a state-centered system of politics.[187] Its emphasis on transformations and the capacity of law and politics to achieve those transformations emphasizes a positive view of politics as effective and world building. Political choices are imagined to be endogenous to a system in which politics and law are closely linked.[188] Democratic theory is also important to this view, since it is only by participation in the political process that public opinion can form and be transformative.[189] Finally, the new public law emphasizes normativity and substance, rather than objective procedural processes alone; and it stresses the need for a flexible approach to law that allows decision makers, especially courts, to adapt statutory meaning to the continual demands of the present.[190]

Like the reinvention approach itself, the new public law results in a pragmatic approach to law and to the use of law to effectuate change.[191] Indeed, much of the deregulation that occurred, especially in the early days of the Reagan administration, was the result of pragmatic public-law interpretations and regulatory choices.[192] When the Reagan administration was unable to achieve its more philosophically based deregulatory goals through Congress, it adopted judicial and executive agency strategies to achieve its ends. Primarily through executive orders, it imposed a rigorous cost-benefit approach to federal-agency rule making aimed at slowing the growth of agency regulation.[193] The administration carefully appointed to regulatory bodies officials who interpreted their statutory powers in ways that encouraged deregulation and other market approaches.[194] Indeed, they were able to achieve substantial deregulation within the very same statutory frameworks that created the very regulatory structures they sought to dismantle.[195] For the most part, courts took a very deferential approach to agency interpretations of their own broad statutory delegations of power, thereby authorizing agencies to use market approaches to achieve their goals.[196] *Chevron v. U.S.A.* was the symbolic embodiment of this judicial approach.[197]

As we saw in chapter 1, the laissez-faire philosophical side of the Reagan deregulatory strategy failed in Congress and in the courts. With few exceptions, Congress refused to repeal outright its regulatory statutes or to abolish regulatory agencies.[198] While the courts took a deferential approach to agency interpretations that favored the market and market approaches as regulatory tools, the Court resisted constitutional approaches that would, in effect, repeal substantial portions of the New Deal.[199] In a series of cases culminating in *Mistretta v. United States,* the Supreme Court rejected approaches to separation-of-power questions that would have put the constitutionality of independent regulatory commissions seriously in doubt.[200] At the same time, the Court's approach to federalism issues in the 1980s as well as state action and takings questions remained relatively stable, despite a growing political debate regarding the appropriate role of the federal government and the courts in a variety of regulatory contexts.[201]

The efficient state, however, was more than a reflection of the Reagan administration's conservatism. The use of market approaches continued, forming the cornerstone of many Clinton administration reforms.[202] Moreover, it was, in many ways, a transition to the globalizing state described below.

Mixing Public and Private Power: The Globalizing State

Let us now turn to the globalizing state—introduced in chapter 2—which differs significantly from the strong and efficient state scenarios discussed above. Those concepts of the state assume a relatively closed system in which the power of states, individually and as members of an international order, is relatively stable.[203] Globalization challenges that assumption. States must now choose new or different strategies to deal with the processes of globalization, be they more market approaches to regulation or more direct resistance to global forces. Even so, most commentators continue to assume (or so it seems) that a bright line exists between the global and the local, or between the domestic and the international, even if these are dynamically linked.

The concept of the globalizing state differs in degree and in kind from such views. In point of fact, as my discussion of the global era suggested in chapter 1, "the global" and "the local" are heuristic devices, not distinct entities or geographies. The global and the local are analytic perspectives on a complex dynamic process (very broadly speaking), not simply an arrangement of parts and a whole. Moreover, though globalization does not by any means imply the disappearance of states, it does emphasize a far greater degree of fragmentation of state power than a state-centered conception of globalization would allow (again, see chapter 2).[204] The fact of transborder activities (such as trade) or phenomena (such as pollution) and the importance of nonstate actors does not render state power meaningless. Rather, under these conditions, levels of power involve layered networks of actors and sets of rules from several (even many) states, as well as from the global legal systems that nonstate actors are developing.[205] These bodies of rules and law often (at least initially) have little to do with the state-centered approaches to law of any one jurisdiction.[206]

More fundamentally, the globalizing state is a dynamic. Indeed the term "globalizing state" is double edged. It means that the state itself is an agent of globalization, furthering certain processes of this emerging new economic order through, for example, policies designed to attract and retain investment. It is also a product of globalization, continually in the process of being transformed by the very processes in which it is involved. The state, like the transnational enterprises with which it deals, is affected by and ultimately changed in fundamental ways by the increased diffusion of its powers, which now must be shared with other states and, as we have seen, with nonstate actors as well. The United States and the states no longer have a monopoly on certain areas of law and policy, and the new combinations of public and private power that are emerging require a redefinition of what is public and what is private. The globalizing state thus differs in kind as well as degree from the states discussed above. Importantly, the globalizing state is not one that rules the world, but rather one that cannot avoid responding to the world. As its role shifts to one in which it seeks primarily to further the kind of competitive environment that results in greater economic prosperity for those who live within its borders, it transforms itself. Changes in approach that increasingly rely on the private sector to carry out what once were conceived of as essentially public responsibilities globalize the state as much as the efficiencies it presumably achieves enable its constituents to compete more effectively in the global economy.

This double-edged aspect of the globalizing state raises serious issues with which institutions at all levels (local, state, national, and international) must grapple. As Philip Cerny has pointedly argued, diffusion of state power and the dilution of democracy are two of the most negative aspects of globalization:[207]

[G]lobalization entails the *undermining of the public character of public goods and of the specific character of specific assets,* i.e., the *privatization and marketization* of economic and political structures. States are pulled between structural pressures and organizational levels they cannot control. Economic globalization contributes not so much to the supersession of the state by a homogeneous global order as to the splintering of the existing political order. Indeed, globalization leads to a growing disjunction between the democratic, constitutional, and social aspirations of people — which are still shaped by and understood through the frame of the territorial state — on the one hand, and the dissipating possibilities of genuine and effective collective action through constitutional political processes on the other.

If the globalizing state defines itself exclusively in terms of its ability to promote efficiency, these negative aspects will be exacerbated. The globalizing state is not natural. It is the product of global forces and its own responses to them. It is continually produced and can, of course, be changed.

Indeed, the contracting out of governmental services to the private sector[208] and extensive use of market structures and approaches to regulation involve very direct uses of private power to achieve public ends. As we have seen, they also involve increasingly common partnerships between the state and private actors that now involve such local services as schools, prisons, and snow and garbage removal.[209] These new partnership approaches also involve links between and among different governmental entities, especially federal and state. As noted above, programs such as welfare now involve new relationships between and among various levels of government and the private sector, as well.[210]

These mixtures of the public and private, as well as of federal, state, and local powers, amount to more than a collection of new governmental approaches to achieving common ends efficiently. They represent some of the ways in which the globalizing state now interacts in an economy that operates as if there were no borders. The changes involved are more than political choices to favor markets over the state or market regulatory approaches over command and control rules; they are structural as well. They are indicative of a decentered state, creating new demands — and new problems — that the state-centered public law of the past (even in its newer more pragmatic forms) cannot fully address.

First and foremost among these problems is what we have called the democracy problem in globalization, which we shall explore more concretely in chapter 4.[211] Given greater delegations of domestic public power to the transnational private sector, how can we institutionally ensure democracy and public participation in decisions that affect the everyday lives of individuals?

A second issue, also explored below, is flexibility: How can states and private entities maximize the impact of various networks of relationships within and beyond state borders?

These questions not only place new issues on lawmakers' agendas, but they require that decisions made on the basis of older models of constitutional and public law be seen in a new light. Neither of the strong-state models, nor the efficient-state model, can accomplish this. Judicial decisions that limit the flexibility of public/private partnerships, as well as decisions that continue to treat the line between the public and the private as constitutive of the strong state, can do more harm to democratic decision making than good. Moreover, decisions designed to constitutionalize traditional forms of state autonomy at the expense of federal power can also substantially undercut the flexibility of governmental policymakers and reinforce aspects of the strong-state approach to public policy that no longer are in accord with global realities. The maximization of political discourse should be over goals and the regular interplay of local, state, federal, and international law making the end result. Chapter 4 will examine various aspects of these mixes of public and private power and their implications for administrative and constitutional law.

4

Implications of the
Globalizing State for Law Reform

As we have seen, the United States (as a globalizing state) approaches problems in ways that often resemble those of the global corporate entities the government seeks to influence. Thus, like global corporations, states downsize, decentralize, maximize flexibility, or deregulate, and call upon the market and private actors to achieve their goals.[1] Contracting out to the private sector is an increasingly common way for states to carry out their public responsibilities. Administrative agencies also use various market structures and market regulatory techniques, with increasing frequency, to carry out their duties.[2] All of these approaches and interactions with the private sector involve aspects of the public/private distinction, but this distinction no longer demarcates two distinct areas as it once did. The democracy deficit is primarily the result of the application of a traditional conception of the public/private distinction that is likely to lessen considerably the public sector's responsibilities for transparency and accountability when private actors perform certain tasks. Justifications often provided for such an approach begin with the assumption that policy making and administration can, in fact, be separated, an assumption that most commentators reject.[3] Even in privatized contexts, private actors inevitably make policy when they carry out their delegated tasks and interpret the contracts under which they operate. The relationship between the globalizing state and its inherent democracy problems underscores the importance of ensuring that courts, policymakers, and citizens understand the complexities of the public/private distinction as it now arises.

A new kind of administrative law can and should be created to respond to the democracy deficit associated with privatization. It need not rely solely on traditional procedural approaches, arguably designed for governmental agencies carrying out regulatory functions. At the same time, it is important to emphasize that what is at stake are the values of public law—transparency, participation, and fairness. Various procedural approaches may be necessary to ensure the realization of these values. The values of the APA (if not precisely the procedural devices it currently employs)[4] should be extended to various hybrid, public/private arrangements if we are to ensure the legitimacy of those partnerships. Given a reorientation of states and markets due to globalization, the next sections set forth some of the key issues that a new administrative law might now address. Toward that end, I argue that the underlying theory and purpose of administrative law should be reconceptualized, in at least three ways.

First, given the tendency of globalization processes to put a premium on market processes and outcomes, it is important to understand the extent to which private interests and legal techniques are involved in reaching public ends, thereby maintaining a state connection to what otherwise may seem to be essentially private activities.

Second, given the new pressures experienced by states and the strength of global markets, the recourse to the private sector need not simply be taken as evidence of agency capture or the triumph of a relatively pure form of global capitalism. Rather, treaties such as NAFTA, the practice of contracting out governmental services, and the use of market regulatory structures and techniques are but the beginnings of new approaches on the part of the globalizing state to embrace public-interest ends within private-interest mechanisms.

Third, the realms of public and private themselves have been and are subject to the processes of globalization. Domestic-law processes that involve the private sector very directly in the law-making process often will be including the global perspective of many of the participants involved in these issues. Similarly, in many areas of regulation and state involvement, the public realm itself does not stop at U.S. borders. For certain kinds of regulation to be effective, the global state must link up with other states on a global or regional basis. Thus, governmental decision makers need to bring a global perspective to issues that may seem to evoke familiar debates over the local and the global, but in fact now require a broader political, economic, and legal framework of analysis.

The global perspective I advocate is a critical one. It interrogates the extent to which decisions by Congress, administrative agencies, and the courts develop opportunities for public participation while advancing public/private partnerships. This perspective is also normative, in that it posits the importance of maintaining a public viewpoint in decision-making processes that might otherwise be private.

The globalizing state highlights the need for encouraging and protecting the norm of democratic decision making, as well as the need for facilitating the kind of flexibility necessary for new kinds of public/private and state/federal partnerships to form. These goals, as well as the more traditional goals of private and public law, are greatly affected by the way courts approach the public/private distinction in the various contexts in which it now exists.[5] The issues are complex because depending upon the context, calling something "private" does not necessarily mean that the legal consequences of that label yield negative results from a policy point of view, even when judged by public-law values such as accountability, transparency, and participation.[6] Similarly, calling something "public" does not mean that such values are always encouraged or furthered.[7] Market and market regulatory approaches can be very effective regulatory tools, and some governmental or public approaches can represent a decision to opt for the status quo.[8]

There are other facets of privatization, besides creative problem solving. The desire on the part of governments at all levels to lower their costs and to create the currency of global competition is one of the main motivating forces for privatization. Lower regulatory costs make it easier to attract new business to a locality or to retain old ones. But quite apart from cost, the decline in public confidence in the ability of government to function efficiently has made governmental recourse to the private sector politically popular—while preempting politics per se. But the need for reform cannot be fulfilled by a rhetoric of global competition. To invoke the language and concepts of the private sector in contexts that are or should remain public diminishes the role of democracy, and unnecessarily so. The pressures of global competition on the state for low-cost regulation or deregulation may be the context in which new mixtures of public and private power are preconceived as essentially private. But these pressures are actually increased when the state plays the "strong laissez-faire" role, actively competing for new investment in its own jurisdiction. As the globalizing state attempts to create additional currency to compete in the global economy, the ways in which courts view the doctrines that allocate power between the public and private sector take on major significance, especially with regard to local issues.

My proposals for reform start from different premises so far as the role of the state is concerned. As explained in chapter 1, I view the public decisions to privatize as political choices and the perceived zero-sum relationship between markets and law as an artifact of a particular historical experience. Globalization has a domestic face, and the democracy problem of the globalizing state is accessible to domestic law and politics. In this chapter, I will now explore some of the ways in which globalization's domestic democracy deficit might be addressed through law reform and a reinvigorated political sphere.

The Limits of Binary Distinctions

Globalization changes fundamentally the relationship of states to markets, and consequently challenges the traditional binary distinctions between public and private, national and international, and global and local. As I have argued in this book, these binaries fail for different reasons, each failure reflecting different aspects of globalization. The public/private binary fails because the globalizing state divests significant public-sector tasks to the private sector. The domestic/international binary fails because states are extensively interconnected and enmeshed with transnational nonstate actors—including a transnational market economy. The global/local binary fails in view of the embeddedness of globalization in the administrative structure of domestic government at every level, as well as in the substantive responses of nonstate actors to a wide range of problems. "Globalization" is all of these causes and effects, and one of this book's purposes has been to demonstrate the importance of including the domestic side of globalization in any analysis of the phenomenon. It is on the domestic side that the particular fusion of the public and private sectors can be understood as a market "force" that determines where democracy deficits are most directly produced.

The shifts in power we explored in chapters 2 and 3 involve governmental entities above and below the nation state, as well as private actors both domestic and international. Those power shifts have one thing in common: they privilege markets over more public forms of governance. They favor economic discourse over law as a normative basis, notwithstanding the fact that legal regulation carried with it affirmative mandates and mechanisms for public participation in the rule-making process. An antiregulatory ethos built on the premise that free markets are inherently democratic only furthers the myth that law and markets are two separate worlds, locked in zero-sum competition. Those who subscribe to this myth imagine markets to be open and fair, while law making is restrictive and "interested"; however, the history of legal regulation of markets suggests otherwise. As we have seen, since the New Deal era, it no longer makes sense to speak of markets and law in this way. Nor does it make sense to assume that it is only the *public* sphere that is subject to cooptation by special interests and rent seekers. The private sector is not free of special interests. Given the new private/public sphere, both sectors are so intertwined that the flaws of one are the flaws of the other. In short, the market is not an alternative to law; rather, these institutions are interdependent, each ideally sustaining key elements of the other's preconditions as democratic institutions. Failure to take these complexities into account can only deepen the democracy deficit.

Addressing the democracy deficit in globalization through law reform takes a conceptual reorientation toward the relationships of the public and private sectors both at home and abroad. Law reform should also be based on the recognition of the important role of nonstate entities, so as to go beyond the traditional public and private binary and create opportunities for meaningful public participation in those milieus. In doing so, we can begin to create the legal architecture necessary to move past the statecentric focus of the New Deal, yet without simply returning to the market and states' rights dominance that existed prior to that time (as some of today's federalists might seem to wish to do). As this book has argued, the recent shifts in the exercise of power are not the result of the political pendulum swinging back towards an earlier (conservative) view of government but a fundamental (and very contemporary) restructuring of the relationship between markets and the state.

Under these new conditions, two aspects of governance are especially relevant to the prospects for reform in the globalizing state. The first is the legitimacy of the public sector. Legitimacy does not—or should not—rest on a simple equation of representation and participation in state decision making, as if state action automatically satisfied the requirements of democracy. The diverse nature of the parties and interests involved, including important nonstate actors, in most regulatory issues means that state representatives of the executive or legislative branches of government cannot effectively claim sole legitimacy.

The second issue involves representation in the private sector. The privatized nature of much of public decision making today means that the public is excluded, except perhaps in their capacity as consumers. Even as consumers, citizens require more than information about the price of a product. The kind of democracy that markets offer is limited to consumers' economic power; this is by no means the same as the powers (and duties) of citizens in relation to deliberative democracy. Law reform is necessary on both of these fronts, to further substantive citizenship in this broader democratic sense.

Beyond the kind of information that can enable an individual consumer to make a rational choice in a domestic market, some types of information are likely to have more collective political effects. For example, information concerning the corporate practices of global firms that pay exceedingly low wages or make extensive use of child labor might be relevant to some consumers. Indeed, such information access has led to global consumer boycotts of such products and state pressures for reform. When reports surfaced that Reebok was purchasing soccer balls stitched by children, the company responded by creating a centralized production facility and establishing independent monitors. After Starbucks Coffee was picketed by activists concerned with its Guatemalan plantations, the firm issued a revised code of conduct and specific action plans for dealing with abuses. Also bowing to public pressure after high-profile consumer protests, The Gap committed itself to third-party monitoring by signing an agreement with the National Labor Committee.[9]

In these instances, the consumer sovereignty the market creates yields an informal global sanction aimed at curbing practices that individual states have been either unable or unwilling to correct on their own initiative. The market, in effect, constitutes a kind of ad hoc legislative oversight at the global level.[10] Given the reliance the globalizing state places on market processes, providing information that encourages consumer sovereignty may enhance new forms of democratic action and create the kind of accountability that democracy requires. Law can and should facilitate such processes whenever possible.

This chapter develops a broad agenda for procedural law reforms of a kind that might expand opportunities for a meaningful politics in the public/private, federal/state, and domestic/international spheres. These reforms depend on more than the kinds of procedures that may be required by courts pursuant to the due process clause of the Constitution. There are limits to how far courts can go in this regard, and those limits have been significantly reinforced by the jurisprudence of the Rehnquist Court over the past twenty years.[11] Moreover, given the underlying legal basis of the public/private distinction reflected in our Constitution, and the retrospective approach inherent in the way courts are likely to deal with cases involving this distinction, much of the procedural law reform discussed below must come primarily through legislative processes. To assure the freedom of the legislative process to accomplish such reforms, some doctrinal judicial change, in the form of greater judicial deference to political processes, will also be in order.

In the global era, as in earlier times, law reform means innovating in ways that accord with the new futures now being imagined. And in the global era (as urgently as before) this means encouraging and acknowledging the multiplicity of those imagined futures. Successful reform is always a blend of the past with a vision of a future that is at once inspiring and within our grasp. What are the visions of the future in the globalizing state? And whose visions are they? Globalization makes ever more pressing the need to close the democracy deficit so that collective commitments can be decided by an open political process. What are our resources for such a project here at home?

The Spirit of the Age

Some observers will say that the age of globalization involves a cultural shift, given its emphasis in the economic sphere on flexibility, networks, and managerial agility that enables organizations to adapt quickly to new circumstances (including competitors). Be that as it may, these qualities are associated with global markets, not law. Law provides a different picture of globalization—for our purposes a more demanding one and at the same time a more hopeful one. Even in the globalizing state, law is expected to be stable and to emphasize continuities in a language of precedents and gradual social change. Law is authoritative. It consists of commands and provides decision makers with authority to render final decisions—and citizens with the means of holding decision makers to account. The appeals process in law depends on a hierarchy of authority. Indeed, the hierarchical nature of law is the source of its finality and certainty. When globalization is imagined as a culture unto itself, the very image of law in this sense would seem to conflict with the entrepreneurial spirit of the age.

But the globalizing state is a nexus of institutions, not a "system" or an intangible world view. In that institutional milieu, the image of law as stable and authoritative is incomplete. The constitutional role of law potentially provides a common language for a public sphere. Law is the means by which we govern ourselves, the processes and forums in which public commitments can be decided in open deliberation and debate. In short, law is a creative idiom that enables us, in deeply practical ways, to ask each other what kind of society we wish to be. Its stability makes it more important to ask whose interests it protects, and for whom it speaks. Its hierarchy makes it more difficult to ignore the institutional locations of the globalizing state—institutions that were created, in large measure, by law. Thus, while there are important effects of globalization (including cultural change), and while law alone cannot close the democracy deficit, law remains an important resource for those who envision globalization as something other than an indomitable and impersonal force.

A major role for law in the global era is to help create the institutional architecture necessary for democracy to work, not only within the institutions of government but also beyond them in the sphere where the private sector governs. Democracy as an end in itself has given its inherently fundamental importance to the liberal ideal. Law is a means of protecting, preserving, and creating forums for democratic deliberation. Even if executives in seclusion reach the same decision as an agency operating in full sunshine, the democracy deficit reflects the lost occasion for the public to participate in the deliberation by which the value regimes that determine outcomes are themselves defined, distinguished, and decided from among plural possibilities. The value of deliberation over values is especially important as globalization broadens and intensifies the contact among different value regimes and (accordingly) social priorities. Perhaps above all, closing the democracy deficit calls for forums in which people can respond to globalization by deciding the price (so to speak) they are willing to pay for efficiency and profitability. Such decisions call for contexts where people can negotiate their priorities with other stakeholders, even stakeholders from other countries, and accordingly hold their own representatives accountable.

Administrative law is especially appropriate as the vehicle for addressing the democracy deficit in this way. It is in administrative law that the rules for public participation in the form of information and input, as well as for government and industry accountability, are set. Administrative law has always been grounded on basic norms. These norms include transparency, participation, and fairness, and they are built upon the norm of democracy. Indeed, it may be that a major contribution of a new administrative law can be to reformulate the criteria of public/private decision-making processes, creating a space for a politics that acknowledges economic and noneconomic values and their limits.

As I have already suggested, reforms are necessary at all levels of government (local, state, federal, and international). New ways of expanding the democratic reach of administrative law are also in order when nonstate actors are involved. I shall explore the prospects for reform more specifically below.

Democracy Deficits and the Purposes of Law Reform

As the previous chapters have argued, it is not fruitful to imagine different levels of governance as if they were layers on a cake, neatly arranged and unified in strict hierarchical fashion.[12] Bright-line distinctions between federal and international, state and federal, or global and local do not capture the complex transnational mixtures of power now involved even in domestic governance. These multiple levels and centers of governance include state and nonstate actors, and public and private settings. In this milieu, we might consider three broad purposes of law reform. First, a primary purpose of law reform should be to facilitate the flow of information between and among these layers of policymakers, maximizing not only coordination but also citizen input into the process in a timely and, thus, politically meaningful way.

Second, the line between public and private must be renegotiated to take account of globalization. As we have seen (especially in chapter 3), markets and law are merged with regulation and the provision of government services such that it is now necessary to extend public-law values such as transparency and participation to private actors. This goal would by no means condemn us to reinventing the worst excesses of administrative bureaucracy. There are various ways to provide for transparency and accountability that can help retain some of the efficiency advantages a private provider of services might bring. Importing public-law values into the private sector should be aimed particularly at ensuring citizen involvement in the policy aspects of private contracts and in the ways in which those contracts are carried out in practice. In other words, an overriding purpose of law is to provide the means for citizen governance of regulatory issues, regardless of the public or private label that may be placed on the institutional body wielding the power.

This kind of involvement need not open floodgates of micro-management. The processes involved may be more informational in nature, for example, where citizens are given a forum in which to contribute to deliberation over privatization of a particular service, the trade-offs involved in achieving cost savings, the nature of the workforce involved, and the like. The goal of such processes is to keep such issues and concern *in politics,* in the broadest sense of that term. In short, another important purpose of the law reforms proposed below is to promote the recognition of the political sphere as well as to enhance the flexibility and range of approaches to problem solving.

Third, law should protect the timeliness of politics. Legal approaches and mechanisms that remove decisions from the political arena for substantial periods of time should be avoided. With the exception of fundamental human-rights issues, each administration and each generation of citizens should have the freedom—and the forums—to maximize opportunities for experimentation and change. Public actions should not be written in stone. Indeed, as Janet McLean has argued, there is a distinction between "the state" and "the government of the day." "The state," she notes, purports to speak for all citizens and is treated, legally speaking, as if it were a unified entity.[13] State action in this sense binds its constituents, and can establish long-term commitments that go well beyond the terms of office of those who make such commitments on the nation's behalf. The idea of "the government of the day," however, offers a contrasting view of such state action. It reflects more fully the value of experimentation and the reality of the tentative compromise nature of many governmental policies.[14] Our political administration should not be allowed to co-opt the politics of the future by binding future generations to particular policies or policy effects. It is this more fluid and changeable idea of state power that animated New Deal courts and their deference to legislative bodies. In the globalizing state, too, whenever possible, legislative policymakers should have maximum discretion to experiment and change regulatory approaches in the face of new conditions and new political perceptions of the problems involved.

Discussing each of these broad purposes of law reform opens up a dialogue over the most serious manifestations of the democracy deficit presented throughout this book. Indeed, each of these purposes just outlined points to a key location in the production of the democracy deficit. First, and perhaps most seriously, the democracy deficit occurs at state and federal sites where private actors are charged with carrying out public responsibilities. The use of this kind of privatization as a tool of governance must be seen clearly for what it is—the use of markets for public ends. Given this reality, these private providers should be accountable to the public, and we need to go beyond that requirement as well. Private providers, whether working for profit or not, should not be allowed to substitute for citizens, either by turning the public at large into mere consumers of their services or, in effect, claiming to be their political representatives. Not only should private providers be held accountable, but they also need to share their policy-making power with the citizens they serve, at least to the extent of creating and sharing information on which their policies are based and according to which those policies might be assessed. This would enable citizens to comment in meaningful ways on both policy making and evaluation. Citizenship turns on the law's ability to provide the forums necessary for individuals, entities, and groups to help shape and influence outcomes in ways such as these.

As we shall see below, some of the state statutes—known as privatization statutes—aimed at providing greater transparency and accountability for privatized aspects of government offer various approaches to democracy problems. Such statutes, as we shall also see, are in sharp contrast to the way privatization is treated at the federal level, i.e., left largely to the discretion of the federal agencies involved. Not only are federal agencies' basic decisions and reasons for privatization or outsourcing often devoid of public input, but the end result of relying so heavily on private providers to carry out core functions of government (involving, for example, coordinating and servicing the military or determining welfare eligibility through Halliburton and Lockheed Martin, respectively) is to understate the size of government.[15] In the federal privatization process, as I argue below, a kind of neocorporatist approach to government is emerging, replete with its own democracy deficit issues.

Second, democracy deficits are also located in and flow from institutional sites where international and domestic law interact. For example, as noted in chapter 2, when rules are harmonized in accord with a WTO treaty, this is the result of, usually, long negotiations involving the executive branch and various other countries. When the outcomes of these negotiations are duly set forth for public notice and comment under the Administrative Procedure Act, the timing is such that the process is little more than a fait accompli. Given that the executive branch has expended considerable time and effort negotiating these rules, and has done so largely in private, it is not likely it will be responsive to requests for significant changes at this stage in the process. The decision-making process treats the WTO and the negotiations that occur there as if it were separate and apart from domestic processes—in effect, comprising a level above domestic decision makers as if countries were member states in a federal system. In consequence, a federalism mindset and approach comes into play, but this fails as a basis for integrating fully the decision making at the WTO with domestic law.

Third, a democracy deficit results when the executive branch or the court deploys legal mechanisms and constitutional principles such that important issues are taken off the political table for generations to come. Depriving the federal government the opportunity to act in certain regulatory capacities by limiting the scope of the commerce clause is one way this outcome occurs. Expanding the scope of executive power, also at the expense of the legislative process, is yet another way. As already noted, there should be a bias in favor of politics and democracy, that is, in favor of opportunities for legislative reconsideration and change. Issues involving structural constitutional questions such as federalism or separation-of-powers questions should be approached with great restraint by the judiciary.

The following sections examine various ways we might reform state and federal law with these purposes and locations in mind. I begin with privatization at the federal level, examining how administrative agencies can be effective sites for governing globalization and mitigating the worst effects of neocorporatism on democracy. In that context, we shall examine Congress itself as a governance site. The next section shifts to the state level, focusing on private prisons as an extended example. The third section considers international governance through the example of the WTO and then focuses on a deferential role for courts to play in these various contexts. The book concludes with a discussion of the prospects for revitalizing citizen participation in the ongoing project of making globalization responsive to democracy. My goals are neither antimarket nor pro–world government. Rather, I hope to contribute to invigorating democratic governance at the local level by checking the practices whereby the forces of globalization have become synonymous with the democracy deficit.

Privatization at the Federal Level

Privatization at the federal level occurs largely at the discretion of the various agencies involved. It may appear that privatization makes government smaller. In fact, the notion that the federal government is shrinking is inaccurate. Most reports on governmental size fail to count the increase in government employees that is now occurring due to grants, contracts, and the number of employees necessary to carry out federal mandates at the state and local levels of government. As Paul Light notes in his annual report on the overall size of the federal government for the Brookings Institution, when one accounts for the growing use of delegations to the private sector or local and state mandates that require the use of state employees, the overall size of government is not shrinking but growing.[16] The age of big government in the form in which we once recognized the public sector may be over, but the actual number of individuals doing the public's business is increasing. At a minimum, a more transparent and publicly accessible accounting for the actual size of government is necessary on the part of the federal government, but even more important is the opportunity for citizens to (1) have input into the basic decisions made by various agencies to privatize in the first place, (2) have some indication of the processes and criteria used to achieve these outcomes, and (3) have an ongoing ability to assess its success or failure. Administrative procedure can play an important role in such reform. Though the Administrative Procedure Act is often associated with a regulatory period far different from the market-dominated era in which we now live, the values of the APA remain vitally relevant to the way we choose to govern ourselves. Openness, accountability, and citizen participation are vital to new governance regimes now emerging.

Though these goals of openness, accountability, and participation may be achieved in a variety of ways, the APA is already available as a platform for procedural reforms that can counter many aspects of the democracy deficit by extending APA values and procedures to the public/private, hybrid decision-making contexts spawned by privatization. The APA need not be applied in old ways, but can be reformulated and reconceptualized so as to address the problems and possibilities of a global era. Perhaps the most important change to be made is the expansion of the APA to include private actors carrying out public responsibilities. Administrative law, as reflected in the APA,[17] is built around the act's assumptions about the market and the state, assumptions that reflect the state-action doctrine in the Constitution.[18] Due process and other constitutional rights apply to states and state actors, not the private sector.[19] Administrative agencies are defined as state actors, and the procedural protections that apply, both constitutional and statutory, are designed for a relatively clearly demarcated public sphere.[20] The APA is, by definition, state centered.

Three main administrative-law theories underlie the implementation of this act and of administrative law as we know it today. They deal with the way the state and agencies act in relation to the private sector and to interest groups' lobbying, and all of them are statecentric. These are pluralism, public-choice theory, and republican theory.[21] Indeed, the major theoretical underpinnings of administrative law assume (incorrectly) that the market and the state are separate worlds. (We have emphasized their interaction and integral intertwining.) Pluralistic theorists see the outcome of state legislative and regulatory action ultimately as the product of voluntary interaction among autonomous interest groups.[22] From this interaction solutions to problems emerge that are in the public interest. Public-choice theorists, on the other hand, posit a political marketplace, not unlike the economic marketplace, where powerful groups demand legislation or regulation that is ultimately supplied by legislators and regulators. Many of these theorists even reject the notion that there is something that can be called the public interest.[23] Republican theorists see legislative and regulatory outcomes as the products of a deliberative process in which a public interest can be defined and achieved.[24]

All of these statecentric theories are designed to account for the way state actions come about, at the legislative and the regulatory agency levels. Agencies are set squarely in the state sphere, but as a guide to administrative law, this map is now incomplete. The "province of administrative law," as we have seen, also includes administration by private entities and hybrid public/private bodies, such as federal corporations.[25] The relationship of the market to the state in such bodies differs from that in earlier notions that assumed a relatively clean division between the public and the private. Rather than private interest groups persuading state actors to undertake a certain course of action, public bodies themselves now often determine who, when, and how to delegate public functions to private actors. Private actors, either alone or in partnership with the state, are important administrators and policymakers.[26] States need them to solve problems and compete effectively in the global economy, and private entities can now provide certain kinds of technical experience and cost-effective management.

When one focuses on such mixes of public and private power from a global point of view, it is apparent that the state's role is changing as is its relationship to global markets and the private sector. Privatized market-oriented approaches to services and regulation raise theoretical questions that go to the heart of the U.S. administrative process, requiring new ways of understanding it as well as highlighting new risks that can arise from a fusion of public and private mechanisms and values. For reasons developed below, the risks of neocorporatism[27] are significant. Its impact on public law values and the democracy deficit are potentially profound.

The Globalizing State and the Risks of Neocorporatism

Corporatist theory involves several aspects of regulatory actions that are relevant to our analysis of the democracy deficit and the potential for addressing it through law reform. First, corporatism denies the basic pluralist idea that policy emerges from the free and voluntary interaction of multiple interest groups. It, in effect, advocates government bargaining with selected, representative interest groups or "peak organizations" with subsequent deal making among those groups with respect to public policy in key areas.[28]

Corporatist theory holds that during the bargaining that ensues, the state is operating with a public-interest goal in mind. It is not a captured entity, but an independent player with a very important seat at the policy-making table.[29] Thus the state does more than simply reflect the sum total of the preferences of its constituents, but rather seeks to assert its view of the public interest in the course of bargaining.

As a result of these state approaches, corporatist theory holds that the state is, by definition, elitist—democratic neither in purpose nor result. From a corporatist perspective, the state enters into bargaining in an attempt to avoid confrontation and to maintain a politics of accommodation. For this degree of consensus to occur, however, normal political processes are usually sidestepped or undermined. Traditional democratic processes are replaced by technocratic and managerial solutions.[30]

Each of these three aspects of corporatist theory describes an important aspect of the current globalizing state, especially in privatized contexts. Neocorporatism also illustrates clearly the risks to democracy in globalization. Correspondingly, it underscores the importance of administrative law as a context where hybrid approaches to government are forged. While it might initially seem that the idea of peak organizations is foreign to U.S. politics, given the wide diversity of views and groups that exist, the reality of the administrative process in the globalizing state has become quite different than it may appear. Once issues are funneled through an administrative process, there is usually a significant drop-off in the number of interest groups with the resources necessary to participate and, therefore, capable of influencing agency decisions. Those that can persist are, in some sense, like peak organizations. They may not have been chosen or selected by the government, but neither are they infinitely diverse. Peak organizations, as such, are not at all typical in the United States, but the economic discourse that increasingly dominates regulation, and provides the raison d'etre for privatization, narrows the policy choices in such a way that any participating group must "speak" the same language as, in effect, a prerequisite to admission. In short, there may be no peak organizations per se, but the discourse the key players engage in is so economically oriented and focused that a distinction between certain selected groups and those that now, in fact, participate is one without a difference.

In most privatization contexts involving contracting out, the number of parties involved is small. Often, for example, just two or three major corporations realistically compete to manage prisons.[31] Once one of these contractors is chosen, as is true in many contractual arrangements, long-term relationships are likely to develop, threatening to diminish even further the actual number of bargaining parties at the table in the future. As Paul Craig observes, "A mutually dependent bargaining relationship emerges between government and the corporate sector, in which favorable policies are traded for co-operation and expertise."[32] Alan Cawson refers to these effects as "the growing inter-representation of the public and the private spheres."[33]

The globalizing state needs not only the political support of only certain groups as well as their know-how and expertise to carry out tasks in cost-effective and, ideally, politically uncontroversial ways. The reliance of the state on the market for these ends make the state to some extent dependent on private interests, as Cawson goes on to note: "the crucial concept is that of public policy as the outcome of a bargaining process between state agencies and those organized interests whose power in the political marketplace means that their co-operation is indispensable if agreed upon policies are to be implemented."[34]

The relationship of private technical expertise to the states' efficacy suggests another neocorporatist element in governance at the domestic level. While technical expertise constitutes an important mode of state legitimation, economic discourse alone may narrow substantive debate so as to call that legitimacy into question. This is especially the case in relation to social services where significant noneconomic values are at stake.[35] When efficiency values are defined solely in terms of accountability measures as legitimizing devices, without an opportunity to temper often short-term economic goals with noneconomic values, technocracy "mask[s] ideological choices"[36] that should be subject to public debate.

The need for the state to enter into bargaining arrangements as a means of achieving realistically enforceable contracts is indicative of the current limits of direct command-control regulations. Those limits go beyond the scope of the deregulation movement. As noted above, globalization restricts a state's regulatory options in various ways, not the least of which is that some industries can move production around the globe relatively easily, avoiding certain costs, and often affecting local politics and employment opportunities in the process. The territorial fixity of the state is a bargaining disadvantage in that capital can easily slip beyond the limits of state jurisdiction—though it can also be an advantage in attracting foreign capital. Corporations are freer to reject the political costs of doing business in any one jurisdiction if they can move production around the globe relatively easily.[37] Furthermore, as the funding of agencies decreases, effective enforcement of the agency regulations increasingly requires the cooperation of the regulated.[38] There are simply not enough staff and resources to enforce regulations that seemingly undercut a company's basic economic goals and make the achievement of the regulatory outcomes sought more costly than the company believes they need to be.

Whether or not corporatist theory adequately accounts for the relationship of the government to interest groups, from a theoretical standpoint, the implications of any parallels should raise serious concerns regarding the new private public sphere, especially when social services are involved. The activities of private providers regarding prisons and welfare, for example, clearly have important public dimensions no matter what label we place on the service providers involved.

The province of administrative law must be broad. Taking account of the global context in which administrative law now functions must mean theorizing afresh the nature of pluralism and republicanism in relation to the administrative process. It is possible to conceive of privatization and democracy in terms of the classical theories, such as pluralism and republicanism, as but one technology of marketization among others, and as one deliberative process among others. As indicated above, though, pluralism and republicanism as currently framed imply a territorialized state, and indeed a nation state that contains all the prospective participants. They also imply that these participants are on more or less equal footing before the state.

As currently framed, these theories cannot account for the highly ambiguous line between the public and private sectors in practice, nor the extent to which key industries or even individual companies might figure in a government's policy planning. It would be naive to imagine that such fusions did not exist, or to imagine that they were not necessary. Absent democratic checks, the current scenario appears to be evolving in a way reminiscent of corporatism, at least to the extent that public-private partnerships are now at the very core of the state's self-legitimating practices. My recommendations for addressing the democracy deficit are aimed not at rolling back the clock but at acknowledging the current state of affairs and exposing that fusion at the core of government to democratic procedures and open political debate. In this way, administrative law can play a vital role in the new governance structures and processes now taking shape, ensuring opportunities for individuals, in their capacities as citizens, to participate in the decisions that significantly affect their lives and the communities of which they are a part. It can and should involve the application of public-law values to private actors and the creation of informal approaches to ensure that a multiplicity of voices can be heard and that noneconomic values as well as monetary costs are considered. It often falls to Congress to initiate these statutory procedural reforms, but Congress itself can also play an even more direct substantive role when it comes to governing globalization, as I shall discuss below.

Emerging Issues for a New Administrative Law

Privatization has been one of the primary forms of marketization in the United States. Some proponents of the trend might say that there is no great trade-off for democracy if snow removal shifts from a city garage to a private contractor or even if a publicly operated prison is now managed by a for-profit private corporation. But the fact that such trends in management are driven by global processes assures us that a larger transformation is underway. The connection between the relatively minor example of snow removal and the more significant change in approach to prisons or welfare is in their common reference to globalization and the structural aspects of their insulation from the public.

Democracy requires more than just market forces and outcomes. It involves and requires more than representation and a chance to hold public officials accountable through the ballot box.[39] Legitimacy comes in many forms and through many forums. Administrative law can facilitate the creation of multiple arenas for policy discussion for the ongoing monitoring and revising of contracts. Focusing on the democracy deficit brought about by globalization does not mean that the traditional legitimacy arguments so common in administrative law are the only relevant arguments.[40] In fact, the major difference between legitimacy concerns expressed in traditional public law terms and today's concerns is that nonstate decision makers must now be accounted for. We have moved from old questions concerning the proper role of judges as opposed to legislators to new questions as to whether policy making will leave room for any public input at all. It is not just a connection with an elected official that matters. What matters more are opportunities for interested individuals to have input in policy-making processes generally as well as in the specific instances that may affect them directly. Again, I emphasize that law enables a public conversation about what kind of society we wish to be.

Beyond traditional notions of electoral accountability, democracy requires the means by which issues can be drawn, information shared and a meaningful politics created. This involves multiple public forums as already noted. Legitimacy requires more than a process designed simply to "check up" on those in positions of responsibility, to see if they are doing their job. It also involves creating the kind of information necessary for citizens to understand the issues involved so that a real debate can ensue and new ideas can be suggested. Administrative law can and should play an important role in making forums available to consider and assess new approaches to issues considered not only by public agencies but by public/private hybrids as well. The public/private distinction should not shield decision-making processes unduly from opportunities for participation and the articulation of values and points of view that enrich our politics and, indeed, make meaningful political discussion possible.

Closely related to these democracy concerns are questions of citizenship. Quite apart from the decision makers involved, how do we conceptualize those affected by these decisions? In addition to being citizens, individuals are increasingly treated as consumers, customers, and clients, as well. Each of these labels (citizen, customer/consumer, and client) carries a different expectation with regard to individual and collective responsibility for the provision of services. At what point does the convergence of market processes, private decision makers, and individuals as consumers, customers, or clients actually undercut our ability as citizens to engage in the broader kinds of participation necessary for a vibrant political process?[41] It is important that the legal discourses triggered by the public/private distinction do not undercut or mask the role that citizens need to play.

A third, related set of issues for the new administrative law involves conflict-of-interest concerns. The statecentric aspects of traditional administrative law have focused primarily on public administrators. When it comes to conflict questions, the law asks questions such as whether there was a personal economic interest tied to the decision involved,[42] or inappropriate ex parte[43] contacts, or whether there was undue bias on the part of the decision maker.[44] Economic gain is a particularly relevant criterion when applied to some forms of privatization, where the decision makers involved are chosen in part because of the incentives provided by their duty to try to make a profit. Clearly, to obviate this problem, the parameters of the delegated task must be set forth with clarity. Delegation-like doctrine requirements can and should surface in this context, since it can only be assumed that a private-prison provider will want to carry out its duties in as profitable a manner as possible. To assure that this does not include riding roughshod over prisoners' rights, legislative and contractual detail is necessary. Such an approach can thus eliminate a financial conflict by making clear the challenges the contractor must meet before any profit is possible.

In contexts covered by the APA, conflict questions turn largely on the nature of the proceedings involved. Are they adjudicatory or legislative? Such a discourse normally would not apply in privatized settings. Private providers are implementing public policies but, of course, new policies and approaches inevitably emerge in the dynamic contexts in which they operate. Moreover, there are some new, deregulated markets in which private bodies and private actors now make decisions with significant public implications. This clearly is one of the lessons of the Enron debacle.[45] More specifically, private providers of public services must keep the profit motive in mind; that is their obligation to their shareholders. Yet, public-policy concerns may require approaches, actions, or the sharing of information in a timely fashion that might further some public goals but increase private costs. What are the conflict-of-interest requirements of such participants in these contexts? The very natures of public and private enterprises differ. The profit motive can be a good incentive, but, in public settings, it is not the sole goal, and it can conflict with other values. Indeed, what happens when market-oriented, bottom-line considerations drive decisions that adversely affect human rights? A private-prison provider may have more incentives to construe as narrowly as possible the due process or Eighth Amendment requirements of the Constitution, even assuming they apply fully in a private setting.[46] Can all such matters be dealt with specifically before they arise, by statute or contract, without unnecessarily burdening public/private decision-making processes?

Reforms

The risks of neocorporatism and the changing relationship of the market to the state suggest various reforms. Engaging in the process requires an understanding of the pluralistic aspects of the law developing in various privatization contexts,[47] but at the same time it also requires recognizing the need for basic democratic values. Democracy and neutrality are essential for the legitimacy of any regime with broad public significance; this is particularly true with regard to social services involving the poor, welfare recipients, and prisoners. By definition, welfare recipients and prisoners fall outside the opportunity structures of the normal economy. But quite apart from giving rise to demands for transparency, participation, and fairness in such contexts, privatization may be nothing short of a quiet revolution in how to cope with public problems.[48] The Administrative Procedures Act of the twenty-first century must find ways to ensure that the values of administrative law remain relevant. To accomplish this, I suggest beginning with three basic federal administrative reforms, each addressing one of the three aspects of democracy deficit discussed earlier.

First, it is important to recognize that the public or private label we place on an actor wielding power over others is less important than the power relationships that are established. To this end, we might take a page from the United Kingdom's approach to natural justice questions.[49] Due process procedural protections apply to powerful entities, whether or not they are state actors. Procedural protections also should be designed to assure that there is a flow of information about the operation of hybrid partnerships and the creation of a meaningful politics. A twenty-first-century APA should apply to some private actors, as well as the state, particularly when private actors have significant power over the constituents with whom they deal and when they are engaged in public functions. Extension of the APA does not mean that the same procedures must be used that were devised for a different era, or that we should overjudicialize hybrid arrangements. Indeed, information flow and the ability of good information to create a politics around an issue is a crucial reform as well. Extending the Freedom of Information Act at least to those private entities engaged in providing services previously provided by government is an important first step. Moreover, informal administrative procedures, as opposed to adjudication, for example, may be all that is necessary to put this information to good work.

At the same time, there are other APA provisions that remain relevant, and should be amended. The contracting-out provision in section 553 is a prime example.[50] Contracts used to outsource social services to the poor or to manage private prisons should be viewed as rules, subject to notice and comment, and as the beginning of a process, not the end of a private negotiation. As I have argued elsewhere,[51] contracts of this kind are part of an evolving process of governance, not the final result of private negotiations. Input on a regular basis is necessary if citizens are to have a meaningful role in the policy-making process. If policy questions arise within the framework of the contract involved, the flexibility necessary to react to them on the part of citizens should exist. Contracts need to be open to such change if participation is to be meaningful.

Moreover, the informal rule-making provision of which the contracting provision is a part can be used to broaden considerably both the scope of our domestic perspective and the range of participants involved. Administrative rule-making processes should include an explicit direction to consider seriously the global implications of proposed rules, similar in principle to the National Environmental Policy Act (NEPA) and its requirement that the environmental consequences of governmental actions be assessed and analyzed. There should, in effect, be a global NEPA statement attached to informal rule-making procedures. This would not only encourage participants to indicate the transboundary effects of a rule but also provide a domestic forum to raise the issue. The participants involved might very well come from parts of the world likely to feel the brunt of the action considered. For example, when the tobacco companies were considering entering into a settlement in which they retained the right to market their products freely in the developing world, it might have been useful to consider the worldwide implications on health such action would have and to do so at the source, so to speak.

Many conflict-of-interest concerns can be addressed in terms of contract reform. Not unlike the constitutionally based delegation doctrine, requiring legislative standards to guide agency discretion, there must be a level of specificity in the contract involved sufficient to make clear the obligations of the provider; to ensure that some efficiencies are not achieved for the wrong reasons, such contracts should specify not only what must be accomplished but also how. Administrative law also needs to further the development of new approaches as well, beyond the extension of well-known procedural types of protections. One approach to conflict-of-interest problems is to involve third parties as auditors in various contexts. What the Government Accounting Office (GAO) does for public policies might be duplicated by private-group certification of the private delivery of social services. For example, as Robert Fischman has noted, "Market certification of sustainable forest management is a new development of the past decade."[52] Professor Fischman describes the Forest Stewardship Council (FSC), "an independent, non-profit coalition of environmental groups, citizens, economic development organizations, and the timber industry" who sponsor private audits of forestry practices.[53] Providing information and the opportunity for input and dialogue by a variety of private parties deeply concerned with all of the issues, economic and environmental, can help further a relatively unbiased approach to policy making. An outgrowth of the Enron debacle is the regulation of accounting firms for conflict-of-interest concerns, but this problem transcends accounting per se. The principles developed in the context of the Sarbanes-Oaxley Act ought to be extended to cover the kinds of conflicts that arise in the hybrid partnerships we have been discussing. Congress should not overlook this significant area of governance as it seeks to reform the accounting industry.

Privatization at the State Level

State legislatures have been much more actively involved in governing privatization than the Congress. Indeed, individual states take various approaches to the privatization issue in general, subjecting private service providers to differing degrees of public accountability. Some individual states have become more involved in the privatization of prisons than in the privatization of possibly any other public service. "By the end of 2000, there were 87,369 state and federal prisoners in private detention facilities in the United States—6.3% of all state and federal prisoners, and 22.7% more than in 1999."[54] Most states have statutes regarding the privatization of prisons, some allowing and encouraging them, some banning their use altogether.[55] Currently, thirty states (as well as Puerto Rico and the District of Columbia) have contracts with private prisons for the housing of state prisoners.[56] Several states (for example, Delaware, Nebraska, and New Mexico) have statutes allowing for prison privatization but do not have any contracts with private providers.[57] Other states (such as Iowa, Maryland, and Minnesota) have private-prison contracts without any specific statutory authorization for such contracts.[58] Many states also have general privatization statutes covering the privatization of any service. These various statutes reflect a variety of views towards privatization. For example, Colorado's privatization statute provides that "it is . . . the policy of this state to encourage the use of private contractors for personal services to achieve increased efficiency in the delivery of government services."[59] At the other end of the spectrum, the Massachusetts privatization statute states that the legislature "hereby finds and declares that using private contractors to provide public services formally provided by public employees does not always promote the public interest."[60] The danger of statutes like Colorado's is that they implied by stating as fact the contentious issue of whether private providers are more efficient; the statute encourages a finding that private companies would more efficiently provide *any* service. This statute can operate as a presumption that privatization is in the public interest, which may stifle debate on any individual privatization decision.

In order to illustrate how public values can be applied to private actors, it is helpful to look at the statutes involved in the privatization of prisons because of both the large number and the variety of such statutes. They are illustrative of the ways in which states attempt to create "global currency"—in effect, the price government is willing to pay to remain economically competitive.[61] The most common form of currency is money, generated from the provision of fewer or more efficiently provided governmental services or both, from lower taxes, from lower regulatory costs, as well as from investments in the infrastructures and human capital necessary to create, stimulate, and sustain economic growth.[62]

Not all forms of global currency are legitimate. For example, allowable trade-offs for cost cutting in privatizing prisons should not include deprivations of private prisoners' constitutional rights.[63] Similarly, if global currency is generated by economic decisions with short-term gain but foreseeable, long-term costs, and information about these trade-offs was not given in a useful way to the affected public, legitimacy problems may arise.[64] Child labor,[65] slave wages,[66] and unsafe working conditions[67] are also arguably illegitimate forms of global currency. They all provide a competitive advantage to a particular location and individuals associated with it, but at a cost borne by people unable to fully choose for themselves or unaware of the true costs of the bargain being struck. For example, the costs of a toxic dump may not be fully apparent to those most likely to bear them (i.e., local residents), or they may have little or no effective power to resist them.[68]

As I stated in chapter 3, there is a continuing debate about whether private prisons offer any real cost benefit at all. It is common, however, for statutes to require a minimum-percentage cost savings from private-prison operators.[69] The Colorado statute explicitly allows private providers to adjust worker wages and benefits: "[t]he general assembly recognizes that such contracting may result in variances from legislatively mandated pay scales and other employment practices that apply to the state personnel system."[70] In contrast, Washington, D.C., requires a private provider to offer displaced workers a right of first refusal for jobs with the private company, and further requires that the private company comply with the government pay scale for six months.[71] The D.C. statute restricts a private provider's ability to meet cost targets by hiring more efficient workers or changing incentive structures; any required efficiency gains must therefore come from the reduction of other costs. The Colorado statute, like many others, provides that "privatization of government services not result in diminished quality in order to save money."[72] When privatizing prisons, however, an important question asks, whose perspective provides the basis for measuring "quality"?

Accountability

One way to increase the accountability of private-prison operators is to limit the length of the privatization contract. The Supreme Court recognized this form of accountability in *Richardson v. McKnight,* where a Tennessee statute limited a contract's term to three years. The majority stated that the firm's "performance is disciplined . . . by pressure from potentially competing firms who can try to take its place."[73] Many states, however, do not specify a maximum contract length; some statutes explicitly allow for long-term contracts. Arkansas, for example, states that contracts with private prisons "may be entered into for a period of up to twenty (20) years."[74] On the other end of the spectrum, Ohio provides that a contract "shall be for an initial term of not more than two years, with an option to renew for additional periods of two years."[75] Shorter contracts increase the potential frequency of public input into the process, which would ideally be encouraged before contract renewal takes place.

A problem with the Court's praise of the short term provided by Tennessee law is that it assumed that there would be a number of firms available in the event the private provider fell short in its performance. The actual competitiveness of the privatized-prison industry, or lack thereof, however, is reflected in its oligopolistic nature. As of December 31, 1998, over 76 percent of the private prison capacity was controlled by just two companies: Wackenhut Corrections Corporation and Corrections Corporation of America.[76] When states privatize they must realize that the benefits of any marketlike effects are concentrated in the period before a contract is entered: "The distinctive feature of contracting out is the element of *ex ante* competition—competition *for* the market as opposed to *in* it."[77] The imposition of long contracts between states and prison providers is likely to further concentrate the industry, by providing fewer opportunities for new companies to enter a market with a very limited number of potential customers.

In addition to the accountability-increasing feature of having a short potential contract period, Tennessee also provides that any private prison "must agree that the state may cancel the contract at any time after the first year of operation, without penalty to the state, upon giving ninety (90) days' written notice."[78] This provision encourages the state to oversee the running of any private prison more closely, because the delegation can easily be reconsidered. Private groups who are interested in the privatization of prisons also have an incentive to monitor the private provider more closely, because at any time after the first year, they can lobby the state to rescind the contract if it becomes apparent that a different provider (either public or private) would be preferable.

Another important issue for accountability is what entity actually makes the contract to privatize, and what involvement other actors have in this process. To the extent that contracts become immutable, often even to later legislatures, it is important that the participation of the public and the public's representatives be maximized as early in the process as possible. Tennessee's statute provides a complex contract-approval procedure involving several individuals and entities, but makes no provisions for the input of the general public.[79] The statute must be approved by the state building commission, the attorney general, and the commissioner of correction.[80] Additionally, all proposals are reviewed by two legislative committees, which can make comments to those responsible for approving contracts before such approval takes place.[81] All approved and proposed contracts are then sent to the state and local government committees of both the Senate and the House.[82] While this procedure involves various members of the legislative and executive branch, it does not provide opportunities for the public to affect these officials' decisions. At least the privatization procedure involves members of both the executive and legislative branches, and includes legislators themselves, who are often very accessible to public input. In Idaho, the decision to enter into a contract with a private prison provider is left solely to the state board of correction, not unlike at the federal level;[83] most of the public would not know whom to contact to affect potential privatization contracts, or whom to hold accountable for the decisions of the board.

While several privatization statutes, such as Tennessee's, provide for some participation from the legislative branch in the contracting phase, few suggest any method for direct involvement from the public. One of the few states to specifically call for a public hearing does so in a statute covering all forms of government privatization. Montana requires an agency to form a privatization plan before any state program can be privatized. Additionally, Montana law makes the following provisions:

> The privatization plan must be released to the public and any affected employee organizations and must be submitted to the legislative audit committee at least 90 days prior to the proposed implementation date. At least 60 days prior to the proposed implementation date, the legislative audit committee shall conduct a public hearing on the proposed

privatization plan at which public comments and testimony must be received. At least 15 days prior to the proposed implementation date, the legislative audit committee shall release to the public a summary of the results of the hearing, including any recommendations of the committee relating to the proposed privatization plan.[84]

Public hearings produce little benefit, however, if the public is not provided with adequate information with which to make informed suggestions. Kentucky law requires the production of information necessary for the public to make informed decisions about the quality and value of privatized services.

> The private provider shall develop and implement a plan for the dissemination of information about the adult correctional facility to the public, government agencies, and the media. The plan shall be made available to all persons. All documents and records, except financial records, maintained by the private provider shall be deemed public records. . . .[85]

Kentucky does not rely solely on voluntary disclosure by the provider to amass information on the functioning of privatized prisons. The legislature has also required that "[t]he department shall annually conduct a performance evaluation of any adult correctional facility for which a private provider has contracted to operate. The department shall make a written report of its findings and submit this report along with any recommendations to the private provider and the Legislative Research Commission."[86] The prison privatization provisions create a large amount of data and attempt to transmit most of the data to the public. They do not, however, provide any mechanism for the public to participate in the privatization decision, nor do they limit the length of contracts, nor include most of the concrete requirements for the actual running of the prisons.

Given their cost-savings requirements, private providers bring economic interests to service delivery that public providers might not. For example, if a provider is not required to educate prisoners in an attempt to reduce recidivism, private prisons might theoretically have an incentive to actually increase recidivism (and thereby increase their potential "market"). Michigan, in its statute allowing the privatization of juvenile-correction facilities, mandates that private providers of prisons require prisoners without high school degrees to receive a general education certificate (GED).[87] Colorado requires that private providers guarantee education services (and other services including dental, medical, psychological, diet, and work program) of at least as high quality as public prisons.[88] However, Colorado's provision does not provide any specific, concrete standards by which a comparison of quality can be judged.

Statutes that clearly specify required elements of any prison privatization contract are preferable to those that establish few (or no) concrete requirements of the private entity in such contracts. In contrast to contract provisions, statutory language is readily accessible to the public; almost all of a state's statutory law can be located, free of charge, through the state's homepage.[89] Additionally, even if the public cannot comment, legislative sessions are often open for the attendance of interested individuals (the Colorado General Assembly website allows the public to listen to the proceedings in the state House and Senate, even including committee meetings).[90] Additionally, incorporating contract terms into a statute allows interested groups to focus their efforts on the design of every privatization contract in the state; trying to influence each contract individually (even if the group would be notified before a contract was finalized) might often prove to be too taxing on an interested group's or individual's resources. Finally, legislatures are directly accountable to the public through elections, while entities such as state corrections boards are not.

Several prison privatization statutes create new commissions to oversee prison privatization; one of the most detailed statutes creating such an entity was passed in Florida.[91] The Florida statute created "[t]he Correctional Privatization Commission . . . for the purpose of entering into contracts . . . for the designing, financing, acquiring, leasing, constructing, and operating of private correctional facilities."[92] The commission is made up of five members appointed by the governor; four of the members must be from the private sector and none may be employed by the Department of Corrections.[93] There is some democratic oversight of the commission: it is required to report to both houses of the legislature yearly "on the status and effectiveness of the facilities under its management."[94] The statute provides no mechanism, however, for direct public input in the commission's decisions. Given the immense power of the commission over decisions to privatize prisons as well as the limited scope of its duties, the commission would appear to be in a particularly good position to benefit from public input. Hearings before the commission would be necessarily focused, and only truly interested members of the public would be likely to contribute. Additionally, in light of the required reports to the legislature, the public already has access to information necessary to make informed contributions to the commission's decisions.

One way to ensure that states' contracts with private prisons meet certain minimum standards of accountability would be for Congress to establish uniform standards for the delegation of this public function to private entities. Congress could also subject private operators in all states to information-provision requirements similar to those provided in Kentucky. Even if the states would welcome such national standards, the Supreme Court's decisions in *Morrison* and *Lopez* would seem to imply that national standards in this area might raise constitutional questions. To the extent that national standards could be set to restrict only unconstitutional deprivations of prisoner's rights by the state, however, Congress's legislation should easily be upheld under the Fourteenth Amendment. In finding the Violence against Women Act (VAWA) unconstitutional, the Court emphasized that the Fourteenth Amendment could be used to correct unconstitutional behavior only by the states, not by individuals.[95] While any unconstitutional activity would arguably consist of the activities of private actors (the prisons), states still retain the ultimate responsibility for ensuring constitutional treatment of prisoners, and Congress should be permitted to guarantee that states do not permit unconstitutional actions by private-prison providers.

Revaluing Global Currency

Global currency is created not only by various attempts on the part of the federal government and individual states to lower their regulatory costs through the use of privatization and public/private partnerships. Labor costs are also a key element when it comes to global competition. Privatization in general, and prison privatization in particular, often results in the removal of employees from the state workforce. This often means that privately employed prison guards (often the same guards who were employed by the state) receive lower wages and benefits. The federal minimum wage law has long been a source of debate nationally. The unwillingness of the Congress to address this issue in a meaningful way has triggered a variety of state and local reforms aimed at controlling just how much global currency is created in the context of low-wage jobs. The last increase in the federal minimum wage occurred in 1997, when it was increased to $5.15 per hour. Even after this increase "the real buying power of the minimum wage after adjusting for inflation was still 30 percent below its peak in 1968."[96]

Despite the reluctance to raise the minimum wage of the federal government, which arguably is responding to competitive pressures aimed at keeping the cost of labor as low as possible, the majority of Americans consistently support raising federal wage levels.[97] Democratic pressures to increase the minimum wage, largely frustrated at the federal level, resulted in a movement to create local minimum-wage—often called "living-wage"—laws in the 1990s. The first city to pass a living wage law was Baltimore in 1994. A major impetus for the passage of Baltimore's law was the privatization of government services: "Baltimoreans United in Leadership Development (BUILD) . . . noticed that many people they served in food banks they operated in churches worked full time in privatized city jobs that once paid decently. . . . BUILD . . . thus focused on raising wages for city contractors, partly to discourage privatization based on wage cutting."[98] There are currently close to ninety living-wage laws in effect in the United States, including such laws in nine of the twenty largest American cities.[99] Many cities are considering minimum-wage laws;[100] San Francisco is considering a city minimum wage even though California has a state minimum wage.[101] At the same time, several states (and some cities) are enacting provisions to prevent the establishment of local minimum-wage rates.[102]

There are many arguments about the benefits or costs of local minimum-wage bills; for example, there is extensive debate about whether such laws raise or lower poverty and unemployment.[103] These arguments are beyond the scope of this book, except with respect to the benefits of allowing local citizen participation concerning these issues. I thus focus on the structure of living-wage laws and analyze how these laws attempt to deal with privatized companies while preserving as much global currency and democratic accountability as possible.

As mentioned above, the first living-wage law (in Baltimore) was passed, in part, in response to the downward effect on wages from privatization. Most of the cities that have passed living-wage laws restrict their scope to one or more of three basic categories of employers, all of which have heightened connections to the city: firms receiving some form of business assistance from the city; city contractors and subcontractors; and municipal employees.[104]

Living-Wage Laws

One of the primary arguments for living wages is that they actually reduce the costs of local government by lessening the need for the provision of public services. When the state contracts out the provision of services and does not require the payment of a "living wage," the increased costs of supporting a private employee can fall on the taxpayers indirectly (through increased Medicare and food-stamp costs) rather than directly through salary provision. These costs to the city, it is argued, are not reflected in the bidding process for city services; consequently, such bids do not reflect the true cost of privatization. Many living-wage ordinances set two wage levels, one for employers who provide health insurance and a higher one for those who do not.[105] The difference may attempt to take into account the increased burdens on the city of residents who do not have health insurance.

One argument against local minimum wages specifically argues against this form of citywide wage control because of negative externalities for other cities. Both Florida's and Tennessee's state laws prohibiting local minimum wages argue that such laws "threaten to drive businesses . . . out of the state in search of a more favorable and uniform business environment."[106] While Tennessee's law applies to all employers, Florida's still allows local minimum wages for employees of the subdivision itself, contractors with the subdivision, or employers receiving a direct tax abatement from the subdivision.[107] Florida's exemptions make sense even if one accepts the negative effects of living-wage ordinances, because "contractors can't flee, and businesses leasing city lands are likely stuck on those locations."[108] These types of employers are thus much less likely to change locations and thereby alter the employment market across the state. Additionally, there is an argument that a city's interests in regulating the wage rate of employers in one of the three categories exempted under Florida law is appropriate because of the extensive government involvement in these areas. The argument that cities should not become involved in this issue because living wages distort the market loses much of its force when the market has already been distorted by, for example, a direct tax abatement from the city to the company in question. Additionally, the public has a much stronger interest in dictating the wages paid by companies that receive their revenue directly from the public's tax dollars than it does in affecting the wages of employers in general. Whether such laws are a good idea or not, the public should be allowed to affect the way private employers treat their employees when the public is in effect paying those workers' salaries through the awarding of a public contract.

There is also an argument that living-wage ordinances actually increase stability for employers once they are enacted, contrary to the assertions of the Florida and Tennessee bills. Many of these ordinances index the level of the living wage to the poverty level; for example, Milwaukee requires employers to pay an employee at least enough to reach the poverty line for a family of three.[109] This type of ordinance provides for a gradual raising of an employee's salary, as contrasted with the sporadic increases of a relatively larger magnitude that occur when the federal minimum wage is increased. Indexing also arguably makes government more accountable, because it allows a citizenry that supports a living wage to make such a wage the status quo, but it still permits opponents to repeal such an act through normal democratic processes. Without indexing, opponents of minimum wages need only to prevent the passage of subsequent minimum wages and let inflation (and increases in the federal minimum) erode the effect of living wage legislation.

Living-wage laws embody issues and approaches not unlike those at the federal and international levels. Race-to-the-bottom concerns arise, as do competitive issues and the ability to retain investment in one location when labor costs may be lower in other locations. These issues are very much at the heart of the World Trade Organization's agenda—a prime connection between domestic law and politics and the transnational sphere. Effective public involvement is necessary, as the next section argues, at the international level as well.

International Harmonization and Domestic Law

Earlier in this book,[110] I argued that an adequate analysis of the domestic democracy impact of international organizations such as the WTO requires that we examine them as integral to domestic legal processes (including administrative processes). I propose that the best likelihood for enhancing democracy within the WTO is by extending the values of the APA to the WTO context. What are the prospects for extending the "APA-like" values into the world trade scenario? The answer to this question would involve shifting attention from post hoc compliance issues to the much earlier stages in the decision-making processes when a dialogue on how best to mesh domestic law making with likely WTO requirements can take place within domestic political institutions. Of course, the earliest points of political intervention are the treaty negotiation stage and later, when the treaty is presented to Congress, where fast-track legislative processes are now involved. Those are important elements of the larger picture, but for my purposes, it is the context after treaty negotiation and congressional approval that I will focus on, since I am especially interested in the creation of forums for communication and contest that might take prior and potential WTO rulings into account. A good place to start is with the harmonization of rules that agencies seek to undertake when conforming to the impact of WTO decisions, current and potential. Can we avoid the rubber-stamp quality of the administrative process at this stage?

I think we can, provided we see the domestic as being in dialogue with the international and recognize that change is possible at both levels of process. If domestic lawmakers realistically have little discretion after a negative WTO ruling, they should use the discretion they have beforehand in full awareness and anticipation of the emerging body of WTO decisions and rules. In effect (to borrow from Stewart Macaulay)[111] they are legislating in the shadow of the WTO, as is also the case when administrative agencies anticipate the potential mandates of the WTO in harmonizing their own rules. Unlike the adjudicatory context of WTO panel decisions, where a specific statute and a specific section of that statute is being contested, prospective rules can be formulated in many ways, both to avoid WTO problems and to achieve the substantive goals of the agency involved. To the extent that, for example, the deregulatory effects of some WTO applications can be resisted, those arguing for such an outcome should have a voice in the process and can most meaningfully do so in the democratic arenas provided for at the agency level. Indeed, it is only within the APA process that conflicting viewpoints can, as they must, join in argument. The participants should include other countries and global NGOs so that all those relevant to the negotiation may, perhaps, be able avoid a WTO challenge at a later date.

WTO issues can involve surprisingly local procedures; local groups interested in the procedures seldom have the ability to affect their resolution. When the WTO generates a set of rules for harmonization purposes, such groups seldom even know of them until a substantial draft already exists. For example, the European Union has raised the prospect of opening up publicly owned, non-profit water systems to private, international competition.[112] The United States has over 60,000 publicly owned and operated water systems.[113] A decision to privatize such systems would have a profound impact on numerous communities. Even if the possibility of water privatization occurring is remote, a process should exist that formally makes known the policy proposals carried out "behind closed doors" at the WTO. Preliminary comments should be solicited as early in the process as possible.

Preliminary debates at the domestic level can help inform the WTO should the dispute move to that level, but, more importantly, they would constitute an important space for democratic input before the matter "goes up," as it were, to the WTO in a later compliance case. The range of possible policy outcomes surely may be limited by an existing trade agreement, but the issues likely to arise in advance of harmonization of rules offer more flexibility than those that emerge after the fact, often after intense litigation involving the particular words of a statute or rule. Processes capable of providing for communication and, if necessary, a political space for contest and conflict, are in order and the time and place for this political space can be those provided for by timely APA rule-making processes. These processes should include representative views from states likely to complain at the WTO level, and the negotiation and compromise processes should begin as early in the process as possible. There should, in effect, be worldwide notice and comment possibilities.

Achieving such reforms requires the separation of democracy and sovereignty. Sovereignty arguments alone are likely to lead to reforms that exacerbate the already-existing democracy deficit both at home and abroad; focusing on a more robust definition of democracy brings the arena of reform "home," so to speak, and the sovereignty issues are also, at least in part, simultaneously addressed. This is particularly apparent when we focus on agency harmonization of rules and equivalency and mutual-recognition agreements. These are ideal arenas for the expression of conflicting views by all relevant actors. To see this as an exclusively domestic or an exclusively international process is to exclude some stakeholders who should have a legitimate voice in the proceedings.

As Lori Wallach[114] has shown, harmonization at the rule-making stage also relies to too great an extent on international standards devised primarily by private organizations without serious consideration of a range of consumer and environmental viewpoints. Making such standards the baseline for harmonization only adds to the democracy deficit. The end result is not only a rubber-stamp procedural model at the WTO panel level but essentially a rubber-stamp model at the domestic rule-making phase as well. It is at the domestic rule-making phase, in particular, that domestic processes already in place, such as APA rule making (or an amendment to the APA to take into account in a uniform way the process necessary for the whole range of harmonization approaches from equivalency to mutual recognition agreements), can create a transparent forum where more voices can be heard.

The American Bar Association (ABA), for example, recommends that agencies should inform the public and periodically invite them to comment on harmonization actions before they have advanced too far; significant harmonization actions should also be referred to an advisory committee and there should also be a public docket of documents and studies available under the Freedom of Information Act on the more significant rules involved.[115]

Shifting our focus to include domestic law-making trends when contemplating reforms for the WTO does not necessarily make the prospects for such reform any easier. The WTO context is not unlike, and indeed is of a piece with, other seemingly purely domestic trends in administrative law. Deregulation, privatization, and increasing executive authority in economic affairs all privilege market processes and outcomes in ways that obviate the need for various administrative forums for contesting individual decisions in matters involving prisons, welfare eligibility, or mental health. The flow of information after the deregulation of such social services is also substantially limited. As we have seen, one important impact of global processes and the economic competition and integration they engender at the local level is the creation of various hybrid public/private partnerships and new governance structures, including the creation of new politics. From this standpoint, the distinctions between public and private, between national and international, or between global and local cannot be readily made. The governance fusions taking place between government and the private sector require that domestic processes be conceptualized in new ways that take the global economy and its institutions into account and do not automatically substitute market processes for those of administrative democracy. In short, the democracy problems that we so readily observe at the international level can be addressed, at least in some measure, at home.

To close the democracy deficit, we must invert the paradox of the strong laissez-faire state thesis, whereby the public sector yields to the market for the sake of defending national prosperity. For strong democracy, we must recognize that the international level is integrally connected to the domestic level. The idea that these are two separate processes must be abandoned. The very fact that separate international processes are involved, however, means that the negotiations involved will inevitably be entrusted to the executive branch of government. Herein lies another area where courts and legislatures have traditionally deferred to executive discretion. Moreover, on a pragmatic level, one can persuasively argue that the number of negotiators must be limited, if they are to be productive. What will or will not be open to negotiation may need to be private in order for negotiations to be maximally successful. But these natural, pragmatic tendencies can be carried too far. More timely input from the public need not foreclose negotiating positions; rather, it may raise issues that should not be ignored. The perspectives provided by the public can, in effect, help negotiations, not undermine them. More importantly, early notice of proposed WTO agreements and the harmonization processes to follow will make some issues controversial at an early stage, but this is at it should be. The ABA proposals are a start and a step in the right direction. As Sidney Shapiro has argued, they should be made mandatory for all participating agencies.[116]

Closely related to the impact of new agreements on domestic rules are so-called equivalency agreements. WTO members are required to accept equivalent regulations in foreign countries as satisfying their own regulatory requirements on a variety of issues. For example, the WTO's Sanitary and Phytosanitary Agreement states,

> Members shall accept the sanitary or phytosanitary measures of other Members as equivalent, even if these measures differ from their own or from those used by other Members trading in the same product, if the exporting Member objectively demonstrates . . . that its measures achieve the importing Member's appropriate level of . . . protection.[117]

WTO equivalency requirements can dramatically undercut democratically accountable domestic decision-making processes. The advocacy group Public Citizen has explained how the Food Safety and Inspection Service's (FSIS) *Salmonella* testing procedure provides a good example of how this comes about.[118] In response to several *Salmonella* outbreaks in the United States, the FSIS in 1996 enacted a regulatory provision, under normal APA procedures, to test for *Salmonella* in raw ground meat from slaughterhouses.[119] The FSIS also provided that its own employees would perform the *Salmonella* testing on-site and sent the samples to government labs.[120] Prior to the United States becoming a member of the WTO in 1994, "[f]oreign meat inspection systems were required to have laws and regulations, and sanitary and quality standards, identical to those of the U.S., including those requiring meat inspectors."[121] The FSIS, at a 1999 meeting (without prior public notice that it planned to declare other countries' procedures equivalent) found twenty-seven countries to have adequate *Salmonella* testing procedures, among several equivalency findings.[122] Twelve of these countries employ private labs for testing; ten permit the slaughterhouse to take its own samples; and one, the Netherlands, does not even test for *Salmonella* (instead testing for enterobacteriaceae).[123] Clearly, if FSIS wanted to alter its requirements in a similar way for American producers, it would have been required to utilize the notice-and-comment rule-making provisions of the APA. Despite the different inspection procedures utilized by these countries, their products are not only admitted into the United States but are also permitted to bear the USDA seal of approval, implying to the consumer that the meat was government inspected.[124] Moreover, even if a consumer was aware of the different standards in other countries, there is no country-of-origin labeling requirement to give consumers control over the countries from which they purchase meat. Under the 2002 farm bill, country-of-origin labeling was supposed to commence in 2004; the time-frame for labeling was extended to 2006 in an omnibus spending bill "in the dead of night without negotiation" less than seven months before it was to go into effect.[125] This suspension passed despite the fact that "[p]olls have shown overwhelming consumer support for origin labeling, which is already practiced by many of America's agricultural trading partners."[126]

Congress as a Site for the Governance of Globalization

Congress is an important site for the kinds of procedural reforms advanced above. More important, it is also the primary site where domestic globalization takes hold. As an institution, it is capable of conceptualizing globalization in various ways; like other sites where globalizations is involved, it can, for example, mandate minimum national standards for the privatization of prisons. It can, in effect, regulate the local creation of global currencies. It can also intervene more directly. When Congress does intervene, it should be given broad constitutional leeway by the courts, as I argued in chapter 2. Even if the legislative outcome is disappointing, it remains a political decision that a change in politics can alter.

An important congressional issue involving both the effects of globalization and various actors' efforts to deal with them is the issue of cross-border prescription drug sales. In 2002, according to a Canadian health agency report by the Patented Medicine Prices Review Board, drug prices in the United States exceeded the price of the same drugs in Canada by 67 percent.[127] The United States is "the last industrialized country with unregulated drug prices, [and] provides half the [drug] industry's revenues . . . and most of its profits."[128] While the debate about drug importation occurred, both the House and the Senate were considering bills to add a prescription drug benefit to Medicare. In both chambers, the proposed bills "envision taxpayers spending $400 billion over the next 10 years on the drug makers' products, while banning government officials from even seeking volume discounts."[129] The profit explosion of drug companies in America has been matched by their increasing involvement in the national political process. In the 1990 election cycle, for example, drug companies gave a total of about $3.2 million; in the 2002 cycle donations had risen to $26.9 million.[130]

A bill, the Save Our Seniors Act, was passed by the House in July of 2003 in order to permit the importation of drugs from Canada immediately and from the European Union within three years.[131] However, "[w]ithin hours of the bill's passage, 53 senators signed a letter opposing the provision"; this letter had been drafted by pharmaceutical lobbyists.[132] This importation provision was left out of the final Medicare reform bill signed by President Bush in December 2003. In fact, the $530 billion legislation not only does not include a re-importation provision, it explicitly prohibits re-importation without FDA approval (though the FDA is instructed to analyze the safety of the re-importation of American drugs sold in Canada). The legislation also "specifically forbids the government to use its influence to negotiate lower drug prices."[133]

The federal government was unable to completely contain the political pressure for cheaper drugs from Canada. Despite administration announcements of possible dangers from Canadian drugs, only 10 percent of Americans believe Canadian drugs are unsafe.[134] Additionally, 64 percent of Americans think that states should be allowed to re-import pharmaceuticals.[135] The day after President Bush signed the new Medicare bill into law both Boston and New Hampshire announced plans to begin importing drugs from Canada.[136] Also considering importation programs are the states of Minnesota, Iowa, Michigan, and Illinois.[137] The governors advancing re-importation include members of both major parties. Cities debating such programs include Burlington, Vermont, and Cambridge, Massachusetts.[138] The city of Springfield, Massachusetts, is already re-importing drugs from Canada, and its mayor believes the city will realize a 50 percent reduction in its annual drug bill for city employees.[139] The FDA has not threatened either Springfield or any American citizen for obtaining drugs through illegal re-importation. The agency has, however, increased its threats to halt city and state re-importation programs, and it has announced that it is "investigating the Canadian supplier of drugs for Springfield rather than prosecuting the city itself."[140] While the governor of Illinois has pledged not to violate the law and will commence importation only if the FDA grants the state a waiver (which Governor Blagojevich claims is within the FDA's power under the new legislation), New Hampshire's governor plans to press forward despite the apparent illegality of the state's program.[141] Governor Blagojevich is attempting to generate pressure to legalize re-importation in other ways; for example, he and the governor of Minnesota, Tim Pawlenty, "have begun planning a Washington Summit on the issue for governors in February."[142] Private companies in the United States have also entered the fray; a Portsmouth, New Hampshire, entrepreneur has established a business to help locals purchase cheaper drugs from Canada.[143]

This issue shows the power of transnational corporations to affect domestic policy at both the national and international levels. In addition to successfully pressuring the Senate not to follow the House's lead, pharmaceutical companies began (or continued) to exert pressure on Canadian pharmacies to stop exporting drugs to the United States. Pfizer, within days of the passage of the Save Our Seniors Act of 2003, sent letters to fifty Canadian pharmacies stating in part that "[i]f Pfizer decides that the pharmacies are ordering more drugs than they need to meet Canadian demand, it will cut off shipments to them."[144] Three other drug companies—GlaxoSmithKline, AstraZeneca, and Wyeth—put similar pressure on Canadian pharmacies.[145] The procedures that drug companies utilize in their efforts to prevent importation of Canadian drugs into the United States involve extensive surveillance and data management:

> Data-tracking companies keep close tabs on doctors' prescriptions, so companies are keenly aware of actual local demand in much of the industrialized world. The companies also closely track buying trends.

When drug orders at a particular pharmacy spike in the absence of a similar jump in nearby doctors' prescriptions, executives investigate.[146]

After the announcements by Boston and New Hampshire, "[t]he trade group representing Canada's largest internet pharmacies told American cities and states to stop planning large-scale prescription drug purchasing plans for employees" because such actions will create drug supply problems.[147] So far, the Canadian government has kept out of the re-importation issue, but authorities have warned that if drug supplies for Canadian citizens are threatened "they will seek to shut down the internet pharmacies."[148]

The new Medicare bill, in addition to banning price negotiation in the United States, seeks to eliminate price negotiation by foreign governments. Preventing such negotiations would not only increase the drug companies' overseas profits; if enough countries eliminate price negotiation, the re-importation drain on profits would also be eliminated. The bill "requires the Bush Administration to apprise Congress on progress toward opening Australia's drug pricing system."[149] The Australian minister for trade stated that after passage of the Medicare reform bill American officials began "pressing to water down the system under which the Australian government negotiates [drug] prices."[150]

The Use of Information

Several Massachusetts legislators have proposed legislation that attempts to help drug consumers through the provision of information. These lawmakers wish to publicize the Canadian prices of prescription drugs in order to help residents obtain the best deals.[151] It is unclear, however, whether such legislation (even if passed) would survive legal challenge, since federal law currently bans drug importation by anyone other than pharmaceutical manufacturers.

The drug industry has communicated its views to the public about the possible ramifications of legalizing the importation of drugs. An industry trade group, along with the Traditional Values Coalition, sent targeted fliers to voters stating that RU-486 (the abortion pill) "may become as easy to get as aspirin" if drug re-importation is legalized, despite the fact that the prescription requirements for any drugs would not change.[152] The infiltration of drug industry–financed interest groups also blurs the message that the public receives about the importation issue: "Mike Naylor, AARP's director of advocacy, said drug representatives miscalculated when they asked AARP to join an anti-importation campaign spearheaded by 'all the phony groups that drive us crazy,' such as the Christian Seniors Association, which rely heavily on industry support."[153] These groups rely on the public's trust that their name reflects the essence of the group's membership (or at least concerns). With the proliferation of advocacy groups on every issue, the public cannot possibly filter out the money behind the message given by groups such as the Christian Seniors Association.

The importance of Congress's willingness to enter the fray in issues like this cannot be underestimated as a positive force for democracy in relation to globalization. At the same time, it is apparent how large, powerful actors can use regulation to prevent the market from operating even while they invoke market metaphors in defense of a "national" industry. Potential federal legislative reforms should promote the institutionalization of various public-participation approaches to internationalization (as in the drugs example) and to privatization (as in the example of private prisons). Federal legislation dealing with prisons might be challenged as an example of federal intrusion into traditional state, police-power issues. As I argued in chapter 2, however, the possibility of such federal/state dialogue should not be cut off. It is necessary to foster a legal interpretive atmosphere such that policymakers at all levels of government have leeway to experiment with new governance approaches. As the next section proposes, this calls for yet another kind of law reform—self-imposed judicial restraint.

Judicial Restraint

Judicial restraint must come, of course, primarily from within the judiciary itself. As chapter 2 has argued, a judicial willingness to constitutionalize federalism issues that might otherwise remain in the political process has a number of adverse effects when it comes to democracy. Not only does it take certain issues out of politics, but it does so in a way that is relatively permanent. The issues are decided for generations to come, and the effects long outlast the government of the day. Federalism issues are a prime example, but so too are separation-of-powers concerns. The more formalistic courts become in the ways in which they apply Congress's doctrines, the less flexible the Congress can be and, as is often the case, the more the power of the executive branch continues to grow. The separation-of-powers concerns in a case involving the flow of information within the executive branch highlights this problem.

Separation of Powers

In early 2001, shortly after President Bush's inauguration, Vice President Cheney presided over the National Energy Policy Development Group in order to formulate the Bush administration's energy policy. Vice President Cheney submitted a report to President Bush that included more than one hundred proposals to increase energy supplies.[154] The administration refused to release much of the information regarding the way the report was developed.[155] The comptroller general, David M. Walker (who oversees the General Accounting Office, which is the investigative arm of Congress), filed suit against Vice President Cheney for not revealing the details of the taskforce's deliberations. Mr. Walker's suit was dismissed because of lack of standing:

> Mr. Walker's interest in this dispute is solely institutional, relating exclusively to his duties in his official capacity as Comptroller General of the United States. Although the Vice President's refusal to disclose the requested documents may have frustrated plaintiff in his efforts to fulfill his statutory role, plaintiff himself has no personal stake in this dispute.[156]

Despite the comptroller general's failure in his lawsuit, an interest-group suit was still ongoing at the time this book was written. Vice President Cheney, in *Judicial Watch, Inc. v. Nat'l Energy Pol'y Dev. Group*, argued that

> requiring [the taskforce] to review documents responsive to plaintiffs' discovery requests, disclose those for which no viable claim of privilege exists, and assert any applicable privileges with respect to specific documents, impermissibly interferes with "core Article II" functions and imposes an unconstitutional burden on the Executive Branch.[157]

The district court, in ordering the vice president to comply with discovery, discounted the asserted constitutional concerns and stated that the harm to the public from preventing discovery was "substantial, likely, and adequately proven."[158] The court noted that "Congress, Executive agencies, and the public have been debating the energy policy developed by defendants without the benefit of the information sought by plaintiffs in this case. In some instances, final actions have already been taken."[159]

The D.C. Court of Appeals rejected an appeal of the district court's ruling allowing discovery. The court stated that the vice president's primary claim of harm was that "extending the legislative and judicial powers to compel a Vice President to disclose to private persons the details of the process by which a President obtains information and advice from the Vice President raises separation of powers problems of the first order."[160] The court was unwilling to accept that there existed a separation-of-powers conflict until the executive branch asserted privilege.[161] The court also rejected another argument based on a separation-of-powers rationale that the president should not be unnecessarily forced to consider whether material is privileged in discovery. The court responded that "executive privilege itself is designed to protect separation of powers."[162]

In dissent, Judge A. Raymond Randolph argued that "[e]ven outside the Executive Office of the President, courts do not allow this sort of discovery into the internal workings of government departments without 'strong preliminary showings of bad faith.'"[163] Judge Randolph further asserted that the taskforce fell into an exemption from the disclosure requirements of the Federal Advisory Committee Act (FACA). FACA exempts committees established by the president that are "composed wholly of full-time . . . officers or employees of the Federal Government."[164] Since the taskforce's committee consisted only of high-level federal officials, it should have been exempted from the act. The majority relied upon the D.C. Court of Appeals' previous case *Ass'n of American Physicians & Surgeons, Inc. v. Clinton,* which held that if private parties were the "functional equivalent" of committee members, then the FACA exception did not apply.[165] The dissent argued that an inquiry into whether "functional equivalence" existed is a question of fact, involving comparative judgment, and therefore such an inquiry will almost always require discovery.[166] Judge Randolph stated that such liberal discovery creates a number of "formidable constitutional difficulties," including "intrusion into the inner workings of the Presidency, the disruption this intrusion is bound to entail, the probing of mental processes of high-level

Cabinet officers . . . , [and] the deleterious impact on the advice the President needs to perform his constitutional duties."

These are serious and complex questions of constitutional law. They show just how difficult it may be to obtain the degree of information necessary for executive-branch transparency to occur. Of course, it is always possible for the executive to waive its privilege in the interest of full disclosure. A lawsuit of this kind certainly highlights that option. At the same time, it also suggests that such questions need not be shrouded from the public on the grounds of a somewhat vague and broad assertion of privilege. The majority was correct to resolve all doubts in favor of disclosure, resisting the constitutionalization of these issues.[167]

Foreign Affairs Preemption

In 2003 the Supreme Court, in a very different context, eroded a state's ability to protect its own citizens in the case *American Ins. Assoc. v. Garamendi*,[168] and, in the process of broadly interpreting issues to be international in scope, also added to executive power. *Garamendi* involved a challenge to California's Holocaust Victim's Relief Act of 1999 (HVIRA). The Court, in an opinion written by Justice Souter, ruled that the HVIRA impermissibly "interferes with the National Government's conduct of foreign relations."[169] The HVIRA required that insurance companies wishing to do business in California disclose insurance policies sold in Europe over a certain period, to ensure that all valid Holocaust-related claims would be paid.[170] The majority stated that this provision interfered with presidential diplomacy, specifically an agreement by President Clinton with Germany and German insurers, and future agreements being pursued with other countries.[171] The German agreements established a foundation to compensate "all those 'who suffered at the hands of German companies during the National Socialist era.'"[172] Justice Souter indicated that the United States promised "to tell courts 'that U.S. policy interests favor dismissal on any valid legal ground'" and noted the U.S. assurance that it would attempt to ensure that state and local governments respect the foundation as the exclusive mechanism to compensate Holocaust victims and their families.[173] As the dissent points out, however, "no executive agreement or other formal expression of foreign policy disapproves state disclosure laws like the HVIRA."[174] Moreover, Justice Ginsburg, writing for the dissent, did not concede that even state litigation should be preempted by the agreement with Germany; she stated that in previous cases agreements had "explicitly extinguished certain suits in domestic courts," while in this case the United States merely agreed to make precatory statements to courts.[175] The dissent rejected the majority's reliance upon the statements of the deputy secretary of the Treasury to articulate the executive branch's objection to California's law, arguing that it is an error to "place the considerable power of foreign affairs preemption in the hands of individual sub-Cabinet members of the Executive Branch."[176] In the following passage, the dissent expressed its view of how foreign affairs preemption should apply:

> We would reserve foreign affairs preemption for circumstances where the President, acting under statutory or constitutional authority, has spoken clearly to the issue at hand. . . . [J]udges should not be the expositors of the Nation's foreign policy, which is the role they play by acting when the President himself has not taken a clear stand. As I see it, courts step out of their proper role when they rely on no legislative or even executive text, but only on inference and implication, to preempt state laws on foreign affairs grounds.[177]

Since the presidential diplomacy that resulted in the invalidation of the HVIRA occurred after passage of the statute, the decision in *Garamendi* raises the possibility that presidents might internationalize issues strategically, to invalidate state provisions with which they do not agree.[178]

The circumstances in *Garamendi* can be usefully compared with the Court's unanimous decision in *Crosby v. Nat'l Foreign Trade Counsel*.[179] *Crosby* involved a challenge to a law passed by Massachusetts that restricted "the authority of its agencies to purchase goods or services from companies doing business with Burma."[180] The Burmese government is a persistent violator of basic human rights, and "a series of strongly worded U.N. resolutions has demanded that the current military regime stop murdering, torturing, imprisoning, and enslaving the population."[181] The Massachusetts law attempted to use the state's spending power to indirectly pressure the Burmese government by discouraging companies from doing business with it. As with the enactment of the HVIRA in California, Massachusetts passed its Burma law before the federal government had taken any similar action. There were also significant differences between the two situations.

Federal action towards Burma involved both the executive and legislative branches of the federal government. The Court quotes an earlier opinion for the proposition that "[w]hen the President acts pursuant to an express or implied authorization of Congress, his authority is at its maximum, for it includes all that he possesses in his own right, plus all that Congress can delegate."[182] When both the legislative and executive branches are involved in establishing a policy, there is less danger of an undemocratic result, and, consequently, less need for additional forums to express the public will.

The state statute "penalize[es] individuals and conduct that Congress explicitly exempted or excluded from sanctions."[183] Therefore, unlike in *Garamendi*, the preemption is based upon a determination by Congress (which is directly responsible to the people), and not a determination by a subcabinet official of the executive branch. Additionally, once the Court has interpreted an action by Congress, Congress's action is only subject to reinterpretation by the Court or Congress itself. In contrast, the opinion of a subcabinet member can be "corrected" by a higher-ranking member of the executive branch.

Foreign governments themselves filed formal protests of Massachusetts's law with the U.S. government and lodged formal complaints with the World Trade Organization.[184] In contrast, only foreign companies challenged California's law. The participation of foreign countries in the Burma dispute solidifies the international nature of the dispute and therefore strengthens the argument that the matter should be left to the national government, if it so chooses. Finally, the California law only required the disclosure of information, while the Massachusetts law on Burma limited the ability of companies contracting with the state to engage in certain activity—for example, providing loans to the Burmese government.

The less restrictive the statute, the weaker the argument that it improperly interferes with the operations of the national government. Judicial doctrines premised on constitutional principles but not constitutional text should be applied with deference to the political branches, especially when the issues at hand are subject to change. The global era is one in which the relationships of power within the government, between the federal government and the states, as well as between and among state and nonstate actors, domestically and internationally, are in flux. This is a time when experimentation and change can be facilitated by law—one of the primary purposes of which is to encourage innovative solutions through continual political dialogue. As explained in chapter 3, current circumstances make it easy to mistake the future for the past—an argument in favor of judicial restraint.

Conclusion

At the peak of the Reagan administration, a ceremony was held marking the end of the Civil Aeronautics Board, a New Deal agency created in 1938. The *Washington Post* reported this event in dramatic fashion on January 1, 1985:

> The Civil Aeronautics Board flew into the sunset yesterday to the soulful notes of a lone Marine bugler playing "Evening Colors," the tune sounded during sunset flag lowering ceremonies at U.S. military bases throughout the world.

> "I declare the Civil Aeronautics Board closed forever," said CAB Chairman Dan McKinnon, banging a gavel that had been given to him by Sam Rayburn, who in 1938 introduced the bill setting up the agency. McKinnon had been a page for the former House Speaker.

> Then Lance Cpl. Robert Gibson of Columbus, Ohio, part of the Marine color guard participating in the closing ceremony, sounded his bugle. When Gibson hit the last notes, Alan M. Pollack, the CAB's public affairs director, took the agency seal down from the wall for donation to the Smithsonian Institution.

> It was a bittersweet final meeting for the CAB, the first federal regulatory agency ever to go out of business.[185]

The dramatic closing of the agency, complete with a color guard and bugler, suggests a high ritual of finality, not only to this agency but to regulation itself. In point of fact, in most contexts, deregulation, privatization, devolution, and internationalization mean new mixtures of regulatory and market approaches, involving state and nonstate actors. These approaches often privilege market competition, but they need not do so at the expense of democracy and nonmarket values. There is nothing permanent or final about such changes or about new mixtures of governmental power and public and private approaches in our regulatory culture. They are all part of a dynamic process, in which law has always played an important role in determining the limits and potential of markets. However extensive the deregulation of a given industry or the privatization of governmental services may be, the simple removal of one regulatory regime does not necessarily create the conditions necessary for a competitive market regime to follow, and it certainly does not ensure that democracy will be enhanced. As this book has argued, if we view such change as somewhat natural and inexorable, the delegations of regulatory power to international organizations and the market (at both the domestic and international levels), coupled with devolutions of power downward to states and localities, can so fragment our democratic structures as to make meaningful citizen participation in the issues of the day increasingly difficult. The challenge for law in the twenty-first century is to create the structures necessary for a new kind of democracy to flourish. We need both more electoral accountability of elected officials and new micro-democratic forums that can test expertise and foster political debate over a variety of issues, large and small. These forums should not be restricted to so-called public bodies.

The proposals suggested in this book are neither "antimarket" nor "prolaw." Nor are they designed to work towards world government. Rather, they are designed in recognition of the fact that the binary distinctions the law has valued to so great an extent no longer capture the complexities of the relationships between and among multiple levels of government and between state and nonstate actors—and now put us at democratic cross-purposes. Rather than some form of world order, what is needed is the democratization of embedded globalization at the domestic level. The purpose of such democratization would be to enable citizens to decide when it is best to further the forces of globalization, how best to transform them, and how to resist them through the institutions of domestic government. This would not only tame globalization, it would also make for a stronger democracy under the rule of law. The proposals I have made would involve no compromise of national interest— nor any single approach. My proposals endorse market regulation (living-wage laws), deregulation (drug imports), accountability of the executive (Cheney), and so forth.

An important theme that thus emerges from deregulation, privatization, and internationalization is that whatever hybrid regulatory regime is created needs timely information if it is to play a meaningful role in decision making. One beneficial side effect of traditional statecentric regulation was that crucial information about regulated industries was available to the public. Are there ways now to require the disclosure of the kinds of information that might provide greater accountability in relation to the markets and new market players? Tools such as the Freedom of Information Act should not be limited to the public sector solely by the private nature of the service provider.

A second theme that cuts across all of the issues we have examined is the fragility of democracy and the ease with which the categorizations of public or private, state or federal, or national or international can, in fact, insulate decision makers not only from accountability but also from valuable input and information as well. A crucial role for law to play is not just as a source of remedies or rights, as important as those are, but as a means for the creation and sustenance of politics. Politics can result in new forms of governance, both substantive and procedural, appropriate to the demands of the times.

A third theme is the need for legal experimentation. The current Supreme Court's approach to constitutional issues involving federalism is illustrative of the constitutionalization of assumptions about states and governance that are no longer true today. Too often the Court's opinions rest on a formalistic separation between state and federal interests. This approach significantly reduces the flexibility needed by policymakers—federal, state, and local—to be responsive to the democracy needs of an interdependent global economy. The global political economy is characterized by multiple levels of interacting governance, rather than the rigid constructions of state power found in most of the Supreme Court's recent federalism decisions. Just as the courts in the New Deal decided they could tolerate legislative experimentation, so too should the courts in the global era be willing to allow for democratic initiatives involving the creation and interrelation of new institutional sites and communication channels. These arenas might link local, state, federal, and international forums for purposes of proposing, debating, and enacting law in more flexible ways. Similarly, separation-of-powers approaches that limit congressional power in favor of empowering the executive branch often can further exacerbate the democracy-deficit problems of globalization, especially when they limit Congress's ability to experiment with new approaches to new mixes of public and private power and privilege executive power in ways that limit democracy to electoral accountability alone.

Though market approaches to problems will always remain important, overreliance on market incentives and values brings its own problems. I have focused on the antidemocratic effects of markets. These risks are exacerbated when we think in either/or terms, as if markets and law were separate worlds. Markets alone cannot be expected to produce a citizen-focused democracy. Citizens can use their power as consumers to try to support certain policy goals (essentially by incentivizing the government through its private side), but this is a highly limited form of power. Restoring democratic citizenship to the new private/public sector calls for a new and broader approach to law, especially administrative law. This is not to suggest that markets and market approaches have no place in governance, nor is it to argue that the public sector of the preglobal era should revive and save the day. Rather, it is to emphasize the embedded quality of globalization, drawing attention to the institutional locations where the values of democracy and public law can be furthered in practice.

My proposals, then, are not intended to attempt to recreate the democratic forums of the past by enlarging the public sphere through regulation, or by localizing it through delegations to private community forums. Restoring democracy to the globalizing state requires furtherance of the interrelationships of public and private sectors through a more innovative, multicentered, and yet integrated approach. In important respects, the market and the state are now one modality, not two separate realms. This is not to deny that local markets may exist outside of the state sphere, but rather to point out (again) that the market and the state are not just rhetorically but also administratively fused in the globalizing state such that the institutions of government are effectively inseparable from the private sector, so called.

Public/private partnerships occur at all levels of government now with such frequency as to require a recognition that part of the challenge for law must be to sort out anew the ways in which the values of democracy (and public law in particular) can be realized in practice. Taking a more pragmatic approach based on functioning power relationships within and beyond government and on the stakes for citizens in those arrangements is a crucial first step in determining how the public and private sectors should be redefined and reformed. Similarly, a realistic view of markets and of the kinds of economic impacts that rise to the level of a public interest is also needed. For example, companies such as Enron or Microsoft may be of such economic significance that they operate, in a sense, like governing bodies and have a correspondingly greater obligation to the public for transparency and accountability relative to smaller business entities. Certainly private companies engaged in social services formerly provided by state entities are also likely to have special public significance; this significance should be recognized by extending public-sector status to those elements of the private sector that carry out public functions. The significance of a new public designation for such elements of the private sector, however, is not that the full panoply of public-law procedures should then automatically be provided. Rather, this designation should mean that there are opportunities for public involvement in policy making, opportunities made meaningful by transparent decision-making procedures and timely access to information. For this to occur, information must be shared, executive power checked, forums for discussion created, and bridges built between those forums and policy-making entities.

Some readers may argue that, realistically, such proposals cannot be implemented. Is there enough interest in this kind of politics to produce the degree of citizen involvement that should be our objective? If we build these bridges and structures, will anyone come? I believe the answer to both questions is "yes." Politics is not limited to partisan maneuvering or spontaneous mobilization in times of crisis. In point of fact, the premise of these proposals and the regulatory agenda set forth in this chapter is that politics requires forums, information, and nurturing. Without the structure and information flows in place, a meaningful politics is not likely to develop.

This, of course, raises an even more serious concern. If public-choice theorists are correct, why would those who benefit from the system as it is currently structured allow such change to occur? Would not an infusion of grass-roots politics suggested here make change more likely and thus necessary to resist? I argue that the breadth and importance of the issues involved—be they issues now entrusted to the private sector or to international organizations—cannot and do not go unnoticed by the population at large. The effects of decisions over which we seemingly have no control are cumulative. The enlargement of the private/public sector and the policy consequences that flow from this on day-to-day life will inevitably bring more citizens into the public sphere than can be predicted by purely economic theories of the political process. Democracy is more than a set of tools or a public apparatus to be manipulated by the elite. It is, in the last resort, embedded deeply in our culture and our legal system.

To date our apparent lack of response is due to the fact that we have not fully grasped the profound ways in which globalization is embedded in our democratic institutions, now necessitating change and a reconceptualization of our basic operating assumptions. Recognizing how globalization has created a new public private sector broadening the range of influential state, nonstate, and interstate actors positions us to reconceptualize administrative law as a resource for reform. Such a reconceptualization is necessary if we are to retain the values on which democracy is based—transparency, accountability, and a body politic of engaged and informed citizens. Globalization highlights the importance of such values, ever more strikingly, as fundamental to the ways in which we govern ourselves, every day, at the domestic level.

Notes

NOTE TO THE PREFACE

1. MATTHEW A. CRENSON & BENJAMIN GINSBERG, DOWNSIZING DEMOCRACY: HOW AMERICA SIDELINED ITS CITIZENS AND PRIVATIZED ITS PUBLIC (Baltimore, MD: Johns Hopkins Univ. Press 2002).

NOTES TO THE INTRODUCTION

1. See Jost Delbrück, Globalization of Law, Politics, and Markets—Implications for Domestic Law—A European Perspective, 1 IND. J. GLOBAL LEGAL STUD. 9 (1993); see also PETER DICKEN, GLOBAL SHIFT: THE INTERNATIONALIZATION OF ECONOMIC ACTIVITY 1–8 (New York: Guilford Press 2d ed. 1992); WILLIAM GREIDER, ONE WORLD, READY OR NOT: THE MANIC LOGIC OF GLOBAL CAPITALISM (New York: Simon & Schuster 1997); KEN'ICHI OHMAE, THE BORDERLESS WORLD: POWER AND STRATEGY IN THE INTERLINKED ECONOMY (New York: Harper Business 1990); SASKIA SASSEN, CITIES IN A WORLD ECONOMY (Thousand Oaks, CA: Pine Forge Press 1994); SASKIA SASSEN, THE GLOBAL CITY: NEW YORK, LONDON, TOKYO (Princeton, NJ: Princeton Univ. Press 1991); Alfred C. Aman, Jr., Symposium: The Globalization of Law, Politics and Markets: Implications for Domestic Law Reform, 1 IND. J. OF GLOBAL LEGAL STUD. 1 (1993); Alfred C. Aman, Jr., The Earth as Eggshell Victim: A Global Perspective on Domestic Regulation, 102 YALE L.J. 2107 (1993); Saskia Sassen, Towards a Feminist Analytics of the Global Economy 4 IND. J. GLOBAL LEGAL STUD. 7 (1997).

2. See RICHARD O'BRIEN, GLOBAL FINANCIAL INTEGRATION: THE END OF GEOGRAPHY 5 (New York: Council on Foreign Relations Press 1992). ("A truly global service knows no internal boundaries, can be offered throughout the globe, and pays scant attention to national aspects. The closer we get to a global, integral whole, the closer we get to the end of geography.") This does not mean one world market for everything. O'Brien describes the emergence of separate networks around foreign exchange, securities, debt, investment, and financial services, and these networks constitute distinct markets. Id. at 32. These ideas

are discussed in Robert Latham, *Globalization and Democratic Provincialism: Re-Reading Polanyi,* 2 NEW POL. ECON. 53 (1997).

3. O'BRIEN, *supra* note 2, at 54–55; *See also* SUSAN STRANGE, THE RETREAT OF THE STATE: THE DIFFUSION OF POWER IN THE WORLD ECONOMY 3–16 (New York: Cambridge Univ. Press 1996). The state, of course, can and often does facilitate the process of globalization by, for example, providing for property rights and other legal regimes that may encourage economic development. Thus, this is not to argue that states have or can have no role in the processes of globalization. Rather, it is to argue that their role is no longer as central as it once was and, to the extent that the state engages in activities that deter globalization, they can often be avoided by multinational actors who simply decide to move aspects of their operations elsewhere or establish parallel, if not competing, legal regimes that cater primarily to their interests. *See* sources cited *supra* note 1.

4. STRANGE, *supra* note 3.

5. DICKEN, *supra* note 1, at 47–59; *See* SASSEN, THE GLOBAL CITY, supra note 1; *see also* ROBERT REICH, THE WORK OF NATIONS: PREPARING OURSELVES FOR 21ST-CENTURY CAPITALISM (New York: Knopf 1991).

6. General Agreement on Tariffs and Trade, Oct. 30, 1947, 61 Stat. A-11, T.I.A.S. 1700, 55 U.N.T.S. 194 [hereinafter GATT].

7. *See, e.g.,* North American Free Trade Agreement, Dec. 8, 1992, Canada-Mexico-U.S. 32 I.L.M. 289 [hereinafter NAFTA].

8. STRANGE, *supra* note 3, at 48 (stating that "over a quarter of all worldwide trade is now intra-firm trade. . . . As much as 40 per cent of Mexico's trade with the US in the early 1990s . . . was done by . . . affiliates of US firms."); *see also* MANUFACTURING MIRACLES: PATHS OF INDUSTRIALIZATION IN LATIN AMERICAN AND EAST ASIA (Gary Gereffi and D. L. Wyman, eds., Princeton, NJ: Princeton Univ. Press 1990).

9. For an example of the transnational politics involved in global warming issues, *see* GARETH PORTER & JANET WALSH BROWN, GLOBAL ENVIRONMENTAL POLITICS 74–78, 92–103 (Boulder, CO: Westview Press 1st ed. 1991); *see generally,* RICHARD ELLIOT BENEDICK, OZONE DIPLOMACY: NEW DIRECTIONS IN SAFEGUARDING THE PLANET (Cambridge, MA: Harvard Univ. Press 1st ed. 1991).

10. *See* SASSEN, THE GLOBAL CITY, *supra* note 1.

11. For an analysis of the global impact of public health problems, *see Symposium: The Public's Health in The Global Era: Challenges, Responses, and Responsibilities,* 5 IND. J. GLOBAL LEGAL STUD. 1 (Issue 1, 1997).

12. *Id.*

13. *See* Gunther Teubner, *Global Bukowina: Legal Pluralism in the World Society, in* GLOBAL LAW WITHOUT A STATE 1 (Gunther Teubner ed., Brookfield, VT: Dartmouth Publ'g 1997); Delbrück, *supra* note 1.

14. *See, e.g.,* STRANGE, *supra* note 3, at 91–97.

15. *Id.* at 43.

16. *See, e.g.,* Teubner, *supra* note 13.

17. *See generally,* GLOBAL PRESCRIPTIONS: THE PRODUCTION, EXPORTATION, AND IMPORTATION OF A NEW LEGAL ORTHODOXY (Yves Dezalay & Bryant G. Garth eds., Ann Arbor, MI: Univ. Michigan Press 2002).

18. For an analysis of how the European Court of Justice fundamentally affects English constitutional and administrative law, *see* Yvonne Cripps, *Some Effects of European Law on English Administrative Law,* 2 IND. J. GLOBAL LEGAL STUD. 213, 219 (1994).

19. Teubner, *supra* note 13; *see also* Francis Snyder, *Governing Economic Globalization: Global Economic Pluralism and EU Law, in* REGIONAL AND GLOBAL REGULATION OF INTERNATIONAL TRADE 1, 8 (Francis Snyder ed., Oxford, UK: Hart Pub. 2002) (stating that "Teubner's principle thesis is that global law develops mainly outside the political structures of nation states and international organizations. The basic device is contract, and the paradigm is *lex mercatoria.*").

20. *See* Linda Bosniak, *Citizenship Denationalized,* 7 IND. J. GLOBAL LEGAL STUD. 447 (2000).

21. *See* Martin A. Rogoff, *The European Union, Germany, and the Länder: New Patterns of Political Relations in Europe,* 5 COLUM. J. EUR. L. 415, 416 (1999).

22. *See* Sidney A. Shapiro, *International Trade Agreements, Regulatory Protection, and Public Accountability,* 54 ADMIN. L. REV. 435 (2002). Many nations are not even involved in the original decisions at the WTO. Steve Charnovitz, *The Emergence of Democratic Participation in Global Governance (Paris, 1919),* 10 IND. J. GLOBAL LEGAL STUD. 45, 49 (2003) (describing the WTO practice in which "officials leading a negotiation will invite selected governments into a room to hammer out a deal that is later presented to the entire membership as a fait accompli.").

23. *See, e.g.,* Tara L. Branum, *President or King? The Use and Abuse of Executive Orders in Modern-Day America,* 28 J. LEGIS. 1 (2002).

24. For a more complete discussion of corporate codes and citizen input, see discussion, *infra* ch. 4, pages 000–000.

25. *See, e.g.,* Jacqueline Peel, *Giving the Public a Voice in the Protection of Global Environment: Avenues for Participation by NGOs in Dispute Resolution at the European Court of Justice and World Trade Organization,* 12 COLO. J. INT'L ENVTL. L. & POL'Y 47 (2001).

26. Jost Delbrück, *Transnational Federalism: Problems and Prospects of Allocating Public Authority beyond the State,* 11 IND. J. GLOBAL LEGAL STUD. (forthcoming 2004) (on file with author).

27. For other analyses of the infiltration of globalization into the states, *see* SASKIA SASSEN, CITIES IN A WORLD ECONOMY (Thousand Oaks, CA: Pine Forge Press 1994); Saskia Sassen, *Transnational and Supranational Democracy: The*

Participation of States and Citizens in Global Governance, 10 IND. J. GLOBAL LEGAL STUD. 5 (2003); *see also* ALFRED C. AMAN, JR., ADMINISTRATIVE LAW IN A GLOBAL ERA (Ithaca, NY: Cornell University Press 1992); Alfred C. Aman, Jr., *The Globalizing State: A Future-Oriented Perspective on the Public/Private Distinction, Federalism, and Democracy*, 31 VAND. J. TRANSNAT'L L. 769, 780–91 (1998).

28. Jonathan R. Macey, *Cynicism and Trust in Politics and Constitutional Theory*, 87 CORNELL L. REV. 280, 295 (2002) (arguing that "government action necessarily displaces private action, and displacing voluntary initiatives to solve social problems has devastating consequences, including the twin evils of rampant corruption and governmental excess."); Gregory S. Alexander, *Playing with Fire*, 87 CORNELL L. REV. 449, 449 (2002); *see also* JERRY L. MASHAW, GREED, CHAOS, AND GOVERNANCE: USING PUBLIC CHOICE TO IMPROVE PUBLIC LAW 24–25 (New Haven, CT: Yale Univ. Press 1997) ("Contemporary reanalysis of the mechanisms of collective choice by public choice theorists mocks our efforts at democratic governance. Majoritarianism is an illusion. Legislation and administrative regulation are little better than private contracts at public expense. . . . The national government, all government, should be constrained radically. Our trust should be instead in the market, in voluntary associations, and in local, community-based governance."); Paul Stephen Dempsey, *Market Failure and Regulatory Failure as Catalysts for Political Change: The Choice between Imperfect Regulation and Imperfect Competition*, 46 WASH. & LEE L. REV. 1, 26 (1989) (stating that

> [p]roponents of the public choice theory embrace the normative conclusion that we would be better off with less regulation and less government. Because politicians respond to pressure groups and the desire to be reelected, politicians often employ the wheels of government to magnify rather than eliminate market imperfections. Blending schools of market economics and political science, public choice theorists adhere to a policy hostile to government and friendly to unconstrained competition.
>
> Public choice theory was the prevailing wisdom in the Reagan Administration. Consistent with public choice theory, Interior Secretary James Watt and Environmental Protection Agency Administrator Ann Gorsuch reduced enforcement of environmental regulation. It was the theory under which Federal Trade Commission Chairman James Miller III gutted the agency's antitrust regulatory staff. Pursuant to public choice theory Federal Communications Commission Chairman Mark Fowler repealed radio and TV programming and advertising regulations. It was the theory under which ICC Chairman Heather Gradison refused to regulate rail rates in monopoly markets. Adhering to the tenets of public choice theory the Department of Transportation under Secretary Elizabeth Dole approved every airline merger proposal submitted to the agency.).

29. *See* Molly Beutz, *Functional Democracy: Responding to Failures of Accountability,* 44 HARV. INT'L L.J. 387, 402 (2003) ("As explained by the Chicago School approach to public choice theory, leaders will be responsive to the needs and desires of the populace primarily when self-interest forces them to respond."). Most public-choice theorists, however, reject the claim that legislatures typically act on behalf of the people. *See, e.g.,* Jonathan R. Macey, *Promoting Public-Regarding Legislation through Statutory Interpretation: An Interest Group Model,* 86 COLUM. L. REV. 223, 223 (1986) ("We live in a time of widespread dissatisfaction with the legislative outcomes generated by the political process. Too often the process seems to serve only the purely private interests of special interest groups at the expense of the broader public interests it was ostensibly designed to serve."). *But see* Frank H. Easterbrook, *The State of Madison's Vision of the State: A Public Choice Perspective,* 107 HARV. L. REV. 1328, 1345 (1994) ("When governments become sufficiently plentiful, and when the scope of laws matches the domain of their costs and benefits (that is, when costs and benefits are all felt within the jurisdiction that enacts the laws), competitive forces should be as effective with governments as they are with private markets.") Judge Easterbrook then states, however, that "the competitive ideal cannot be achieved—there are not enough governmental units, the populations of jurisdictions are not sufficiently homogenous, and externalities are common." *Id.*

30. *See, e.g.,* JOHN HART ELY, DEMOCRACY AND DISTRUST: A THEORY OF JUDICIAL REVIEW 73–88 (Cambridge, MA: Harvard Univ. Press 1980) (arguing against an activist judiciary and instead for a judicial approach that reinforces the representative nature of the other, more democratic, branches).

NOTES TO CHAPTER I

1. The deference to the executive branch has increased after the September 11 attacks. *See* Odah v. U.S., 321 F.3d 1134 (D.C. Cir. 2003) *petition for cert. granted sub nom;* Rasul v. Bush, 72 U.S.L.W. 3171 (U.S. Nov. 10, 2003) (holding that Guantanamo Bay, Cuba, is not U.S. territory and therefore aliens detained there are not protected by the Constitution); Global Relief Foundation v. O'Neill, 315 F.3d 748 (7th Cir. 2002) *cert. denied sub nom;* Global Relief Foundation v. Snow, 72 U.S.L.W. 3092 (U.S. Nov. 10, 2003) (upholding secretary of Treasury's freezing of charitable corporation's assets without hearing).

2. An earlier version of this argument appeared in ALFRED C. AMAN, JR., ADMINISTRATIVE LAW IN A GLOBAL ERA (Ithaca, NY: Cornell Univ. Press 1992), some portions of which appear in chapter 1 in revised form.

3. Felix Frankfurter, *Social Issues before the Supreme Court,* 22 YALE REV. 476 (1933).

4. 198 U.S. 45 (1905).

5. *Id.* at 75.

6. For example, the Court struck down virtually all of the New Deal legislation that came before it in 1935. *See, e.g.,* Louisville Joint Stock Land Bank v. Radford, 295 U.S. 555 (1935) (Frazier-Lemke Act); A.L.A. Schecter Poultry Corp. v. United States, 295 U.S. 495 (1935) (section 3 of National Industrial Recovery Act); R.R. Ret. Bd. v. Alton R.R., 295 U.S. 330 (1935) (Railroad Retirement Act); Panama Ref. Co. v. Ryan, 293 U.S. 388 (1935) (section 9 of National Industrial Recovery Act). *But see* Perry v. United States, 294 U.S. 330 (1935) (sustaining validity of Joint Resolution of June 5, 1933, which declared gold payment contracts illegal); Nortz v. United States, 294 U.S. 317 (1935) (same); Norman v. Baltimore & Ohio R.R., 294 U.S. 240 (1935) (same).

7. 295 U.S. 495 (1935).

8. 293 U.S. 388 (1935).

9. 300 U.S. 379 (1937).

10. *See, e.g.,* West Coast Hotel Co. v. Parrish, 300 U.S. 379 (1937); Nebbia v. New York, 291 U.S. 502 (1934).

11. United States v. Darby, 312 U.S. 100 (1941).

12. *Id.*

13. Home Bdng. & Loan Ass'n v. Blaidsdell, 290 U.S. 398 (1934).

14. It was not until Justice Rehnquist's dissent in *Indus. Union Dep., AFL-CIO v. Am. Petroleum Inst.,* 448 U.S. 607, 671–88 (1980) that the doctrine began to experience a revival. Yet, there still is not a majority in the Court that would apply it as Justice Rehnquist has advocated. *See* Whitman v. Am. Trucking Ass'ns, 121 S. Ct. 903 (2001).

15. Oliver Wendell Holmes, quoted in Frankfurter, *supra* note 3, at 478.

16. *Id.* at 480.

17. 304 U.S. 144, 152 n.4 (1938).

18. *Id.* at 152.

19. *Id.*

20. *Id.* at 152 n.4.

21. *Id.*

22. President Franklin D. Roosevelt, *The Second Inaugural Address (January 20, 1937), reprinted in* 6 THE PUBLIC PAPERS AND ADDRESSES OF FRANKLIN D. ROOSEVELT, 1, 5 (Samuel I. Rosenman ed., New York: Random House 1941).

23. *See* Martin M. Shapiro, *The Constitution and Economic Rights, in* ESSAYS ON THE CONSTITUTION OF THE UNITED STATES 74 (M. Judd Harmon ed., Port Washington, NY: Kennikat Press 1978); Bruce A. Ackerman, *The Storrs Lectures: Discovering the Constitution,* 93 YALE L.J. 1013, 1056–57, 1064–65 (1984).

24. This is not to imply that the New Deal consisted only of economic regulation. Important New Deal legislation dealt with social issues such as unemployment compensation and social security. *See* ARTHUR M. SCHLESINGER, JR., 2

THE AGE OF ROOSEVELT: THE COMING OF THE NEW DEAL 263–81, 297–315 (Boston: Houghton Mifflin 1959); *see also* Social Security Act, ch. 531, 49 Stat. 620 (1935) (codified as amended at 42 U.S.C. §§ 301–1399 (2000).

25. Securities Act of 1933, ch. 38, tit. I, 48 Stat. 74 (codified at 15 U.S.C. §§ 77a–77aa (2000)); Natural Gas Act, ch. 556, 52 Stat. 821 (1938) (codified at 15 U.S.C. §§ 717a–717w (2000)); National Labor Relations Act, ch. 372, 49 Stat. 448 (1935) (codified at 29 U.S.C. §§ 151–66 (2000)); Federal Communications Act of 1934, ch. 652, 48 Stat. 1164 (codified in various sections of 47 U.S.C.); Air Carrier Economic Regulation Act, ch. 601, tit. IV, §§ 401–16, 52 Stat. 987 (1938), repealed by Federal Aviation Act of 1958, Pub. L. No. 85-726, 72 Stat. 731 (current version at 49 U.S.C. §§ 481–96 (2000)).

26. *See* ELLIS WAYNE HAWLEY, THE NEW DEAL AND THE PROBLEM OF MONOPOLY: A STUDY IN ECONOMIC AMBIVALENCE 472–94 (Princeton, NJ: Princeton Univ. Press 1966); *see also* BARRY D. KARL, THE UNEASY STATE: THE UNITED STATES FROM 1915 TO 1945 153–54 (Chicago, IL: Univ. Chicago Press 1983); HOWARD ZINN, NEW DEAL THOUGHT 398 (Indianapolis, IN: Bobbs Merrill 1966).

27. 295 U.S. 495 (1935). *See also* HAWLEY, *supra* note 26, at 398.

28. *See* Bruce A. Ackerman & William T. Hassler, *Beyond the New Deal: Coal and the Clean Air Act,* 89 YALE L.J. 1466 (1980). *See* Robert L. Rabin, *Federal Regulation in Historical Perspective,* 38 STAN. L. REV. 1189, 1263 n.236 (1986).

29. *See, e.g.,* Steven E. Rhoads's discussion of THE FEDERALIST NOS. 9, 10 (Alexander Hamilton), No. 57 (James Madison) *in* STEVEN E. RHOADS, THE ECONOMIST'S VIEW OF THE WORLD: GOVERNMENT, MARKETS, AND PUBLIC POLICY 203 (New York: Cambridge Univ. Press 1985); *see also* J. G. A. POCOCK, THE MACHIAVELLIAN MOMENT: FLORENTINE POLITICAL THOUGHT AND THE ATLANTIC REPUBLICAN TRADITION 506–52 (Princeton, NJ: Princeton Univ. Press 1975); Cass R. Sunstein, *Interest Groups in American Public Law,* 38 STAN L. REV. 29, 47 (1985).

30. For an example and discussion of common law rhetoric, see E. H. LEVI, AN INTRODUCTION TO LEGAL REASONING 1–6 (Chicago: Univ. Chicago Press 1958).

31. *See, e.g.,* Phillips Petroleum Co. v. Wisconsin, 347 U.S. 672 (1952).

32. Ch. 324, 60 Stat. 237 (1946) (current version codified in 5 U.S.C. §§ 551–59, 701–6, 1305, 3105, 3344, 5372, 7521 (2000)).

33. For a discussion of the Court's history of favoring the functional approach to separation-of-powers issues, John M. Burkoff, *Appointment and Removal under the Federal Constitution: The Impact of Buckley v. Valeo,* 22 WAYNE L. REV. 1335, 1358 n.108 (1976) (citing cases prior to Buckley that reflect the functional approach); *see also* Peter L. Strauss, *Formal and Functional Approaches to Separation-of-Powers Questions: A Foolish Inconsistency?,* 72

CORNELL L. REV. 488, 516–22 (1987); Phillip B. Kurland, *The Rise and Fall of the "Doctrine" of Separation of Powers,* 85 MICH. L. REV. 592, 593 (1986) (discussing Madison's perception of "checks and balances" as a result, in part, of the indeterminacy of governmental functions); Envtl. Def. Fund, Inc. v. Ruckelshaus, 439 F.2d 584, 597–98 (D.C. Cir. 1971).

34. Increasing national power, whether through administrative agencies or congressional pronouncements, has been a continuing trend. As Professor Kurland has noted, "[l]imited government, or minimalist government, in Lockean or Harringtonian terms, is a matter of ancient history; its demise is probably coincident with the growth of the idea of implied powers." Kurland, *supra* note 33, at 604.

35. *Id.*

36. *Id.* at 603.

37. *Id.* at 604.

38. For an illuminating discussion of the difficulties involved in repealing old statutes, see GUIDO CALABRESI, A COMMON LAW FOR THE AGE OF STATUTES (Cambridge, MA: Harvard Univ. Press 1982).

39. Calvert Cliffs' Coordinating Comm. v. Atomic Energy Comm'n., 449 F.2d 1109, 1111 (D.C. Cir. 1971).

40. *See, e.g.,* Clean Air Act 1970, 4–7 (2000); Clean Water Act of 1977, Pub. L. No. 95-217, 91 Stat. 1566 (codified in various 33 U.S.C. sections); *see also* MARTIN M. SHAPIRO, WHO GUARDS THE GUARDIANS? JUDICIAL CONTROL OF ADMINISTRATION 79–87 (Athens, GA: Univ. of Georgia Press 1988); Ackerman & Hassler, *supra* note 28, at 1468–70, 1475.

41. S. P. HAYS, *The Politics of Environmental Administration, in* THE NEW AMERICAN STATE: BUREAUCRACIES AND POLICIES SINCE WORLD WAR II 22–25 (Louis Galambos, ed., Baltimore, MD: Johns Hopkins Univ. Press 1987).

42. *Id.* at 27. Contrast this consumer-oriented view with the producer-oriented view represented by the New Deal statutes.

43. A superb example is the Alaskan pipeline proceeding, 58 F.P.C. 810 (1977); 58 F.P.C. 1127 (1977) (commission decision).

44. *See, e.g.,* Tanners' Council of America v. Train, 540 F.2d 1188, 1193 (4th Cir. 1976).

45. *See, e.g.,* Baltimore Gas & Elec. Co. v. NRDC, 462 U.S. 84 (1983) (upholding a Nuclear Regulatory Commission rule, but only after a contextual approach that required an examination of a number of interrelated factors).

46. 449 F.2d 1109, 1111 (D.C. Cir. 1971). *See also* Ethyl Corp. v. EPA, 541 F.2d 1 (D.C. Cir. 1976), cert. denied, 426 U.S. 941 (1976). The opinions in this Clean Air Act case highlight some important differences in the judicial role through the debate between Chief Judge Bazelon and Judge Leventhal. In separate concurring opinions, the chief judge argued for more procedural control of agency decision making and New Deal–style deference when it came to agency

expertise involving substantive matters (*Id.* at 66), while Judge Leventhal argued for more direct, substantive judicial review. *Id.* at 68. Judge Leventhal's view eventually prevailed. For an example of the increased complexity of judicial review under the hard-look doctrine, see Sierra Club v. Costle, 657 F. 2d 298 (D.C. Cir. 1981).

47. *See* William F. West & Joseph Cooper, *The Rise of Administrative Clearance, in* THE PRESIDENCY AND PUBLIC POLICY MAKING 192, 207–8, (G. C. Edwards III, S. A. Shull, and N. C. Thomas, eds. Pittsburgh, PA: Univ. of Pittsburgh Press 1985). *See also* RICHARD P. NATHAN, THE PLOT THAT FAILED: NIXON AND THE ADMINISTRATIVE PRESIDENCY (New York: Wiley 1975).

48. *See* West & Cooper, *supra* note 47, at 208; Theodore Lowi, *The Constitution and Contemporary Political Discourse* 115 (unpublished paper on file with *Cornell Law Review*) (listing the new statutes passed from 1969 to 1976).

49. 347 U.S. 483 (1954).

50. *See, e.g.,* Shapiro v. Thompson, 394 U.S. 618, 634 (1969) (fundamental right to travel) ("[I]n moving from State to State . . . appellees were exercising a constitutional right, and any classification which serves to penalize the exercise of that right, unless shown to be necessary to promote a compelling governmental interest, is unconstitutional"); Hunter v. Erickson, 393 U.S. 385, 392 (1969) (fair housing law).

51. This is the second tier of the two-tiered approach to the judicial review of agency actions referred to earlier in this chapter.

52. *See, e.g.,* David P. Currie, *Relaxation of Implementation Plans under the 1977 Clean Air Act Amendments,* 78 MICH. L. REV. 155, 155 (1979) (stating that "[t]he most striking feature of this scheme is its absoluteness. . . ."); *see also* WILLIAM H. RODGERS, JR., 1 ENVIRONMENTAL LAW: AIR AND WATER § 1.2 (St. Paul, MN: West Pub. Co. 1986). This is not to suggest that there were no examples of absolutist legislation in the past, *see, for example,* the Delaney amendment to the Food and Drug Act, mandating a no-risk approach to carcinogenic substances: Food Additives Amendment of 1958, Pub. L. No. 85-929, 72 Stat. 1784 (codified as amended at 21 U.S.C. §§ 321, 331, 342 (2000)).

53. See National Environmental Policy Act of 1969, Pub. L. No. 91-190, 83 Stat. 852 (codified in various sections of 42 U.S.C. (2000)); Clean Water Act of 1977, Pub. L. No. 95-217, 91 Stat. 1566 (codified in various sections of 33 U.S.C. (2000)); Clean Air Amendments of 1970, Pub. L. No. 91-604, 84 Stat. 1676 (codified in various sections of 42 U.S.C. (2000)); Federal Water Pollution Act Amendments of 1972, Pub. L. No. 92-500, 86 Stat. 816 (codified at 12 U. S. C. sec. 24, 15 U.S.C. 633, 636 (2000); Water Quality Improvement Act of 1970, Pub. L. No. 91-224, 84 Stat. 91 (codified in various sections of 33 U.S.C. (2000)); Environmental Quality Improvement Act of 1970, Pub. L. No. 91-224, 84 Stat. 114 (codified at 42 U.S.C. 4371–74 (2000)).

54. *See* RODGERS, *supra* note 52, at § 1.3(c).

55. *See, e.g.,* Am. Textile Mfrs. Inst. V. Donovan, 453 U.S. 490 (1981) (cotton dust); Indus. Union Dep't v. Am. Petroleum Inst., 448 U.S. 607 (1980) (benzene). These cases are disputes surrounding the removal of benzene and cotton dust from the work place and litigation over just how risk free an environment Congress had authorized.

56. *See* Sherbert v. Verner, 374 U.S. 398 (1963) (free exercise of religion); Brown v. Bd. of Educ. 347 U.S. 483 (1954) (school desegregation).

57. *But see* R. SHEP MELNICK, REGULATION AND THE COURTS: THE CASE OF THE CLEAN AIR ACT (Washington, DC: Brookings Institution 1983) (describing how the courts sometimes tempered these statutes through interpretation, allowing cost to be factored into the approach taken.)

58. Clean Water Act of 1977, Pub. L. No. 95-217, 91 Stat. 1566 (codified in various sections of 33 U.S.C. (2000)).

59. Brown v. Bd. of Educ., 349 U.S. 294, 301 (1955) (Brown II).

60. *See* RODGERS, *supra* note 52, at 19. ("Among the more salient examples of absolutism in environmental law are the goals in the Clean Water Act calling for fishable/swimmable water everywhere by July 1, 1983 and no discharges anywhere by January 1, 1985. These two missions impossible . . . are among the most thoroughly denounced actions taken by any twentieth-century Congress.")

61. *See* William H. Rodgers, Jr., *Benefits, Costs, and Risks: Oversight of Health and Environmental Decisionmaking,* 4 HARV. ENVTL. L. REV. 191 (1980).

62. *See, e.g.,* Envtl. Def. Fund, Inc. v. Corps of Eng'r of the United States Army, 492 F.2d 1123 (5th Cir. 1974); Sierra Club v. Froehlke, 486 F.2d 946 (7th Cir. 1973); Conservation Council of N. Carolina v. Froehlke, 473 F.2d 664 (4th Cir. 1973); Envtl. Def. Fund, Inc. v. Corps of Eng'r of the United States Army, 470 F.2d 289 (8th Cir. 1972), cert. denied, 412 U.S. 931 (1973); Calvert Cliffs' Coordinating Comm. v. Atomic Energy Comm'n, 449 F.2d 1109 (D.C. Cir. 1971); Envtl. Def. Fund, Inc. v. Tennessee Valley Auth., 371 F. Supp. 1004 (E.D. Tenn. 1973), *aff'd on other grounds,* 492 F.2d 466 (6th Cir. 1974).

63. *See, e.g.,* Envtl. Def. Fund, Inc. v. EPA, 548 F.2d 998 (D.C. Cir. 1976) (supp. opinion 1977), *cert. den. sub nom,* Velsicol Chemical Corp. v. EPA, 431 U.S. 925 (1977); *see also* E. F. Roberts, *The Right to a Decent Environment: Progress along a Constitutional Avenue, in* LAW AND THE ENVIRONMENT 134 (Malcolm F. Baldwin & James K. Page, Jr., eds., New York: Walker 1970).

64. *See, e.g.,* New York Times v. United States, 403 U.S. 713, 714 (1971).

65. *See, e.g.,* the cases cited in the introduction at note 9 and *supra* note 62. *See also* Richard B. Stewart, *The Development of Administrative and Quasi-Constitutional Law in Judicial Review of Environmental Decisionmaking: Lessons from the Clean Air Act,* 62 IOWA L. REV. 713, 750–54 (1977).

66. HAYS, *supra* note 41, at 23. *See also* Occupational Safety and Health Act of 1970, 29 U.S.C. 651–78 (2000).

67. *See id.* at 25–27.

68. *Id.*

69. *See* Jackson County v. Jones, 571 F.2d 1004, 1013 (8th Cir. 1978); County of Suffolk v. Sec'y of the Interior, 562 F.2d 1368, 1384 (2d Cir. 1977); Envtl. Def. Fund, Inc. v. Corps of Eng'r of the United States Army, 492 F.2d 1123, 1139–40 (5th Cir. 1974); Sierra Club v. Froehlke, 486 F.2d 946, 953 (7th Cir. 1973); Silva v. Lynn, 482 F.2d 1282, 1284 (1st Cir. 1973); Conservation Council of N. Carolina v. Froehlke, 473 F.2d 664, 665 (4th Cir. 1973). For cases involving a judicial hard look independent of the National Environmental Policy Act of 1969, see Nat'l Lime Ass'n v. EPA, 627 F.2d 416, 453 (D.C. Cir. 1980); Columbia Gas Transmission Corp. v. Fed. Energy Regulatory Comm'n, 628 F.2d 578, 593 (D.C. Cir. 1979); United States v. Nova Scotia Food Prods. Corp., 568 F.2d 240, 251–52 (2d Cir. 1977); H & H Tire Co. v. DOT, 471 F.2d 350, 355 (7th Cir. 1972); *see also* William H. Rodgers, Jr., *A Hard Look at Vermont Yankee Environmental Law under Close Scrutiny,* 67 GEO. L.J. 699, 704–8 (1979). Note, *The Least Adverse Alternative Approach to Substantive Review under NEPA,* 88 HARV. L. REV. 735 (1975), H. J. Yarrington, *Judicial Review of Substantive Agency Decisions: A Second Generation of Cases under NEPA,* 19 SAN DIEGO L. REV. 279 (1974).

70. *See, e.g.,* cases cited in note 69, *supra.*

71. This is particularly true if one includes, along with *Chevron,* recent developments in constitutional law taking a formalistic approach to separation-of-power issues and an expansive and protective view of executive power. There are, of course, exceptions to these trends. *See, e.g.,* Morrison v. Olson, 108 S. Ct. 2597 (1988) (appointment of independent counsel by federal court not violative of appointments clause or separation-of-powers concerns). Moreover, the Court's approach in *Chevron* has not necessarily taken hold completely. In other contexts, the Court has shown some reluctance to defer to presidential power in quite the way *Chevron* would suggest. *See, e.g.,* Mississippi Power & Light Co. v. Mississippi, 108 S. Ct. 2428 (1987); INS v. Cardozo-Fonseca, 480 U.S. 421 (1987); Bd. of Governors of the Fed. Reserve Sys. v. Dimension Fin. Corp., 474 U.S. 361 (1986). *But see* Young v. Cmty. Nutrition Inst., 476 U.S. 974 (1986).

Nevertheless, the long-term trend seems very much in the direction of increasing executive power over the administrative process. This is very much of a piece with the general trend of increased presidential power and conforms to some of the reasons Justice Jackson noted for the inevitable increase in executive power in his concurrence in *Youngstown Sheet & Tube Co. v. Sawyer,* 343 U.S. 579, 653–54 (1952). *See also* Kurland, *supra* note 34, at 607–10. As far as the administrative process is concerned, the need for executive coordination has been increasing along with the increase in the policy-making power of the bureaucracy.

72. The unicameral legislative veto, a means by which this could have occurred, was struck down in *INS v. Chadha,* 462 U.S. 919 (1983).

73. *See, e.g.,* Exec. Order No. 12,291, 3 C.F.R. 127 (1981), *reprinted in* 5 U.S.C. 601(1982) (imposing cost-benefit analysis); Exec. Order No. 12,248, 3 C.F.R. 291 (1980) (mandating regulatory planning). For a more current example *see* Exec. Order No. 12,630, 53 Fed. Reg. 8859 (1988). Entitled "Governmental Actions and Interference with Constitutionally Protected Rights," this order suggests a constitutional approach to regulatory takings that arguably is more stringent than what current case law would allow. It is another means of encouraging agencies to be very wary of extending their regulatory authority. Indeed, it is interesting to note that before this order was issued, Congress tried but failed to pass a reformed Administrative Procedure Act that would have added similar cost-benefit analysis provisions. Though Congress failed to pass these reforms, they nevertheless became the centerpiece of the Reagan administration through the issuance of Exec. Order No. 12,291.

74. *See, e.g.,* Heckler v. Chaney, 470 U.S. 821 (1985); UAW v. Brock, 783 F.2d 237 (D.C. Cir. 1986); *see also* Cass R. Sunstein, *Reviewing Agency Inaction after Heckler v. Chaney,* 52 U. CHI. L. REV. 653 (1985) (advocating judicial review of agency inaction); Hon. Patricia M. Wald, *The Contributions of the D.C. Circuit to Administrative Law,* 40 ADMIN. L. REV. 507, 522 (1988) (describing recent years as an era of "nonregulation" in which agencies have failed to enforce existing rules or to promulgate rules where the statute appears to contemplate rules).

75. *See, e.g.,* Chevron v. NRDC, 467 U.S. 837 (1984) (bubble approach).

76. *See, e.g.,* Tax Reform Act of 1986, 26 U.S.C. § 1 (2000).

77. *See* Motor Vehicles Mfrs. Ass'n v. State Farm Mut. Auto. Ins. Co., 463 U.S. 29 (1983).

78. *See generally,* SUSAN STRANGE, THE RETREAT OF THE STATE: THE DIFFUSION OF POWER IN THE WORLD ECONOMY 46 (New York: Cambridge Univ. Press 1996); SASKIA SASSEN, LOSING CONTROL? SOVEREIGNTY IN AN AGE OF GLOBALIZATION 28 (New York: Columbia Univ. Press 1996); Alfred C. Aman, Jr., *The Globalizing State: A Future-Oriented Perspective on the Public/Private Distinction, Federalism, and Democracy,* 31 VAND. J. TRANSNAT'L L. 769, 780–91 (1998) [hereinafter: Aman, *The Globalizing State*].

79. *See, e.g.,* Bruce A. Ackerman & Richard B. Stewart, *Reforming Environmental Law: The Democratic Case for Market Incentives,* 13 COLUM. J. ENVTL. L. 171 (1988).

80. In *Carter v. Carter Coal Co.,* 298 U.S. 238 (1936), the Supreme Court invalidated the Bituminous Coal Conservation Act as an unconditional delegation of legislative power to private parties, specifically large coal producers. The Court stated,

> The power conferred upon the majority is, in effect, the power to regulate the affairs of an unwilling minority. This is legislative delegation in its most obnoxious form; for it is not even delegation to an official or official

body, presumptively disinterested, but to private persons whose interests may be and often are adverse to the interests of others in the same business. . . . [I]n the very nature of things, one person may not be entrusted with the power to regulate the business of another, and especially of a competitor. And a statute which attempts to confer such power undertakes an intolerable and unconstitutional interference with personal liberty and private property.
Id. at 873. As one commentator has noted, the Supreme Court has not invalidated legislation on delegation grounds since the Carter Coal case, and the private exercise of governmental power delegated by state or local governments has not been a federal constitutional issue since the 1920s. David M. Lawrence, *Private Exercise of Governmental Power,* 61 IND. L.J. 647, 648 (1986); *see also* Whitman v. American Trucking Ass'ns, 121 S. Ct. 903 (2001) (upholding delegations of authority to EPA). *But see* Lisa Schultz Brusman, *Schecter Poultry at the Millennium: A Delegation Doctrine for the Administrative State,* 109 YALE L.J. 1399 (2000); Jody Freeman, *The Private Role in Public Governance,* 75 N.Y.U. L. REV. 543, 584 (2000) ("While the federal judiciary may decline to resurrect the non-delegation doctrine to invalidate delegations to administrative agencies . . . it might still invalidate private delegations in future cases, especially if the delegated authority implicates 'core' public powers. A delegation could prove so sweeping that it deprives the executive of its Article II powers, thereby raising a separation of powers concern."); Harold J. Krent, *Fragmenting the Unitary Executive: Congressional Delegations of Administration Authority outside the Federal Government,* 85 NW. U. L. REV. 62 (1990); Whitman v. American Trucking, 121 S. Ct. at 903 (Thomas, J., concurring.)

81. Hon. Patricia M. Wald, *Looking Forward to the Next Millennium: Social Previews for Legal Change,* 70 TEMP. L. REV. 1085, 1098 (1997).

82. *See* Lester M. Salamon, *The New Governance and the Tools of Public Action: An Introduction,* 28 FORDHAM URB. L.J. 1611 (2001).

83. *See Symposium: Redefining the Public Sector: Accountability and Democracy in the Era of Privatization,* 28 FORDHAM URB. L.J. 1307 (2001).

84. The Airline Deregulation Act of 1978, codified before repeal at 49 U.S.C. app. §§ 1301–1557 (1988), repealed in part by Pub. L. No. 103-272, 108 Stat. 745 (2000) and recodified in various sections of 49 U.S.C. (2000).

85. BARBARA STURKEN PETERSEN & JAMES GLAH, RAPID DESCENT: DEREGULATION AND THE SHAKEOUT IN THE AIRLINES 77 (New York: Simon & Schuster 1994). Airline Deregulation Act, Pub. L. No. 95-904, 92 Stat. 1705–54 (1978) (codified as amended at 49 U.S.C. §§ 1303–1552 (2000) [hereinafter ADA]. For a general discussion of the efforts to deregulate the airline industry, *see* Stephen G. Wood et al., *Regulation, Deregulation and Re-Regulation: An American Perspective,* 1987 B. Y. U. REV. 381 (1987).

86. Wood et al., *supra* note 85, at 390–91.

87. *See, e.g.,* Mark Green & Ralph Nader, *Economic Regulation v. Competition: Uncle Sam the Monopoly Man,* 82 YALE L.J. 871 (1973) (discussing problems with unguided regulatory systems that lead to situations where "regulated industries are often in clear control of the regulatory process."); Alfred C. Aman, Jr., *The Globalizing State: A Future-Oriented Perspective on the Public/Private Distinction, Federalism, and Democracy,* 31 VAND. J. TRANSNAT'L L. 769, 780–91 (1998).

88. *But see* Stephen G. Breyer, *Antitrust, Deregulation, and the Newly Liberated Marketplace,* 75 CAL. L. REV. 1005, 1012 (1987) (stating that "[p]roponents of deregulation did not rest their case on likely deconcentration. They argued instead that competition, including potential competition, would force prices down and increase traveler choice, irrespective of whether the industry became more, or less, concentrated.").

89. Stephen Breyer, now Justice Breyer, was one of the primary staff architects of these proposals. *See* STEPHEN G. BREYER, REGULATION AND ITS REFORM 317–40 (Cambridge, MA: Harvard Univ. Press 1982).

90. For a discussion of how the bureaucracy actually grew during the Reagan years, *see* IAN AYRES & JOHN BRAITHWAITE, RESPONSIVE REGULATION: TRANSCENDING THE DEREGULATION DEBATE 7–10 (New York: Oxford University Press, 1992).

91. PAUL KENNEDY, THE RISE AND FALL OF THE GREAT POWERS: ECONOMIC CHANGE AND MILITARY CONFLICT FROM 1500 TO 2000 416–18, 425–27 (New York: Random House 1st ed. 1980).

92. RICHARD N. ROSECRANCE, THE RISE OF THE TRADING STATE: COMMERCE AND CONQUEST IN THE MODERN WORLD 137–38 (New York: Basic Books 1986).

93. *Id.* at 141.

94. The Reagan administration was not successful at repealing any significant statutory programs. Instead, it adopted a court- and agency-oriented strategy. AMAN, *supra* note 2, at 43–44; the success of this strategy depended in large part on the nature of the regulation and the agency itself. The Reagan administration lost its major court battles in health and safety areas, while it was more successful in communication and commercial areas. *See infra* notes 146–47 and accompanying text.

95. *See* Duane Chapman, *Environmental Standards and International Trade in Automobiles and Copper: The Case for a Social Tariff,* 31 NAT. RESOURCES J. 449 (1991).

96. *Id.*

97. *See generally,* BREYER, *supra* note 89.

98. *See, e.g.,* Alan B. Morrison, *OMB Interference with Agency Rulemaking: The Wrong Way to Write a Regulation,* 99 HARV. L. REV. 1059 (1986); Christo-

pher C. DeMuth & Douglas H. Ginsburg, *White House Review of Agency Rule-making*, 99 HARV. L. REV. 1075 (1986).

99. *See, e.g.*, Motor Vehicles Mfrs Assoc. v. State Farm Mutual, 463 U.S. 29 (1983). For an earlier rejection of market approaches to regulatory problems, *see* FPC v. Texaco, 377 U.S. 33 (1964) (holding that the statutory mandate of just and reasonable rates required regulation and not a determination that the market price would suffice).

100. *See, e.g.*, Chevron v. Nat'l Res. Def. Council, 467 U.S. 837 (1984).

101. *Id. See* Alfred C. Aman, Jr., *Administration in a Global Era: Progress, De-Regulatory Change, and the Rise of the Administrative Presidency*, 73 COR-NELL L. REV. 1101, 1223–25 (1988).

102. *See, e.g.*, Motor Vehicles Mfrs. Assoc. v. State Farm Mutual, 463 U.S. 29 (1983).

103. *Compare* Motor Vehicles Mfrs. Assoc. v. State Farm Mutual, 463 U.S. 29 (1983) (strong review of auto safety, deregulation) *with* Black Citizens for Fair Media v. F.C.C., 719 F.2d 407 (1983) (deferential reviews of F.C.C. regulations streamlining licensing procedures).

104. *See, e.g.*, Heckler v. Chaney, 105 S. Ct. 1649 (1985); Sunstein, *supra* note 29.

105. *See* Chevron v. Nat'l Res. Def. Council, 467 U.S. 837 (1984).

106. *See, e.g.*, West & Cooper, *supra* note 47, at 192, 207–8.

107. *See, e.g.*, Bowsher v. Synar, 478 U.S. 714 (1986); Morrison v. Olson, 108 S. Ct. 2596, 2625 (1988) (Scalia dissenting).

108. *See, e.g.*, Occupational Safety and Health Act, 29 U.S.C. § 651 (1970).

109. *See* note 73, *supra.*

110. *Id.*

111. 467 U.S. 837 (1984).

112. *Id.* at 865–66.

113. *See* Alfred C. Aman, Jr., *Symposium: How Separation of Powers Protects Individual Liberties*, RUTGERS L. REV. 41 796–805 (1989).

114. *See* Bowsher v. Synar, 478 U.S. 714 (1986). Though footnote 4 of Bowsher expressly states that this issue was not decided, the implications of this opinion were tested again in Morrison v. Olson, 108 S. Ct. 2597 (1988). Once again, the Court refused to rule in a manner that made the "headless fourth branch" unconstitutional. In fact, it seems to have put the issue to rest once again. *But see* 108 S. Ct. at 2622 (Scalia, J., dissenting).

For commentary criticizing the role of administrative agencies in our constitutional system, *see* Geoffrey P. Miller, *Independent Agencies*, 1986 SUP. CT. REV. 41 (1986); David P. Currie, *The Distribution of Power after Bowsher*, 1986 SUP. CT. REV. (1986). For an overview of these important constitutional issues, *see* Peter L. Strauss, *The Place of Agencies in Government: Separation of Power and the Fourth Branch,* 84 COLUM. L. REV. 573 (1984). For an application of this analysis to Bowsher v. Synar and other recent cases, *see* Strauss, *supra* note 33.

115. Strauss, *supra* note 33.

116. 462 U.S. 919 (1983).

117. 478 U.S. 714 (1986).

118. *See* Peter L. Strauss, *Was There a Baby in the Bathwater? A Comment on the Supreme Court's Legislative Veto Decision,* 1983 DUKE L.J. 789 (1983), who addresses the Court's inability in *Chadha* to distinguish the use of the veto in political and regulatory contexts. For a study of legislative vetoes in general and their effect on the administrative process, see Harold H. Bruff & Ernest Gellhorn, *Congressional Control of Administrative Regulation: A Study of Legislative Vetoes,* 90 HARV. L. REV. 1369 (1977).

119. *But see* 462 U.S. at 968–74 (White, J., dissenting) (noting the various kinds of legislative vetoes that have developed over time). *See also* Strauss, *supra* note 118, at 804–12 (analyzing Justice White's "intellectual" approach to the legislative veto question).

120. *Cf.* Chevron v. NRDC, 467 U.S. 837 (1984), which demonstrates the rhetorical, all-or-nothing aspect of the formalistic approach. In that case, Justice Stevens set forth, as a condition of judicial intervention, the requirement that Congress speak *precisely* to the issue then before the Court. According to Stevens, courts should resolve all doubts in favor of agency discretion in the face of statutory silence or ambiguity.

121. 462 U.S. at 951 ("Although not 'hermetically' sealed from one another, the powers delegated to the three Branches are functionally identifiable.") (internal citation omitted).

122. *See* Strauss, *supra* note 118, at 794–801.

123. Chadha, 462 U.S. at 945–46.

124. JAMES M. LANDIS, THE ADMINISTRATIVE PROCESS 11 (New Haven, CT: Yale Univ. Press 1938).

125. This is not to say that the veto provision in *Chadha* was not, in fact, unconstitutional, but rather to emphasize that if unconstitutional, it was so for reasons more subtle and complicated than those articulated by the sweeping opinion of the majority. *See, e.g.,* 462 U.S. at 959 (Powell, J., concurring); *see also* Strauss, *supra* note 118, at 817; Cass R. Sunstein, *Constitutionalism after the New Deal,* 101 HARV. L. REV. 421, 496 (1987) (concluding that a functional approach to *Chadha* would yield the same result).

It is also important to note that, despite the impression of almost mechanical rigidity, formalism is also capable of flexibility and ambiguity. Judges have discretion when characterizing the nature or function of the official under review. The discretion involved in the labeling approach gives courts a great deal of power, not only because it makes legislation more vulnerable constitutionally but also because of confusion regarding the definitions of legislative, executive, and judicial functions. Once the court defines and applies these labels, the analysis appears very simple. But the process of judicial definition behind this approach is by no means clear cut. *See, e.g.,* Bowsher v. Synar, 478 U.S. 714, 748–49 (1986) (Stevens, J., concurring); *see also* Strauss, *supra* note 118, at 797–98 (discussing what is legislative); Kurland, *supra* note 33, at 603 (commenting on "[t]he inefficacy of resorting to a general notion of separation of powers to resolve contests between two branches of government. . . .").

126. Chadha, 462 U.S. at 958–59.

127. Pub. L. 99-177, 99 Stat. 1038, 2 U.S.C. 901–7, 921–22 (2002).

128. For a similar problem that arises when the First Amendment is arguably overextended to certain kinds of commercial or regulatory speech, see Thomas Jackson & John Jeffries, Jr., *Commercial Speech: Economic Due Process and the First Amendment,* 65 VA. L. REV. 1 (1979); *see also* Alfred C. Aman, Jr., SEC v. Lowe: *Professional Regulation and the First Amendment,* 1985 SUP. CT. REV. 93 (1985).

129. 295 U.S. 602 (1935).

130. Synar v. United States, 626 F. Supp. 1374, 1398 (D.C. Cir. 1986).

131. *Id.*

132. *Id.*

133. *Synar,* 626 F. Supp. at 1399 (citation omitted).

134. *Id.*

135. The lower court noted,

Under subsection 251(b) (1), the Comptroller General must specify levels of anticipated revenue and expenditure that determine the gross amount which must be sequestered; and he must specify which particular budget items are required to be reduced by the various provisions of the Act . . . and in what particular amounts. The first of these specifications requires the exercise of substantial judgment concerning present and future facts that affect the application of the law—the sort of power normally conferred upon the executive officer charged with implementing a statute. The second specification requires an interpretation of the law enacted by Congress, similarly a power normally committed initially to the Executive under the Constitution's prescription that he "take Care that the Laws be faithfully executed" Art. II, 3. *And both of these specifications by the Comptroller General are, by the present law, made binding upon the President in the latter's application of the law. . . .* In our view, these cannot be regarded as anything but executive powers in the constitutional sense.

Synar, 626 F. Supp. at 1400 (emphasis in original) (internal citation omitted).

136. *Id.*

137. *Id.* at 1401 (quoting Buckley v. Valeo, 424 U.S 1, 129 (1976)).

138. Bowsher v. Synar, 478 U.S. 714 (1985).

139. 478 U.S. at 726.

140. *See* Strauss, *supra* note 33, at 489.

141. As the majority noted,

The statutes establishing independent agencies typically specify either that the agency members are removable by the President for specified causes, . . . or else do not specify a removal procedure. . . . This case involves nothing like these statutes, but rather a statute that provides for direct congressional involvement over the decision to remove the Comptroller General.

478 U.S. at 725 n.4 (internal citations omitted).

142. 108 S. Ct. 2597 (1988).

143. *Id.* at 2369 (Scalia, J. dissenting).

144. As Justice Scalia noted,

That is what this suit is about. Power. The allocation of power among Congress, the President, and the courts in such fashion as to preserve the equilibrium the Constitution sought to establish—so that "a gradual concentration of the several powers in the same department," . . . can effectively be resisted.

Id. at 2623 (Scalia, J., dissenting) (citation omitted).

145. *See, e.g.,* Office of Communication of the United Church of Christ v. FCC, 707 F.2d 1413 (D.C. Cir. 1983). This case concerned the FCC's decision to deregulate the commercial radio industry by eliminating quantitative processing guidelines for nonentertainment programming, formal ascertainment procedures, commercialization processing guidelines, and programming log requirements. *Id.* at 1419. The FCC's deregulation was based on the belief that "current conditions in the radio marketplace permit the Commission to reduce direct government control of licensees while still remaining faithful to its statutory mandate to regulate in the public interest." *Id.* at 1420.

The court agreed, upholding all of the deregulation decisions except the elimination of the program log requirement. *Id.* at 1443. The court found nothing in the Federal Communications Act, 47 U.S.C. §§ 151–610 (2000), the FCC's enabling statute, to prevent deregulation. The statute's mandate of a broad-based public-interest standard gives the FCC a great deal of discretion to formulate its public policy goals. 707 F.2d 1432.

Like the FCC, the Interstate Commerce Commission (ICC) also has been fairly successful at deregulation. When the ICC was founded, Congress was primarily concerned with the railroads' monopoly power. Interstate Commerce Act of 1887, ch. 104, 24 Stat. 379 (1887) (current version in scattered sections of 49 U.S.C.). By the mid-1900s, however, the railroads no longer held such a dominant position. In 1980, Congress responded to this change by passing legislation designed to increase the flexibility of action under the current regulatory scheme. *See* Staggers Rail Act of 1980, Pub. L. No. 96-448, 94 Stat. 1895 (1980).

Congress believed that decreased regulation would translate into increased competition, thus enabling the rail industry to provide services more effectively. *See* H.R. CONF. REP. NO. 1430, 96th Cong., 2d Sess. 79 (1981). Congress also passed several statutes to effectuate its deregulation goals. *See, e.g.,* 49 U.S.C. §§ 11343(e), 10505(a) (2000).

For the most part, the ICC's deregulation has been upheld. *See, e.g.,* Baltimore & O.R.R. v. ICC, 826 F.2d 1125 (D.C. Cir. 1987) (holding that in measuring the potential harm to users of railroad track that the railroad sought to abandon, the ICC could consider the possibility of the user purchase of or subsidy to the railroad's operation); Illinois Commerce Comm'n v. ICC, 819 F.2d 311 (D.C. Cir. 1987) (upholding ICC exemption for trackage rights agreements); Baltimore Gas & Elec. Co. v. United States, 817 F.2d 108 (D.C. Cir. 1987) (upholding ICC's promulgation of regulations for competitive access hearings).

There are some exceptions to the cases listed above. *See, e.g.,* Regular Common Carrier Conference v. United States, 820 F.2d 1323 (D.C. Cir. 1987) (holding that ICC impermissibly granted an exemption from a prior approval hearing to a railroad seeking to acquire six trucking companies); General Chem. Corp. v. United States, 817 F.2d 844 (D.C. Cir. 1987) (holding that ICC's determination that railroads were not market dominant was arbitrary and capricious).

Commentators point out that there seems to be some tension between the courts and the ICC concerning deregulation, but this tension is not based on philosophical grounds. Instead, the courts are constrained to permit certain deregulation because it conflicts with statutes that remain in force. Until Congress clarifies the situation by repealing the conflicting statutes, the courts will be forced to abide by them. For a detailed commentary on the ICC's deregulation efforts, *see* Mary A. Wallace, *The D.C. Circuit Review September 1986–August 1987: Interstate Commerce Commission,* 56 GEO. WASH. L. REV. 937 (1988). President Clinton has proposed to abolish the ICC altogether. *See generally,* Robert Pear, *The Clinton Budget: The Overview,* N.Y. TIMES, Feb. 3, 1995, at A1.

146. *See* Motor Vehicle Mfrs. Ass'n v. State Farm Mutual Auto. Ins., 463 U.S. 29 (1983). In this case, the Supreme Court upheld the D.C. Circuit's holding that the National Highway Transportation Administration (NHTSA) had failed to provide an adequate explanation for repealing the passive restraint standard. This standard required automobile manufacturers to install passive restraint devices in all new automobiles over a three-year period beginning in September 1981. Shortly after assuming office, the Reagan administration decided to delay implementation of the rule for one year, citing numerous cost and compliance problems. In addition, the delay was designed to give the NHTSA time to review the entire passive restraint issue, opening up the possibility that the standard would be completely rescinded. Because of this possibility, several insurance companies and consumer groups brought legal action to challenge NHTSA's rescission of the standard. *See* AMAN, *supra* note 2, at 63–77; *see also* Larry W.

Thomas et al., *The Courts and Agency Deregulation: Limitations on the Presidential Control of Regulatory Policy,* 39 ADMIN. L. REV. 27, 32–34 (1987).

For other cases adverse to the Reagan administration's deregulation attempts at the agency level, see Public Citizen v. Steed, 733 F.2d 93 (D.C. Cir. 1984) (invalidation of NHTSA's indefinite suspension of treadware grading standards); Int'l Ladies' Garment Workers' Union v. Donovan, 722 F.2d 795 (D.C. Cir. 1983) (invalidation of the rescission of a thirty-nine-year-old regulation prohibiting homework in the knitted outerwear industry); Pub. Citizen Health Research Group v. Auchter, 702 F.2d 1150 (D.C. Cir. 1983) (holding that the Occupational Safety and Health Administration had abused its discretion in not issuing an emergency standard reducing worker exposure to ethylene oxide.)

147. See AMAN, *supra* note 2, at 9–13.

148. One way of highlighting the impact of deregulation at the agency level is by noting the significant shift in the numbers of administrative law judges (ALJs) functioning in economic regulatory agencies such as the FCC or the ICC, which were often the targets of the deregulatory reforms of the 1970s and 1980s:

> Shortly after the APA was passed, there were 196 ALJ's, 64% (125) of whom were assigned to economic regulatory agencies and 6.6% (or 13) to the Social Security Administration. By 1984, there were 1121 ALJ's. Only 6.5% (or 73) ALJ's were in the twelve economic regulatory agencies, while 67.8% (or 760) ALJ's were in Social Security.

ALFRED C. AMAN, JR., & WILLIAM T. MAYTON, ADMINISTRATIVE LAW, 200 n.7 (St. Paul, MN: West Pub. 1st ed. 1993) (relying on a study by Jeffrey Lubbers of the United States Administrative Conference).

149. *See, e.g.,* cases cited in note 145, *supra.*

150. President Bush's memorandum imposing a moratorium on a new regulation and a review of old regulations sought to eliminate costs and advance economic growth, thereby furthering America's global competitiveness. President Bush first announced this moratorium in his 1992 State of the Union Address, stating,

> I have this evening, asked major Cabinet departments and Federal agencies to institute a 90-day moratorium on any new Federal regulations that could hinder growth. In those 90-days, major departments and agencies will carry out a top-to-bottom review of all regulations old and new, to stop the ones that will hurt growth and speed up those that will help growth.

The President's Address before a Joint Session of the Congress on the State of the Union, 28 WKLY. COMP. PRES. DOC. 170, 172 (January 28, 1992). Bush extended the moratorium for another 120 days and then again, until the expiration of his term. The President's Remarks on Regulatory Reform, 28 WKLY. COMP. PRES. DOC. 726, 727 (April 29, 1992); Remarks Accepting the Presidential

Nomination for the Republican National Convention in Houston, 28 WKLY. COMP. PRES. DOC. 1462, 1466 (August 24, 1992).

151. Alfred C. Aman, Jr., *A Global Perspective on Current Regulatory Reforms: Rejection, Relocation, or Reinvention?*, 2 IND. J. GLOBAL LEGAL STUD. 429, 445–47 (1995).

152. AMAN, *supra* note 2, at 43–44.

153. *See, e.g.*, takings legislation, risk-assessment legislation, and the two-house veto. These provisions would make agency action difficult, if not practically impossible, but they seek to restrain rather than replace the federal regulation to which they apply. As has already been noted, some agencies have been singled out for abolition; *see also* Contract with America, *available at* http://www.townhall.com/documents/contract.html (last visited Oct. 15, 2003); Christopher Georges, *Senate Republicans Begin to Give Details on Spending Cuts They Intend to Seek*, WALL ST. J., Mar. 13, 1995, at A4 (stating that Texas Senator Phil Gramm and Senate Majority Leader Bob Dole separately proposed abolishing the Department of Education).

154. Vice President Al Gore, Report of the National Performance Review, *From Red Tape to Results: Creating a Government That Works Better and Costs Less* (Sept. 7, 1993) [hereinafter National Performance Review]. For a discussion of this report, see Jeffrey S. Lubbers, *Better Regulations: The National Performance Review's Regulatory Reform Recommendations*, 43 DUKE L.J. 1165 (1994); Daniel B. Rodriguez, *Management, Control, and the Dilemmas of Presidential Leadership in the Modern Administrative State*, 43 DUKE L.J. 1180 (1994); Susan Rose-Ackerman, *Consensus versus Incentives: A Skeptical Look at Regulatory Negotiation*, 43 DUKE L.J. 1206 (1994).

155. *See* Vice President Dan Quayle, Remarks to the Food and Drug Law Institute Conference Regarding the President's Council on Competitiveness, Fed. News Service, Dec. 11, 1991, *available in* LEXIS, News Library, CURNWS File.

156. PAUL C. LIGHT, THE TRUE SIZE OF GOVERNMENT 1 (Washington, DC: Brookings Institution 1999) (noting that there are almost 11 million employees of private companies performing contracted-out public tasks).

157. For an expansive list of recent social security privatization proposals, see Colleen E. Medill, *Challenging the Four "Truths" of Personal Social Security Accounts: Evidence from the World of 401(k) Plans*, 81 N.C. L. REV. 901, 904–6 (2003). For a detailed discussion of the debate over potential drilling for oil in the Arctic National Wildlife Refuge (ANWR), the possible environmental effects of such drilling, and an argument that development of ANWR would violate international law, see Bonnie Docherty, *Challenging Boundaries: The Arctic National Wildlife Refuge and International Environmental Law Protection*, 10 N.Y.U. ENVTL. L.J. 70 (2001).

158. *See* discussion *supra* ch. 2, pp. 000–000.

159. For a detailed discussion of "unfunded mandates," see MATTHEW A.

CRENSON & BENJAMIN GINSBERG, DOWNSIZING DEMOCRACY: HOW AMERICA SIDELINED ITS CITIZENS AND PRIVATIZED ITS PUBLIC 32–44 (Baltimore, MD: Johns Hopkins Univ. Press 2002).

NOTES TO CHAPTER 2

1. HENRY COWELL & SIDNEY COWELL, CHARLES IVES AND HIS MUSIC 144–45 (New York: Oxford Univ. Press 1969).

2. Our statutes allow for the rejection of such WTO rulings, but as a practical matter, this does not occur. *See* Uruguay Round Agreements Act, 19 U.S.C. § 3512(a)(1) (2000) (denying effect to WTO rulings "inconsistent with any law of the United States.").

3. *See, e.g.,* Gregory C. Shaffer, *The World Trade Organization under Challenge: Democracy and the Law and Politics of the WTO's Treatment of Trade and Environment Matters,* 25 HARV. ENVTL L. REV. 1 (2001).

4. *See, e.g.,* Sidney A. Shapiro, *International Trade Agreements, Regulatory Protection, and Public Accountability,* 54 Admin. L. Rev. 435 (2002).

5. Alfred C. Aman, Jr., *The Earth as Eggshell Victim: A Global Perspective on Domestic Regulation* 102 YALE L.J. 2107, 2117 (1993).

6. *See* WOLFGANG H. REINICKE, GLOBAL PUBLIC POLICY 102–34 (Washington, DC: Brookings Institution Press 1998).

7. ROBERT B. REICH, THE WORK OF NATIONS: PREPARING OURSELVES FOR 21ST-CENTURY CAPITALISM (New York: Knopf 1991).

8. With the growth of vast transnational corporations, corporate national identity has become an increasingly malleable concept. For example, U.S. corporations are increasingly willing to change their corporate nationality, to take advantage of lower corporate taxes. *See* David Cay Johnston, *U.S. Companies File in Bermuda to Slash Tax Bills,* N.Y. TIMES, Feb. 18, 2002, at A1. As a further step towards decentralization, some companies have taken to forming "virtual corporations"; a virtual corporation is defined as a "temporary network or loose coalition of manufacturing and administrative services that comes together for a specific business purpose and then disassembles when the purpose has been met." P. Maria Joseph Christie & Reuven Levary, *Virtual Corporations: Recipe for Success,* INDUSTRIAL MANAGEMENT, July 1, 1998, at 7.

9. For an analysis of welfare devolution, see Matthew Diller, *The Revolution in Welfare Administration: Rules, Discretion, and Entrepreneurial Government,* 75 N.Y.U. L. REV. 1121 (2000).

10. *See* Phillip Kurland, *The Role of the Supreme Court in American History: A Lawyer's Interpretation* 14 BUCKNELL REVIEW 16 (Fall 1966).

11. *See* West Coast Hotel Co. v. Parrish, 300 U.S. 379 (1957) (the so-called switch-in-time-that-saved-nine case); *see also* Felix Frankfurter, *Mr. Justice*

Roberts, 104 U. Pa. L. Rev. 311, 314–15 (1955) (showing vote in *West Coast Hotel* was taken before legislation to expand court was proposed).

12. 452 U.S. 264 (1981) (emphasis in original) (internal citation omitted).

13. *Id.* at 307 (quoting U.S. Const. art. I, § 8, cl. 3).

14. *Id.*

15. *See, e.g.,* New York v. U.S., 505 U.S. 144 (1992); Gregory v. Ashcroft, 501 U.S. 452 (1991).

16. U.S. v. Lopez, 115 S. Ct. 1624 (1995).

17. For a discussion of federalism advocating an alternate view, i.e., that federalism is an empowerment of the national government, *see* Erwin Chemerinsky, *The Value of Federalism,* 47 Fla. L. Rev. 499, 504 (1995) ("It is desirable to have multiple levels of government all with the capability of dealing with the countless social problems that face the United States as it enters the 21st century.").

18. 529 U.S. 598 (2000).

19. *Id.* at 653.

20. *Id.* at 661 (citations omitted).

21. *Id.* at 654 (emphasis in original).

22. *Id.* at 662.

23. *See, e.g.,* Richard C. Revesz, *Rehabilitating Interstate Competition: Rethinking the "Race to the Bottom" Rationale for Federal Environmental Regulation,* 67 N.Y.U. L. Rev. 1210 (1992). *But see* Daniel C. Esty, *Toward Optimal Environmental Governance,* N.Y.U. L. Rev. 1495 (1999).

24. *See, e.g.,* Martha C. Nussbaum, *Patriotism and Cosmopolitanism, in* For Love of Country: Debating the Limits of Patriotism 2 (Joshua Cohen ed., Boston, MA: Beacon Press, 1996); *see also* Kwame Anthony Appiah, *Cosmopolitan Patriots, Id.* at 21.

25. *See* Alfred C. Aman, Jr., *The Globalizing State: A Future-Oriented Perspective on the Public/Private Distinction, Federalism, and Democracy,* 31 Vand. J. Transnat'l L. 769 (1998). Portions of chapters 2 and 3 are based on arguments made in this article and appear here in a revised and expanded form. *See also* Alfred C. Aman, Jr., *A Global Perspective on Current Regulatory Reforms: Rejection, Relocation, or Reinvention?,* 2 Ind. J. Global Legal Stud. 429, 435–37 (1995). For an argument that much of what courts claim are rationales for federalism are, in reality, an argument for decentralized management instead, *see* Edward L. Rubin & Malcolm Feeley, *Federalism: Some Notes on a National Neurosis,* 41 UCLA L. Rev. 903, 914 (1994).

26. *See* Richard Elliot Benedick, *Ozone Diplomacy: New Directions, in* Safeguarding the Planet (Cambridge, MA: Harvard Univ. Press 1st ed. 1991).

27. *See* Robert Perrucci, Japanese Auto Transplants in the Heartland: Corporatism and Community 41–76 (New York: de Gruyter 1994).

28. *Id.* at 125–45.

29. *Id.* at 17.

30. *Id.* at 131–34.

31. Alfred C. Aman, Jr., *Administrative Law for a New Century, in* THE PROVINCE OF ADMINISTRATIVE LAW 101 (Michael Taggart ed., Oxford, UK: Hart Pub. 1997).

32. PERRUCCI, *supra* note 27.

33. MATTHEW A. CRENSON & BENJAMIN GINSBERG, DOWNSIZING DEMOCRACY (Baltimore, MD: Johns Hopkins Univ. Press 2002).

34. For example, private prisons' costs should not be lower because there are fewer constitutional protections available to prisoners.

35. *See, e.g.,* Esty, *supra* note 23; Diane P. Wood, *United States Antitrust Law in the Global Market,* 1 IND. J. GLOBAL LEGAL STUD. 409 (1994).

36. *See* Daniel C. Esty, *Stepping Up to the Global Environmental Challenge,* FORDHAM ENVTL. L.J. 103, 108–11 (1996); *see also* J. William Hicks, *Protection of Individual Investors under U.S. Securities Laws: The Impact of International Regulatory Competition,* 1 IND. J. GLOBAL LEGAL STUD. 431 (1994).

37. For example, according to the Multilaterals Project at Tufts University, at least thirty-six major multilateral environmental treaties have opened for signature since 1972. Information about this project can be viewed at http://fletcher.tufts.edu/multilaterals.html (last visited Oct. 8, 2003).

38. *Id. See also* WORLD COMMISSION ON ENVIRONMENT AND DEVELOPMENT, OUR COMMON FUTURE (Geneva: Center for Our Common Future 1992).

39. *See, e.g.,* the debate over sovereignty that occurred when the World Trade Organization was established; *see also* Senate Committee on Commerce, Science, and Transportation hearing on fast-track legislation, 1997 WL 605646 (F.D.C.H.) (Sept. 30, 1997) (comments by Senator Ernest F. Hollings, D-SC).

40. For a public-choice perspective on this overall increase in international agreements, *see* Enrico Columbatto & Jonathan R. Macey, *A Public Choice Model of International Economic Cooperation and the Decline of the Nation State,* 18 CARDOZO L. REV. 925 (1997).

41. *See, e.g.,* the Trade Act of 2002, which granted President Bush fast-track authority (referred to as trade promotion authority) to negotiate trade agreements without providing for congressional amendments. Pub. L. No. 107-210, §§ 2101–13, 116 Stat. 933, 992–1022 (2002); *see also* Chantal Thomas, *Constitutional Change and International Government,* 52 HASTINGS L.J. 1, 17–21 (2000) (citing congressional opposition to fast-track authority and reviewing fast track's history).

42. Of course, it can be horizontal as well, when, for example, states try to take advantage of other states. *See, e.g.,* dominant commerce clause cases such as Kassel v. Consolidated Freightways Corp. 450 U.S. 662 (1981). These issues,

however, involve only states and are controlled by the relationship of the state law to the commerce clause.

43. For a discussion of the power of transnational corporations and their impact on politics, see Susan Strange, The Retreat of the State: The Diffusion of Power in the World Economy 44–54 (New York: Blackwell 1986) ("the progressive integration of the world economy has shifted the balance of power away from states toward world markets. That shift has led to the transfer of some powers in relation to civil society from territorial states to TNC's."). *Id.* at 46.

44. Strange, Casino Capitalism (New York: Blackwell 1986).

45. *See* Group of Lisbon Report, Limits to Competition (Cambridge, MA: MIT Press 1995).

46. *See* Strange, *supra* note 44, at 54 (arguing that if one excludes war and peace, and focuses more broadly on day-to-day economic issues, TNC's have come to play a significant role in determining "who gets what" in the world system.)

47. *See generally,* Ellis W. Hawley, The New Deal and the Problem of Monopoly: A Study in Economic Ambivalence (Princeton, NJ: Princeton University Press 1966). *See also* Archibald Cox, The Court and the Constitution (Boston, MA: Houghton Mifflin 1987).

48. *See, e.g.,* New York v. United States, 505 U.S. 144 (1992); Gregory v. Ashcroft, 501 U.S. 452 (1991); United States v. Lopez, 115 S. Ct. 1624 (1995); Printz v. United States, 117 S. Ct. 2365 (1997); and United States v. Morrison, 529 U.S. 598 (2000).

49. *See* Anne-Marie Slaughter Burley, *International Law and International Relations Theory,* 87 Am. J. Int'l L. 205 (1995).

50. *See generally,* Joseph A. Camilleri & Jim Falk, The End of Sovereignty? The Politics of a Shrinking and Fragmenting World (Brookfield, VT: Elgar 1992); *Cf.* United States v. Morrison, 529 U.S. 598, 655 (2000) (Souter, J., dissenting):

> The facts that cannot be ignored today are the facts of integrated national commerce and a political relationship between States and Nation much affected by their respective treasuries and constitutional modifications adopted by the people. The federalism of some earlier time is no more adequate to account for those facts today than the theory of laissez-faire was able to govern the national economy 70 years ago.

51. *See, e.g.,* United States v. Lopez, 514 U.S. 549, 577 (1995) ("Were the Federal Government to take over the regulation of entire areas of traditional state concern, areas having nothing to do with the regulation of commercial activities, the boundaries between the spheres of federal and state authority would blur and political responsibility would become illusory."); *see also* Printz v.

United States, 117 S. Ct. 2365, 2377 (1997) ("The Framers' experience under the Article of Confederation had persuaded them that using the States as the instruments of federal governance was both ineffectual and provocative of federal-state conflict. . . . [T]he Constitution thus contemplates that a State's government will represent and remain accountable to its own citizens.").

52. *Id.*

53. 501 U.S. 452 (1991).

54. *Id* at 457 (internal citation omitted).

55. *Id.*

56. *See* Alexander B. Murphy, *The Sovereign State System as Political and Territorial Ideal: Historical and Contemporary Considerations, in* STATE SOVEREIGNTY AS SOCIAL CONSTRUCT 81, 81–93, 100–102 (Thomas J. Biersteker & Cynthia Weber, eds., Cambridge: Cambridge Univ. Press 1996).

57. *Id.* at 181.

58. *Id.* at 182.

59. 501 U.S. at 458.

60. *Id.*

61. Consider, for example, the power of private drug companies over potential reimportation efforts by Congress and the states, discussed *infra*, ch. 4, pp. 000–000.

62. 535 U.S. 743 (2002).

63. *Id* at 760.

64. *Id.* at 777.

65. *Id.* at 785–86 (internal citation omitted).

66. *See, e.g.,* Dennis Conway, *Are There New Complexities in Global Migration Systems of Consequence for the United States "Nation-State"?,* 2 IND. J. GLOBAL LEGAL STUD. 31, 35–43 (1994) (discussing international mobility, the world as an interconnected community, and the way individuals relate to and identify with more than one country at a time).

67. *See generally,* GARY TEEPLE, GLOBALIZATION AND THE DECLINE OF SOCIAL REFORM 69–74 (Atlantic Highlands, NJ: Humanities Press 1st ed. 1995); *see also* WILLIAM GREIDER, ONE WORLD, READY OR NOT: THE MAGIC LOGIC OF GLOBAL CAPITALISM 360–87 (New York: Simon & Schuster 1997).

68. *See generally,* SASKIA SASSEN, CITIES IN A WORLD ECONOMY (Thousand Oaks, CA: Pine Forge Press 1994).

69. *See* Daniel C. Esty, *Revitalizing Environmental Federalism,* 95 MICH. L. REV. 570, 627–38 (1996).

70. Rubin & Feeley, *supra* note 25.

71. 505 U.S. 144 (1992).

72. As Justice White described it, concurring in part and dissenting in part, [The Act] resulted from the efforts of state leaders to achieve a state-based set of remedies to the waste problem. They sought not federal pre-emption

or intervention, but rather congressional sanction of interstate compromises they had reached.

[The] 1985 Act was very much the product of cooperative federalism, in which the States bargained among themselves to achieve compromises for Congress to sanction. . . . Unlike legislation that directs action from the Federal Government to the States, the [Congressional action] reflected hard-fought agreements among States as refereed by Congress.
Id. at 189–90, 194.

73. Adam Babich, *Our Federalism, Our Hazardous Waste, and Our Good Fortune,* 54 MD. L. REV. 1516 (1995).

74. *Id.* at 1533.

75. 505 U.S. at 152.

76. *Id.* at 154.

77. Writing for the majority, Justice O'Connor noted,
The actual scope of the Federal Government's authority with respect to the states has changed over the years, therefore, but the constitutional structure underlying and limiting that authority has not. In the end, just as a cup may be half empty or half full, it makes no difference whether one views the question at issue in these cases as one of ascertaining the limits of the power delegated to the Federal Government under the affirmative provisions of the Constitution or one of discerning the core of sovereignty retained by the States under the Tenth Amendment. Either way, we must determine whether any of the three challenged provisions of the Low-Level Radioactive Waste Policy Amendments Act of 1985 oversteps the boundary between federal and state authority.
Id at 159.

78. *Id.* at 166 (internal citations omitted).

79. *Id.* at 175. It is interesting to note that New York was, of course, involved in the political process that produced this result. The Supreme Court, however, rejected arguments to the effect that New York had, in effect, consented to these federal regulations. ("Where Congress exceeds its authority relative to the States the departure cannot be ratified by the 'consent' of state officials.") *Cf.* dissent by White.

80. 117 S. Ct. 2365 (1997).

81. *Id.* at 2383.

82. *Id.* at 2384.

83. *Id.* at 2386.

84. *Id.* at 2403.
At least some other countries, facing the same basic problem, have found that local control is better maintained through application of a principle that is the direct opposite of the principle the majority derives from the

silence of our Constitution. The federal systems of Switzerland, Germany, and the European Union, for example, all provide that constituent states, not federal bureaucracies, will themselves implement many of the laws, rules, regulations, or decrees enacted by the central "federal" body.

85. 115 S. Ct. 1624.

86. *Id.* at 1626 (quoting 18 U.S.C. § 922(g)(1)(A) (1988 ed. Supp. V)).

87. *Id.* at 1630.

88. *Id.* at 1632.

89. *Id.* at 1627.

90. *Id.* at 1638.

91. *Id.*

92. *Id.* at 1657.

93. *Id.* at 1660.

94. *Id.*

95. *Id.*

96. *Id.*

97. *Id.* at 1661 (emphasis in original).

98. 317 U.S. 111 (1942) (upholding the application of the Agricultural Adjustment Act to the planting and consumption of homegrown wheat).

99. 115 S. Ct. at 1661 (quoting majority opinion).

100. One could argue that Justice Breyer's approach proves too much, i.e., that the links between global and domestic economies are so apparent as to assure a federal result. As this book has argued, the distinction between the global and various forms of the local has collapsed; this does not mean Congress must automatically act. It is not compelled to act. Rather, the issues are now political issues to be acted on in the political process, without such judicial intervention, as contemplated in *Lopez*. Justice Stevens argues that state sovereignty is protected through the political process: "[i]t is the Framers' compromise giving each State equal representation in the Senate that provides the principal structural protection for the sovereignty of the several States." Kimel v. Florida Bd. of Regents, 528 U.S. 62, 93 (2000) (Stevens, J., dissenting in part and concurring in part). He adds,

> Federalism concerns do make it appropriate for Congress to speak clearly when it regulates state action. But when it does so . . . we can safely presume that the burdens the statute imposes on the sovereignty of the several States were taken into account during the deliberative process leading to the enactment of the measure.

Id. at 96.

101. CRENSON & GINSBERG, *supra* note 33, at 232.

102. *Id.* at 212.

103. Varamon Ramangkura, *Thai Shrimp, Sea Turtles, Mangrove Forests*

and the WTO: Innovative Environmental Protection under the International Trade Regime, 15 GEO. INT'L ENVTL. L. REV. 677, 682 (2003).

104. CLAUDE E. BARFIELD, FREE TRADE, SOVEREIGNTY, DEMOCRACY: THE FUTURE OF THE WORLD TRADE ORGANIZATION 143–45 (Washington, DC: AEI Press 2000) (proposing the creation of a bipartisan congressional commission to "inform [Congress] not only of individual actions, policies, or cases but also of the overall trends within international organizations that will have an impact on the normal workings of the U.S. political system").

105. *See, e.g.,* John O. McGinnis & Mark L. Movesian, *The World Trade Constitution,* 114 HARV. L. REV. 511 (2000). *But see* Daniel Bodansky, *The Legitimacy of International Governance: A Coming Challenge for International Environmental Law?,* 93 AM. J. INT'L L. 596 (1999).

106. *See* Curtis A. Bradley, *International Delegations, the Structural Constitution, and Non-self Execution,* 55 STAN. L. REV. 1557 (2003).

107. *See, e.g.,* United States v. Morrison, 529 U.S. 598, 654 (2000) (Souter, J., dissenting) ("It is, then, not the least irony of these cases that the states will be forced to enjoy the new federalism whether they want it or not. For with the Court's decision today, Antonio Morrison, like *Carter Coal*'s James Carter before him, has 'won the states' rights plea against the states themselves.'") (citation omitted).

108. College Sav. Bank v. Florida Prepaid Postsecondary Educ. Expense Rd. 527 U.S. 666, 703 (1999).

109. *Id.* at 640.

110. BARFIELD, *supra* note 104, at 37–69.

111. *See, e.g.,* Larry A. DiMatteo et al., *The Doha Declaration and Beyond: Giving a Voice to Non-Trade Concerns within the WTO Trade Regime,* 36 VAND. J. TRANSNAT'L L. 95 (2003); Steve Charnovitz, *WTO Cosmopolitics,* 34 N.Y.U. J. INT'L L. & POL. 299 (2002); Jeffery Atik, *Democratizing the WTO,* 33 GEO. WASH. INT'L L. REV. 451 (2001).

112. *See, e.g.,* Claude E. Barfield, *Free Trade, Sovereignty, Democracy: The Future of the World Trade Organization,* 2 CHI. J. INT'L L. 403, 408 (2001) (arguing that "alternatives should be pursued that will reintroduce some of the former elements of 'diplomatic' flexibility that characterized the earlier GATT regime.").

113. BARFIELD, *supra* note 104.

114. The United States' implementing legislation denies effect to WTO rulings that are inconsistent with domestic law. 19 U.S.C. §3512(a)(1) (2000).

115. *See, e.g.,* Eric L. Richards & Martin A. McCrory, *The Sea Turtle Dispute: Implications for Sovereignty, the Environment, and International Trade Law,* 71 U. Colo. L. Rev. 295 (2000) (discussing the difficulties of conforming regulations enforcing section 609 of Public Law 101-162 with the statute and WTO appellate body decision).

116. *See, e.g.,* Barfield, *supra* note 104.

117. *See, e.g.,* McGinnis & Movesian, *supra* note 105.

118. Thomas, *supra* note 41.

119. Philippe C. Schmitter, *What Is There to Legitimize in the European Union . . . and How Might This Be Accomplished?,* at http://www.iue.it/SPS/People/Faculty/CurrentProfessors/bioSchmitter.shtml (last updated Sept. 30, 2003).

NOTES TO CHAPTER 3

1. Though nationalization is rare in the United States, there are some exceptions. The Tennessee Valley Authority was created as a government corporation to undertake the building and operation of dams. See Richard Wirtz, *The Legal Framework of the Tennessee Valley Authority,* 43 Tenn. L. Rev. 573 (1976).

2. Airline Deregulation Act, Pub. L. No. 95-504, 92 Stat. 1705 (1978).

3. See, e.g., Bruce A. Ackerman & Richard B. Stewart, *Reforming Environmental Law,* 37 Stan. L. Rev. 1333, 1341 (1985).

4. 5 U.S.C. § 551, *et seq.* (2000).

5. See Motor Vehicles Mfrs. Assn. v. State Farm Mut. Auto Ins. Co., 463 U.S. 29 (1983).

6. *See* cases listed *supra* ch. 1, note 146.

7. Lester M. Salamon, *The New Governance and the Tools of Public Action: An Introduction, in* The Tools of Government: A Guide to the New Governance 1, 1–2 (Lester M. Salamon ed., New York: Oxford Univ. Press 2002) [hereinafter cited as Salamon, *The Tools of Government*].

8. *Id.* at p. 33. In addition to tools for providing governmental services, agencies utilize similar market approaches, such as regulatory contracts to carry out their statutory duties. See Jody Freeman, *The Contracting State,* 28 Fla. St. U. L. Rev. 155, 189–201 (2000). For excellent analysis of various public/private forms of governance, and the relationships between public and private actions, see Jody Freeman, *The Private Roles in Public Governance,* 75 N.Y.U. L. Rev. 543 (2000); Jody Freeman, *Private Parties, Public Functions and the New Administrative Law, in* Recrafting the Rule of Law: The Limits of Legal Order 331 (David Dyzenhaus ed., Oxford, UK: Hart Pub. 1999).

9. For an interesting discussion of the differences between privatization and deregulation in the United States and Europe, see Giandomenico Majone, *Paradoxes of Privatization and Deregulation,* J. Eur. Pub. Pol'y 4 (1994).

10. *Id.*

11. *See* Shymeka L. Hunter, *More Than Just a Private Affair: Is the Practice of Incarcerating Alaska Prisoners in Private Out-of-State Prisons Unconstitutional?,* 17 Alaska L. Rev. 319, 327–28 (2000).

Given the way the federal government and states like Alaska have supported the private sector's prison ventures and the booming market, it is perhaps not surprising that by 1996 there were more than one hundred private jails and prisons located across twenty-seven states. As of 1997, the private prison industry was grossing 550 million dollars annually; Alaska is among the twenty-five states that make use of private prisons. Thirty-one states, the Federal system, and Washington, D.C., reported a housing total of 71,208 prisoners in private facilities in 1999. Specifically, Alaska housed thirty-five percent of its prison population in private facilities during 1999, making it second only to New Mexico's thirty-nine percent.

12. Lewis D. Solomon, *Reflections on the Future of Business Organizations,* 20 Cardozo L. Rev. 1213, 1216 (1999). ("Virtually any asset or service that a local government owns or provides has been privatized somewhere in the United States in some manner, including fire protection, police protection, waste water treatment, street lighting, tree trimming, snow removal, parking structures, railroads, hospitals, jails, and even cemeteries.")

13. Matthew Diller, *The Revolution in Welfare Administration: Rules, Discretion, and Entrepreneurial Government,* 75 N.Y.U. L. Rev. 1121 (2000).

14. There are many exceptions. For example, when agencies rely on tradable pollution permits, they create incentives on the part of the private parties involved to undertake the enforcement of those who cheat. The government is, in effect, not involved in the enforcement of the requirements of these permits and the choice of tradable permits rather than command control regulations lessens the direct involvement of the state in the enforcement process.

15. For the most part, agency deregulation in the form of market incentives largely overlaps with what might be called the reinvention-of-government approach to reform. For a discussion of how this approach differs from privatization in an ideological sense and privatization in the sense of market tools for public purposes, see Salamon, *The Tools of Government, supra* note 7, at 14–16. For a discussion of some of the legal issues presented by reinvention of government approaches, see Alfred C. Aman, Jr., *A Global Perspective on Current Regulatory Reforms: Rejection, Relocation or Reinvention?,* 2 Ind. J. Global Legal Stud. 429 (1995).

16. *See, e.g.,* Carlos Manuel Vázquez, *Sovereign Immunity, Due Process, and The Alden Trilogy,* 109 Yale L.J. 1927, 1957–62 (2000).

17. For a discussion of the various ways that competition in a global economy can affect state entities, politics, and the law they apply *see* Alfred C. Aman, Jr., *The Globalizing State: A Future-Oriented Perspective on the Public/Private Distinction, Federalism, and Democracy,* 31 Vand. J. Transnat'l L. 769, 780–91 (1998). Portions of chapter 3 represent a revised and expanded form of the arguments that first appeared in this article.

18. *See, e.g.,* David J. Kennedy, *Due Process in a Privatized Welfare System,* 64 Brook. L. Rev. 231, 259–61 (1998) (arguing that welfare reform often results in higher costs).

19. *See, e.g.,* Contract with America, *available at* http://www.townhall.com/ documents/contract.html (last visited Oct. 15, 2003). This document, emphasizing a minimalist role for the federal government in economic areas, was signed by a majority of Republican Congresspeople prior to Republicans taking control of the House of Representatives after the 1994 election. *See also* Unfunded Mandate Reform Act of 1995, Pub. L. No. 104-4, 109 Stat. 48 (1995); Private Property Protection Act of 1995, H.R. 925, 104th Cong., 1st Sess. (1995); Risk Assessment and Cost-Benefit Analysis Act of 1995, H.R. 690, 104th Cong., 1st Sess. (1995).

20. Contract with America, *supra* note 19.

21. *See, e.g.,* the Private Property Protection Act of 1995, H.R. 9, 104th Cong., 1st Sess. (1995), which was the most prohibitive of the legislative proposals dealing with the compensation of property rights. It required that the federal government "compensate an owner of property whose use of any portion of that property has been limited by an agency action, under a specified regulatory law, that diminishes the fair market value of that portion by 20 percent or more. The amount of the compensation shall equal the diminution in value that resulted from the agency action." *Id.* at § 203(a).

22. *See, e.g.,* Mark A. Hofman, *Nader Faults EPA as Lax on Enforcement,* 29 Bus. Ins., May 1, 1995, at 47.

23. A prime example is Vice President Al Gore, Report of the National Performance Review, *From Red Tape to Results: Creating a Government That Works Better and Costs Less* (1993) [hereinafter *National Performance Review*]. For a discussion of this report, see Jeffery S. Lubbers, *Better Regulations: The National Performance Review's Regulatory Reform Recommendations,* 43 Duke L.J. 1165 (1994); Daniel P. Rodriguez, *Management, Control, and the Dilemmas of Presidential Leadership in the Modern Administrative State,* 43 Duke L.J. 1180 (1994); Paul R. Verkuil, *Is Efficient Government an Oxymoron?,* 43 Duke L.J. 1221 (1994).

24. Hindy Lauer Schacter, Reinventing Government or Reinventing Ourselves: The Role of Citizen Owners in Making a Better Government (Albany, NY: SUNY Press 1997).

25. *Id. See also* Mark Sagoff, The Economy of the Earth: Philosophy, Law, and the Environment (New York: Cambridge Univ. Press 1988).

26. *See* Saskia Sassen, The Mobility of Labor and Capital: A Study in International Investment and Labor Flow (New York: Cambridge Univ. Press 1988).

27. *Id.*

28. Alfred C. Aman, Jr., Administrative Law in a Global Era 42–62 (Ithaca, NY: Cornell Univ. Press 1992).

29. *See, e.g.,* congressional testimony in support of fast-track authority by Robert W. Holleyman, II, president of Business Software Alliance (1995 WL

293530 (F.D.C.H.), May 11, 1995) and by Marc Curtis of the American Soybean Association (1997 WL 592041 (F.D.C.H.), Sept. 23, 1997). *See also* the various legislative proposals to scale back, reregulate, or repeal aspects of various regulatory regimes in the Contract with America, by the 104th Congress. *E.g.,* Unfunded Mandates Reform Act of 1995, Pub. L. No. 104-4, 109 Stat. 48; Thomas O. McGarity, *The Clean Air Act at a Crossroads: Statutory Interpretation and Longstanding Practice in the Shadow of the Delegation Doctrine,* 9 N.Y.U. ENVTL. L.J. 1, 17 (2000) (stating that "[t]he 104th Congress very nearly enacted legislation imposing a cost-benefit 'supermandate' on all federal health and environmental agencies as part of the 'Contract with America' implementing legislation.").

30. It is assumed, however, that the antitrust laws still apply when, for example, pricing regulations are removed.

31. *See* Elizabeth Bailey & Dong Liu, *Airline Consolidation and Consumer Welfare,* 21 E. ECON. J. 463 (1995) ("While it was recognized that regional carriers had a higher cost structure than national carriers, it was thought that this would be eliminated by permitting free entry and exit. As Alfred Kahn once expressed it, airplanes are marginal costs with wings that can readily be deployed in newly opened markets.").

32. Pub. L. No. 95-504, 92 Stat. 1705 (codified in 49 U.S.C. § 1301, *et seq.* (2000)).

33. Executive Order No. 12, 287, 3 L.F.R. 124 (1981) (reprinted in 15 U.S.C. § 757 (2000)).

34. 15 U.S.C. § 753(a) (1976).

35. The Trucking Deregulation Act and the Abolition of the ICC Act.

36. *See, e.g.,* Mark Green & Ralph Nader, *Economic Regulation vs. Competition: Uncle Sam the Monopoly Man,* 82 YALE L.J. 871 (1973).

37. In fact, the deregulation imposed by the agency itself ultimately led to a "deregulation" bill that sought to regulate this area. *See* Aman, *supra* note 17, at 31.

38. AMAN, *supra* note 28; Aman, *supra* note 17, at 821–22.

39. *See, e.g.,* Clark C. Havighurst, *American Health Care and the Law,* in THE PRIVATIZATION OF HEALTH CARE REFORM: LEGAL AND REGULATORY PERSPECTIVES (M. Gregg Bloche ed., New York: Oxford Univ. Press 2003) (promoting market privatization in health care provision).

40. *See* Telecommunications Act of 1996, Pub. L. No. 104-104, 110 Stat. 56 (codified in scattered sections of 47 U.S.C. (2000)); *see generally,* Michael I. Meyerson, *Ideas of the Marketplace: A Guide to the 1996 Telecommunications Act,* 49 FED. COMM. L.J. 251 (1996).

[The Telecommunications Act of 1996] represents a vision of a telecommunications marketplace where the flexibility and innovation of competition replaces the heavy hand of regulation. It is based on the premise that

technological changes will permit a flourishing of telecommunications carriers, engaged in head-to-head competition, resulting in a multitude of
communications carriers and programmers being made available to the
American consumer.
Creation of the markets necessary for this act to work has been a major task facing the Federal Communications Commission. *See, e.g.,* Charles M. Oliver, *The
Information Superhighway: Trolls at the Tollgate,* 50 FED. COMM. L.J. 53, 61
(1997) ("[T]he core of the Telecommunications Act of 1996 is a quid pro quo:
the RBOCs [Regional Bell Operating Companies] will be allowed to get into the
long distance and manufacturing businesses, in return for which they must open
their markets to local competition.").

41. *See* Michael A. Carrier, *All Aboard the Congressional Fast Track: From
Trade to Beyond,* 29 GEO. WASH. J. INT'L L. & ECON. 687 (1996).

42. *See* Hon. Dana Rohrabacher, *Pennies for Thoughts: How GATT Fast
Track Harms American Patent Applicants,* 11 ST. JOHN'S J. LEGAL COMMENT
491 (1996) (arguing that in an effort to harmonize U.S. patent law with international laws, the U.S. Patent Office traded away critical patent protection American inventors had come to expect); *see also* Patti Goldman, *The Democratization of the Development of United States Trade Policy,* 27 CORNELL INT'L L.J.
631 (1994) (proposing revision of the fast-track process to allow social values
and consumer concerns to be considered when trade agreements are proposed).
Many commentators argue that fast track does provide ample opportunities to
debate and deliberate fully. The president is required to notify Congress of his intent to enter into a trade agreement and has ninety days from that date to con-
sult with Congress on the terms of the agreement. 19 U.S.C. § 2902 (2000). Because amendments are not permitted under the fast-track process, this consulta-
tion period serves as an opportunity for the executive and legislative branches to
discuss the issues and make changes to the proposal before the final vote. For a
detailed description of this process see Janet A. Nuzum, *Comments on the Fast-
Track Process for Congressional Consideration of NAFTA,* 1 U.S.-MEX. L.J. 339
(1993). In addition, Congress has the power to choose to "derail" fast track and
follow the usual approach of congressional deliberations. Carrier, *supra* note 40;
19 U.S.C. § 2903 (2000).

43. For a statistical illustration of the increased use of executive agreements
when compared with the use of treaties (which require two-thirds approval from
the Senate), see Terry M. Moe & William G. Howell, *The Presidential Power of
Unilateral Action,* 15 J. L. ECON. & ORG. 132, 164 (1999). There has also been a
movement away from treaties towards congressional-executive agreements
(which require simple majority approval by both the Senate and House). For an
argument that such agreements are unconstitutional, see Laurence H. Tribe, *Taking Text and Structure Seriously: Reflections on Free-Form Method in Constitutional Interpretation,* 108 HARV. L. REV. 1221, 1267 n.156 (1995). *Contra* Bruce

Ackerman & David Golove, *Is NAFTA Constitutional?*, 108 HARV. L. REV. 799 (1995).

44. *See, e.g.,* AMAN, *supra* note 28, chs. 1 & 2 (reviewing the decisions of the FCC and the ICC and the manner in which courts allowed these changes to occur).

45. *See generally,* Bruce Ackerman & Richard Stewart, *Reforming Environmental Law,* 37 STAN. L. REV. 1333, 1341 (1985):

Our basic reform would respond to these deficiencies by allowing polluters to buy and sell each other's permits—thereby creating a powerful financial incentive for those who can clean up most cheaply to sell their permits to those whose treatment costs are highest. This reform will, at one stroke, cure many of the basic flaws of the existing command-and-control regulatory systems discussed earlier.

See also Marshall Breger, Richard Stewart, et al., *Providing Economic Incentives in Environmental Regulation* 8 YALE J. ON REG. 463, 468–69 (1991) ("I am persuaded that the endless proliferation of command-and-control regulations is not, in general, a workable or appropriate long-run way of dealing with this problem.").

46. Ackerman & Stewart, *supra* note 3, at 1341.

47. See discussion, *supra* ch. 2, pp. 000–000.

48. *See, e.g.,* Alec Stone Sweet, *Judicialization and the Construction of Governance,* 32 COMP. POL. STUD. 147 (1999) (discussing the effect of private entities on rule making at the international level as a result of private litigation in international forums).

49. *See, e.g.,* Christopher L. Bell, *Bench Test,* ENVTL. FORUM, Nov./Dec. 1997, at 24 (describing the International Organization for Standardization's environmental management standard, "ISO 14000.") This is a voluntary standard, devised privately, that is meant to provide uniform approaches to environmental management for companies operating around the world. *See also* Jeff Gerth, *Where Business Rules: Forging Global Regulations That Put Industry First,* N.Y. TIMES, Jan. 9, 1998, at D1 (stating that "[t]he final automotive standards agreement is expected by March [1998] but few consumer advocates will have had a say. There were 62 government regulators and 26 industry representatives who took part in the Geneva auto committee last November, under United Nations rules, but only one consumer representative from London and one auto club member from France."); Peter J. Spiro, *New Global Communities: Nongovernmental Organizations in International Decision-Making,* WASH. Q., Winter 1995, at 45.

50. For an excellent, thorough analysis of harmonization in the environmental area, *see* Daniel C. Esty & Damien Geradin, *Market Access, Competitiveness, and Harmonization: Environmental Protection in Regional Trade Agreements,* 21 HARV. ENVTL. L. REV. 265 (1997).

51. IAN HARDEN, THE CONTRACTING STATE (Philadelphia, PA: Open Univ. Press 1992).

52. *Id.* at 10–11.

53. *Id.* at 11–12.

54. *See* Clayton P. Gillette, *Opting Out of Public Provision,* 73 DENV. U. L. REV. 1185 (1996).

55. *See generally,* RICHARD W. HARDING, PRIVATE PRISONS AND PUBLIC ACCOUNTABILITY (New Brunswick, NJ: Transaction Publishers 1997).

56. The pressure to move prisoners back to Mexico is created predominantly by cost. Currently, Arizona spends approximately $66 million a year to house thirty-three hundred Mexican nationals. Barrett Marson, *Plan: Ship Mexican Inmates Back,* ARIZ. DAILY STAR, Oct. 20, 2003, at A1.

57. *See, e.g.,* Rep. Philip Crane's proposals to privatize the U.S. Postal Service ("The performance of the post office can only be improved by transferring it to the private sector.") 135 Cong. Rec. E547–48 (Feb. 28, 1989).

58. *See supra* text accompanying notes 52–55.

59. *See* HARDING, *supra* note 55.

60. McKnight v. Richardson, 521 U.S. 399, 405–7 (1997); James Theodore Gentry, Note, *The Panopticon Revisited: The Problem of Monitoring Private Prisons,* 96 YALE L.J. 353 (1986).

61. *See* HARDING, *supra* note 55, at 3.

62. *Id.*

63. Gentry, *supra* note 60, at 357–58.

64. If, for example, prison guards can simply tie up inmates with straightjackets (as in *Richardson*) and leave them for days at a time, certainly Eighth Amendment and Fourteenth Amendment concerns should arise. Without the possibility of constitutional oversight in the federal courts, these fundamental rights—already litigated and settled in the federal courts—would be rendered moot by a nationwide wave of such "outsourcing." The system may soon have an opportunity to address these questions in the context of abuse in privately run juvenile prisons. The Tallulah Correctional Center for Youth, a privately run detention facility in Tallulah, LA, came under harsh criticism amid allegations of physical abuse by guards, failure to educate and counsel the youths, and arbitrary and severe punishments for misbehavior. Louisiana's juvenile prison system is just one of a series being investigated by the U.S. Justice Department. Kentucky, Puerto Rico, and Georgia are also under investigation, and "private juvenile prisons in Colorado, Texas, and South Carolina have been successfully sued by individuals and groups or forced to give up their licenses." Fox Butterfield, *Profits at a Juvenile Prison Come at a Chilling Cost,* N.Y. TIMES, July 15, 1998, at A1.

65. *See, e.g.,* Note, *Limits of Competition, Accountability in Government Contracting,* 112 YALE L.J. 2465 (2003).

66. *See* Douglas W. Dunham, *Inmates' Rights and the Privatization of Prisons*, 86 COLUM. L. REV. 1475 (1986); *see also* Warren L. Ratliff, *The Due Process Failure of America's Prison Privatization Statutes*, 21 SETON HALL LEGIS. J. 371 (1997).

67. *See, e.g.*, Edmonson v. Leesville Concrete Co., 500 U.S. 614 (1991); Lugar v. Edmonson Oil Co., 457 U.S. 922 (1982). *But see* Corr. Servs. Corp. v. Malesko, 534 U.S. 61, 81 (2001) (Stevens, J., dissenting) (arguing that majority improperly exempted corporation operating a private prison from lawsuit by a former inmate, stating that if such a suit were allowed "both private and public prisoners would be unable to sue the principal (i.e., the Government), but would be able to sue the primary federal agent (i.e., the Government official or the corporation).").

68. Of course, one can imagine a more positive view of private prisons as well, one where a more efficiently trained workforce runs a cleaner, more effective facility. But even the more positive political rhetoric that can surround this reform is implicitly negative vis-à-vis the state. It reinforces the laissez-faire conception of the state noted above, by its implication that the market can handle prisons more effectively than government.

69. 521 U.S. 399, 404 (1995).

70. *Id.* at 405.

71. *Id.* at 408.

72. *Id.* at 404–5.

73. *Id.* at 410–11.

74. *Id.* at 407.

75. *Id.* at 409.

76. *Id.* at 408.

77. *Id.* at 407–8.

78. *Id.*

79. *Id.* at 408.

80. *Id.*

81. *Id.* at 414.

82. *Id.* at 414–15.

83. *Id.* at 415.

84. *Id.*

85. *Id.* at 418–19 (internal citation omitted).

86. *Id.* at 419.

87. *Id.*

88. *Id.* at 419–22.

89. *Id.* at 419.

90. *Id.* at 421–22.

91. *Id.* at 422–23.

92. *Id.* at 421–22.

93. *Id.*
94. *Id.* at 421.
95. *Id.* at 422.
96. *See* Gillette, *supra* note 54.
97. HARDEN, *supra* note 51, at 7–8.
98. Mark Aronson, *A Public Lawyer's Responses to Privatization and Outsourcing, in* THE PROVINCE OF ADMINISTRATIVE LAW 40, 62 (Michael Taggart ed., Oxford, UK: Hart Pub. 1997).
99. *Id.*
100. *Id.* at 56–58. *But see* current tax reform proposals that seek to differentiate between policy and administration. The Internal Revenue Service Restructuring and Reform Act of 1997, H.R. 2676, 105th Cong., 2d Sess. (1998), passed the House on November 5, 1997. Section 101 of that measure would create a new Internal Revenue Service Oversight Board to oversee the IRS's "[a]dministration, management, conduct, direction, and supervision of the executive and application" of the tax laws. However, it would have no authority as to "the development and formulation of federal tax policy."

This proposal emanated from the Report of the National Commission on Restructuring the Internal Revenue Service: A Vision for a New IRS, *reprinted in* TAX NOTES TODAY (June 26, 1997) (§ 1, recommendation 2 of the report). However, skeptics have expressed doubts whether such distinctions could be maintained in practice were the proposal enacted. *See id.* (dissenting statement of Commissioner Larry Irving) ("The line being drawn between oversight and tax policy and management will, in my opinion, be almost impossible to police or maintain, and ultimately will raise serious accountability and jurisdictional questions.").

101. *See* HARDEN, *supra* note 51, 44–45, 75–77.
102. *See, e.g.,* JOHN HART ELY, DEMOCRACY AND DISTRUST: A THEORY OF JUDICIAL REVIEW (Cambridge, MA: Harvard Univ. Press 1980). *But see* CHRISTOPHER L. EISGRUBER, CONSTITUTIONAL SELF-GOVERNMENT (Cambridge, MA: Harvard Univ. Press 2001).
103. *See generally,* Susan Marks, *The End of History? Reflections on Some International Legal Theses,* 8 EUR. J. INT'L. LAW 449 (1997).
104. *See, e.g.,* Michael J. Graetz, *The Decline (and Fall?) of the Income Tax* 271 (New York: Norton 1997) ("Because capital, in particular, is extremely mobile across international boundaries, every nation's sovereignty over its own tax policy is constrained. As nations compete for investments, they tend to reduce their taxes on capital to make such investments more attractive."); *see also* discussion *supra* ch. 2, pp. 000–000.
105. *See generally,* DANIEL C. ESTY, GREENING THE GATT: TRADE, ENVIRONMENT, AND THE FUTURE 108–11 (Washington, DC: Inst. for International Economics 1994).

106. *See, e.g.,* Harold J. Berman, *The Law of International Commercial Transactions (lex mercatoria), in* A LAWYER'S GUIDE TO INTERNATIONAL BUSINESS TRANSACTIONS: THE LAW OF INTERNATIONAL COMMERCIAL TRANSACTIONS (LEX MERCATORIA), Part III, folio 3 (W. S. Surrey & D. Wallace, Jr., eds., Philadelphia, PA: American Law Institute 1983); J. H. Baker, *The Law Merchant and the Common Law before 1700*, 38 CAMBRIDGE L.J. 295 (1979); Yves Dezalay & Bryant G. Garth, DEALING IN VIRTUE: INTERNATIONAL COMMERCIAL ARBITRATION AND THE CONSTRUCTION OF A TRANSNATIONAL LEGAL ORDER (Chicago, IL: Univ. Chicago Press 1996) (analyzing commercial arbitrators). *See also* Esty & Geradin, *supra* note 50, at 285. Global law is developed outside the framework of any one state and largely outside the framework of states at all. *See* Gunther Teubner, *"Global Bukowina": Legal Pluralism in the World Society, in* GLOBAL LAW WITHOUT A STATE 1 (Gunther Teubner ed., Brookfield, VT: Dartmouth Publ'g 1997).

107. *See, e.g.,* Lewis Rosman, Note, *Public Participation in International Pesticide Regulation: When the Codex Commission Decides, Who Will Listen?*, 12 VA. ENVTL. L.J. 329 (1993).

108. Various mixtures of public and private power, and the constitutional problems some of them can cause, of course, long predate the rise of the global state. *See, e.g.,* Note, *Law Making by Private Groups*, 51 HARV. L. REV. 201 (1937). More recently, commentators have discussed a variety of potential constitutional problems that could arise when law-making power is delegated to private groups. *See, e.g.,* Harold J. Krent, *Fragmenting the Unitary Executive: Congressional Delegations of Administrative Authority outside the Federal Government*, 85 NW. U. L. REV. 62 (1990); Harold I. Abramson, *A Fifth Branch of Government: The Private Regulators and Their Constitutionality*, 16 HASTINGS CONST. L.Q. 165 (1989); David M. Lawrence, *Private Exercise of Governmental Power*, 61 IND. L.J. 647 (1986).

109. *See* WILLIAM WINSLOW CROSSKEY, 1 POLITICS AND THE CONSTITUTION IN THE HISTORY OF THE UNITED STATES 93 (Chicago, IL: Univ. of Chicago Press 1953).

110. *Id.* at 82.

111. *See generally,* JEAN DRÈZE & AMARTYA SEN, INDIA: ECONOMIC DEVELOPMENT AND SOCIAL OPPORTUNITY 13–16 (New York: Oxford Univ. Press 1995).

112. *See generally,* JOSEPH A. CAMILLERI & JIM FALK, THE END OF SOVEREIGNTY? THE POLITICS OF A SHRINKING AND FRAGMENTING WORLD 166–67 (Brookfield, VT: Elgar 1992); *see also* SUSAN STRANGE, THE RETREAT OF THE STATE: THE DIFFUSION OF POWER IN THE WORLD ECONOMY 21–23 (New York: Cambridge Univ. Press 1996).

113. *See generally,* JOHN LEWIS GADDIS, WE NOW KNOW: RETHINKING COLD WAR HISTORY (New York: Oxford Univ. Press 1997).

114. *See, e.g.,* WILLIAM GREIDER, ONE WORLD, READY OR NOT: THE MANIC LOGIC OF GLOBAL CAPITALISM 172 (New York: Simon & Schuster 1997).

115. *Id.* at 369–70. Many argue that this model is peculiarly American. *See, e.g.,* Martin Shapiro, *The Globalization of Law,* 1 IND. J. GLOBAL LEGAL STUD. 37 (1993); but others note that this model is more common to global capitalism in general. *See* JEAN-MARIE GUÉHENNO, THE END OF THE NATION STATE 30–31 (Victoria Elliot trans., Minneapolis, MN: Univ. of Minnesota Press 1995). ("Certainly, the United States pushes to the limit the logic of the confrontation of interests in which the idea of a general good is dissolved. . . . But the extreme case can help to shed light on the average situation, and the American crisis is an indication of our future.").

116. *See, e.g.,* GREIDER, *supra* note 114, at 35–38.

117. *Id. See also* PAUL R. KRUGMAN, POP INTERNATIONALISM 15–21 (Cambridge, MA: MIT Press 1996).

118. *See* Philip G. Cerny, *What Next for the State?, in* GLOBALIZATION: THEORY AND PRACTICE 123, 132–33 (Eleonore Kofman & Gillian Youngs eds., New York: Pinter 1996). ("The main focus of the competition state in the world . . . is the promotion of economic activities, whether at home or abroad, which will make firms and sectors located within the territory of the state *competitive in international markets.*"); *see also A Competitive Strategy for America, Second Report to the President and Congress,* Competitiveness Policy Council, Washington, D.C. (March 1993).

119. See generally, THE PROVINCE OF ADMINISTRATIVE LAW, *supra* note 98. *See also* JANE KELSEY, ECONOMIC FUNDAMENTALISM (East Haven, CT: Pluto Press 1995) (analyzing the shift to corporatist approaches in New Zealand); Symposium, *Privatization: The Global Scale-Back of Government Involvement in National Economies,* 98 ADMIN. L. REV. 435 (1996).

120. For a discussion of how state regulatory approaches often borrow from private forms and structures, *see* Alfred C. Aman, Jr., *The Earth as Eggshell Victim: A Global Perspective on Domestic Regulation,* 102 YALE L.J. 2107 (1993); *see also* Alfred C. Aman, Jr., *Administrative Law for a New Century, in* THE PROVINCE OF ADMINISTRATIVE LAW 90, 90–91 (Michael Taggart ed., Oxford, UK: Hart Pub. 1997).

121. *See generally,* GUÉHENNO, *supra* note 115, at 23.

122. *See* ROBERT B. REICH, THE WORK OF NATIONS: PREPARING OURSELVES FOR 21ST-CENTURY CAPITALISM 301–15 (New York: Knopf 1991) (asking the question "who is us?" in light of an increasingly denationalized global economy).

123. *Id.* at 119–35; *see also* PETER DICKEN, GLOBAL SHIFT: THE INTERNATIONALIZATION OF ECONOMIC ACTIVITY 13–14 (New York: Guilford Press 2d ed. 1992).

124. REICH, *supra* note 122, at 119–35.

125. The state, despite its diversity, has a distinct role to play. *See, e.g.,* BRINGING THE STATE BACK IN (Peter B. Evans et al. eds., New York: Cambridge Univ. Press 1985); *see also* STATES AGAINST MARKETS: THE LIMITS OF GLOBALIZATION (Robert Boyer & Daniel Drache eds., New York: Routledge 1996). *But see* PETER SELF, GOVERNMENT BY THE MARKET? THE POLITICS OF PUBLIC CHOICE 4–20 (Boulder, CO: Westview Press 1993).

126. *See, e.g.,* Cass R. Sunstein, *Interest Groups in American Public Law,* 38 STAN. L. REV. 29 (1985).

127. For a discussion of corporatist theory, *see* PAUL P. CRAIG, PUBLIC LAW AND DEMOCRACY IN THE UNITED KINGDOM AND THE UNITED STATES OF AMERICA 148–53 (New York: Oxford Univ. Press 1990); *see also* ALAN CAWSON, CORPORATISM AND POLITICAL THEORY 22–46 (New York: Blackwell 1986), at 22–46.

128. ROBERT PERRUCCI, JAPANESE AUTO TRANSPLANTS IN THE HEARTLAND: CORPORATISM AND COMMUNITY 81 (New York: de Gruyter 1994).

129. *See, e.g.,* Robert Pear, *Federal, State Officials Spar over Welfare Spending,* L.A. DAILY NEWS, Dec. 29, 1996, at B22.

130. *Id.*

131. *See* PERRUCCI, *supra* note 128, at 1–20 (describes and analyzes the competition among various Midwestern states for Japanese auto plants, noting that a kind of corporatism characterized the decision-making processes at the state and local levels that led to the financial incentives necessary to attract this investment).

132. As noted in the Lisbon Report,
Competing in the global economy, characterized today by the emergence of new competitors, especially from South and Southeast Asia has become the everyday slogan of multinational corporation advertisers, business school managers, trendy economists, and political leaders. People are told that a new global economy is in the making, the main players being North American, Western European, and Japanese-based multinational corporations. Through localization and transplants of production facilities and fierce competition or alternatively, via strong alliances to enable more successful competition at the world level the global networks of multinational corporations are reshaping the sectoral and territorial configuration of the world economy, from the automobile industry to telecommunications, electronics to pharmaceuticals, textiles to civilian air transport. The new global economy looks like a battle among economic giants where no rest or compassion is allowed the fighters. The globalization of the economy seems an inexorable process enabling world networks of financial and industrial firms to amass an unparalleled power of decision-making and influence over the destiny of millions of people throughout the world.

GROUP OF LISBON REPORT, LIMITS TO COMPETITION xiii (Cambridge, MA: MIT Press 1995) [hereinafter Lisbon Report].

133. *See* Cerny, *supra* note 117, at 124 ("[W]hile the state has always been to some extent a promoter of market forces, state structures today are being transformed into more and more market-oriented and even market-based organizations themselves. . . ."). For a discussion of how the state has turned to the private sector for structural and procedural examples of administration, see Aman, *supra* note 15. *See also infra* text accompanying notes 172–82.

134. *See supra* text accompanying notes 56–67.

135. *See supra* text accompanying notes 11–14.

136. Lisbon Report, *supra* note 132, at 121–40.

137. *Id.* at xvi–xvii.

138. KRUGMAN, *supra* note 117, at 5.

139. *See generally*, SCHACTER, *supra* note 24.

140. *Id.* at 7–8.

141. *Id.* at 9.

142. For an analysis of how markets for municipal services differ from other markets for goods, *see* HARDEN, *supra* note 51.

143. *Id.* at 1–6. *See also* Aronson, *supra* note 98.

144. Aronson, *supra* note 98, at 53.

145. *Id.*

146. *See* ROBERT GILPIN, THE POLITICAL ECONOMY OF INTERNATIONAL RELATIONS (Princeton, NJ: Princeton Univ. Press 1987); *see also* JOSEPH S. NYE, BOUND TO LEAD: THE CHANGING NATURE OF AMERICAN POWER (New York: Basic Books 1990).

147. *See* ROBERT NOZICK, ANARCHY, STATE, AND UTOPIA (New York: Basic Books 1974).

148. *Id. See, e.g.,* Jack Kemp's assertion in October 1996 vice presidential debate, "the U.S. economy is overtaxed and over regulated," *quoted in* James Gerstenzang & Marc Lacey, *Gore, Kemp Clash on Tax Cuts and Economic Growth Politics,* L.A. TIMES, Oct. 10, 1996, at A1.

149. CRAIG, supra note 127, at 153–57.

150. *See, e.g.,* Chief Justice Rehnquist's approach to state action in *Moose Lodge 107 v. Irvis,* 407 U.S. 163 (1972); *Jackson v. Metropolitan Edison Co.,* 419 U.S. 345 (1974); *Flagg Bros., Inc. v. Brooks,* 436 U.S. 149 (1978); *Blum v. Yaretsky,* 457 U.S. 991 (1982); *Rendell-Baker v. Kohn,* 457 U.S. 830 (1982); *NCAA v. Tarkanian,* 488 U.S. 179 (1988). *See also* Cerny, *supra* note 118, at 130 ("[G]lobalization entails *the undermining of the public character of public goods and of the specific character of specific assets,* i.e. the *privatization and marketization* of economic and political structures.").

151. *See* MILTON FRIEDMAN, CAPITALISM AND FREEDOM (Chicago, IL: Univ. Chicago Press 1962).

152. *Id.*

153. H.R.J. Res. 52, 105th Cong. (1997).

154. For example, many strong-state laissez-faire advocates in the economic sphere often support state intervention on social issues. *See, e.g.,* ANDREW GAMBLE, THE FREE ECONOMY AND THE STRONG STATE: THE POLITICS OF THATCHERISM 35 (Durham, NC: Duke Univ. Press, 1st ed. 1988); *see also School Prayer Delayed by GOP Squabbles,* 54 CONG. Q. WKLY. REP. 2529 (Sept. 7, 1996) (discussing social conservatives' proposed constitutional amendment to protect school prayer).

155. *See, e.g.,* the isolationist positions of some conservative senators, found in proposals such as Jesse Helms's proposed Foreign Relations Revitalization Act (S.908), which would have eliminated the Agency for International Development, the U.S. Arms Control and Disarmament Agency, and the U.S. Information Agency (Proceedings and Debates of the 104th Congress, 1st sess., Dec. 14, 1995) (14 CONG. REC. S18617-02); *see also* Helms's opposition to the International Chemical Weapons Convention (143 CONG. REC. S3570-628) (daily ed. Apr. 24, 1997); some of the more extreme APA cost-benefit reforms of the 104th Congress are designed more to ensure agency inaction than any real reform, such as the Comprehensive Regulatory Reform Act of 1995 (S. Res. 343).

156. Using process to achieve substantive results that prevent governmental intervention is a kind of laissez-faire proceduralism. *See* Paul R. Verkuil, *The Emerging Concept of Administrative Procedure* 78 COLUM L. REV. 258 (1978). As Professor Verkuil has noted with respect to early United States administrative law,

> [t]he substantive values of the nineteenth-century liberal, non-interventionist state and the procedural values of the common-law, adversary model of decision-making have a common core and are mutually supportive. Both sets of values reflected a common philosophical premise that the correct result would be achieved by the free clash of competing forces in the marketplace, or in the courtroom. As Jerome Frank noted, the "fight [or adversary] theory of justice is a sort of laissez-faire."

Id. at 264 *quoting from* JEROME FRANK, COURTS ON TRIAL: MYTH AND REALITY IN AMERICAN JUSTICE 92 (Princeton, NJ: Princeton Univ. Press 1949). For a case study of how Congress used procedure and agency structure to constrain the abilities of a regulatory agency, the Department of Energy, *see* Alfred C. Aman, Jr., *Institutionalizing the Energy Crisis: Some Procedural and Structural Lessons,* 65 CORNELL L. REV. 491 (1980).

157. *See generally,* SELF, *supra* note 125, 48–69.

158. *See, e.g.,* Uruguay Round Agreements of the Gen. Agreements on Tariffs and Trade: Hearing before the House Small Business Comm., 103d Cong. (1994) (testimony of Ralph Nader) [hereinafter Nader], *available at* 1994 WL 230684 ("[D]ecisions arising from [international] governance can pull down our

higher living standards in key areas or impose trade fines and sanctions until such deregulation is accepted.").

159. *Id.*

160. *See* Alissa J. Rubin, *Buchanan's Protectionism Slows Trade Agenda*, 54 CONG. Q. WKLY. REP. 532 (March 2, 1996) (discussing Patrick Buchanan's anti-trade rhetoric in the context of the 1995 trade deficit); *see also Eat Your NAFTA*, ECONOMIST, Nov. 13, 1995, at 15 (discussing Ross Perot's anti-NAFTA stance).

161. *See* Nader, *supra* note 158.

162. *See, e.g.,* Ralph Nader's Public Citizen Watch assertion that a recent outbreak of hepatitis among Michigan school children caused by Mexican strawberries is the result of weak Mexican regulation (*Clinton Wants on the Fast Track with Latin America*, Assoc. Press Release, Apr. 12, 1997).

163. *See* Aman, *supra* note 17, at 806; *see also* Lee v. Weisman, 505 U.S. 577 (1992) (discussing separation of church and state); Roe v. Wade, 410 U.S. 113 (1973) (discussing right of privacy).

164. The late Senator Paul Wellstone (D-MN) adopted this position in the 1995 welfare debates opposing block granting to the states, noting that block grants would "lower the floor of federal protection." (114 CONG. REC. S11,735-03) (Aug. 7, 1995).

165. *See, e.g.,* the differences on this issue among liberal democrats who otherwise support national legislation; *see also* Senate Comm. on Commerce, Science, and Transp. Hearing on Fast Track Negotiating Authority, 1997 WL 605646 (F.D.C.H.) (Sept. 30, 1997).

166. *See, e.g.,* the testimony of Deputy U.S. Trade Representative Charlene Barshefsky before the Trade Subcomm., House Ways & Mean Comm.: Hearing on NAFTA Membership for Chile, 1995 WL 373535 (F.D.C.H.) (June 21, 1995) ("expanding trade is critical to our efforts to create good, high wage jobs").

167. *See Nader Blasts GATT*, FIN. POST, Dec. 23, 1997, at 1 (arguing that "GATT sets up an apparatus that is secretive, inaccessible and unappealing to decide disputes and harmonize standards in our case downward by subordinating and therefore subjugating critical health and safety consumer issues, environmental issues and workplace issues to the imperatives of commercial trade.").

168. *See, e.g., Is Free Trade Good or Bad for America?*, STAR-LEDGER, Sept. 14, 1997, available in 1997 WL 12560888 (containing comments made by AFL-CIO president Charles Wowkaneck explaining the AFL-CIO's opposition to fast-track legislation: "[American labor] can't compete with $2 wages.").

169. *See, e.g.,* All Things Considered: Richard Gephardt Announces Opposition to NAFTA (National Public Radio broadcast, Sept. 21, 1993): "[M]embers of Congress who come to oppose or vote to oppose this NAFTA are not protec-

tionist and we're not against Mexico. We simply believe that passing a NAFTA that fails to ensure sensible Mexican wage increases . . . is worse than no NAFTA at all."

170. In some ways, these strong-state views are somewhat akin to the realists' position vis-à-vis the state in international relations theory. The state is viewed as a unified whole. *See* Anne-Marie Slaughter, *Liberal International Relations Theory and International Economic Law,* 10 AM. U. J. INT'L L. & POL'Y 717, 722 (1995).

171. *See, e.g., A New French Twist,* TIME, June 16, 1997, at 54 (discussing the effects of Lionel Jospin's job-creation proposals on France's plan to join the single European currency). *See also France Still Trapped,* 344 ECONOMIST, July 5, 1997, at 51 (July 5, 1997).

172. For an analogy to this view of the state, *see* Slaughter, *supra* note 170, at 727 (describing a liberal theory of international relations).

173. *See* Gore Commission, *supra* note 23; *see also* Aman, *supra* note 15.

174. An example of this on the international level is the private standards called ISO 14000. *See supra* note 49.

175. *See generally,* PHILIP G. CERNY, THE CHANGING ARCHITECTURE OF POLITICS: STRUCTURE, AGENCY, AND THE FUTURE OF THE STATE 227–29 (Newbury Park, CA: Sage Publications 1990).

176. *See* AMAN, *supra* note 28, at 13.

177. *See* JAMES M. LANDIS, THE ADMINISTRATIVE PROCESS 10–12 (New Haven, CT: Yale Univ. Press 1938).

178. DICKEN, *supra* note 122, at 212–23.

179. *Id.*

180. *Id.*

181. Perhaps the ultimate political example of this was President Clinton's statement in his 1996 State of the Union Address that "the era of big government is over." State of the Union Address, 32 WKLY. COMP. PRES. DEC. 90, 91 (Jan. 23, 1996). The political left had a sharp reaction to this. *See* David Kusnet, *Feeling His Way,* MOTHER JONES, Jan.–Feb. 1997, at 46.

182. *See* SCHACTER, *supra* note 24, at 9.

183. *See generally,* SAGOFF, *supra* note 25.

184. For a discussion of the similarities and the differences between the cost-benefit approaches in the executive orders issued by the Clinton administration and the Reagan-Bush administration, see Ellen Siegler, *Executive Order 12866: An Analysis of the New Executive Order on Regulatory Planning and Review,* 24 ENVTL. L. REP. 10,070 (1994).

185. Ch. 3, *supra* pp. 000–000.

186. *See generally,* Symposium, *The New Public Law,* 89 MICH. L. REV. 707 (1991).

187. See William N. Eskridge, Jr. & Gary Peller, *The New Public Law Movement: Moderation as a Postmodern Cultural Form,* 89 MICH. L. REV. 707, 742, 749 (1991).

188. *Id.*

189. *Id.* at 733–34.

190. *Id.* at 746–47.

191. *Id.* at 749–50.

192. *See* AMAN, *supra* note 28, at 47–62 (showing how deregulatory economic approaches by agencies were approved by courts, pursuant to broad public-interest statutory language).

193. *Id.* at 81–82.

194. *Id.* at 1.

195. Deregulation was particularly effective at the Federal Communications Commission. *Id.* at 54–59. Overall, however, the size of the bureaucracy increased during the Reagan administration. *See* IAN AYRES & JOHN BRAITHWAITE, RESPONSIVE REGULATION: TRANSCENDING THE DEREGULATION DEBATE (New York: Oxford Univ. Press 1992).

196. *See* AMAN, *supra* note 28, at 53–62.

197. 467 U.S. 837 (1984). For an analysis of *Chevron* and its relationship to deregulation, *see* AMAN, *supra* note 28, at 108–21.

198. AMAN, *supra* note 28, at 2.

199. *Id.* at 91–103.

200. *Id.* at 102–3.

201. See Peter M. Shane, *Structure, Relationship, Ideology; or, How Would We Know a "New Public Law" If We Saw It?,* 89 MICH. L. REV. 837, 844–45 (1991).

202. For an analysis of why there were far fewer differences between the regulatory approaches of the Bush I and Clinton administrations, *see* Aman, *supra* note 15.

203. For an analysis critiquing this closed-system approach, *see* GUÉHENNO, *supra* note 115, at 49–65.

> We are entering into the age of open systems, whether at the level of states or enterprises, and the criteria of success are diametrically different from those of the institutional age and its closed systems. The value of an organization is no longer measured by the equilibrium that it attempts to establish between its different parts, or by the clarity of its frontiers, but in the number of openings, of points of articulation that it can organize with everything external to it.

Id. at 49.

204. *See* Cerny, *supra* note 118, at 130. *But see* Geoffrey Garrett & Peter Lange, *Political Responses to Interdependence: What's "Left" for the Left?,* 45 INT'L ORG. 539 (1991).

205. *See* Tun Myint, *Democracy in Global Environmental Governance: Issues, Interests, and Actors in the Mekong and the Rhine,* 10 IND. J. GLOBAL LEGAL STUD. 287 (2003).

206. *See, e.g.,* Gerth, *supra* note 49, at D1. (discussing the global, informal, harmonized rules suggested for governing worldwide auto safety standards by industry in United Nations rule-making proceedings.

In the interest of breaking down trade barriers, negotiations like these are trying to harmonize or create common regulations for products to be sold around the world. At the dawn of this new worldwide regulatory machinery, it is premature to predict its impact. But corporate executives are generally ecstatic, consumer advocates are increasingly critical and many regulators from the U.S. have mixed feelings.

207. Cerny, *supra* note 118, at 130.

208. *See generally,* HARDEN, *supra* note 51; *see also* PATRICK BIRKENSHAW ET AL., GOVERNMENT BY MOONLIGHT: THE HYBRID PARTS OF THE STATE (Boston, MA: Unwin Hyman 1990).

209. For a discussion of schools, see Gary Peller, *Public Imperialism and Private Resistance: Progressive Possibilities of the New Private Law,* 73 DENV. U. L. REV. 1001 (1996).

210. *See, e.g.,* The Personal Responsibility and Work Opportunity Reconciliation Act of 1996, Pub. L. No. 104-193, 110 Stat. 2105 (codified as amended in scattered sections of the U.S.C.) (welfare reform).

211. *See* discussion *infra* ch. 4, at 000–000.

NOTES TO CHAPTER 4

1. *See, e.g.,* Note, *Much Ado about $26 Million: Implications of Privatizing the Collection of Delinquent Federal Taxes,* 16 VA. TAX REV. 699 (1997).

2. *See* Alfred C. Aman, Jr., *A Global Perspective on Current Regulatory Reform: Rejection, Relocation, or Reinvention?,* 2 IND. J. GLOBAL LEGAL STUD. 429, 454–62 (1995).

3. Jody Freeman has described the actual cumulative process of policy making and subsequent implementation and enforcement as "fluid." She explains that "[a]dministrative law scholars tend to take 'snapshots' of specific moments in the decision-making process (such as the moment of rule promulgation) and analyze them in isolation. Rules develop meaning, however, only through the fluid processes of design, implementation, enforcement, and negotiation." Jody Freeman, *The Private Role in Public Governance,* 75 N.Y.U. L. REV. 543, 572 (2000). *See also* Mark Aronson, *A Public Lawyer's Responses to Privatization and Outsourcing, in* THE PROVINCE OF ADMINISTRATIVE LAW 40, 50–58 (Michael Taggart ed., Oxford, UK: Hart Pub. 1997).

4. For purposes of this book, references to the APA are intended to suggest

the use of procedures for hybrid decision making that may or may not be the same as the procedures found in the APA. In many instances, if the APA is to apply it must be amended to fit the needs of hybrid arrangements involved, such as the provisions dealing with contracting out agency duties; in others, it is important to determine which types of private entities should be affected by APA extensions. For a discussion of the scope and coverage of the Freedom of Information Act, as it relates to the private sector, *see, e.g.,* Alfred C. Aman, Jr., *Information, Privacy, and Technology: Citizens, Clients or Consumers?, in* FREEDOM OF EXPRESSION AND FREEDOM OF INFORMATION 325, 333–36 (Jack Beatson & Yvonne Cripps eds., New York: Oxford Univ. Press 2000).

5. *See, e.g.,* private prisons, *supra* text accompanying notes 54–96. *See generally,* Symposium, *The New Private Law,* 73 DENV. U. L. REV. 993 (1996).

6. *See* Gary Peller, *Public Imperialism and Private Resistance: Progressive Possibilities of the New Private Law,* 73 DENV. U. L. REV. 1001 (1996) (discussing public schools and various reform proposals); *see also* Aronson, *supra* note 3.

7. Peller, *supra* note 6, at 1004–5.

8. *Id.*

9. *See* Debora L. Spar, *The Spotlight and the Bottom Line: How Multinationals Export Human Rights,* 77 FOREIGN AFF., Mar.–Apr. 1998, at 7. In response to pressure over labor issues, U.S.-based transnational corporations have created codes of conduct that address workers' rights. A Reebok spokesman has stated, "[c]onsumers today hold companies accountable for the way products are made, not just the quality of the product itself." See Lance Compa & Tashia Hinchliffe-Darricarrere, *Enforcing International Labor Rights through Corporate Codes of Conduct,* 33 COLUM. J. TRANSNAT'L L. 663 (1995); see Jeff Manning, *Nike Battles Back, but Activists Hold the High Ground,* PORTLAND, OREGONIAN, November 19, 1997, at A7 *available at* 1997 WL 13136566 (reporting that New Jersey schoolchildren staged an anti-Nike play on Broadway, and that a 1996 consumer survey listed "bad labor practises" as the third most applicable phrase describing Nike); Gerard Aziakou, *US Nike,* AGENCE FRANCE PRESSE, April 10, 1998, Advisory Section (reporting that labor rights groups are planning a worldwide day of protest on April 18, 1998, to highlight Nike's workers' rights violations at its overseas facilities); Rosalind Rossi, *Poshard Joins Protest at Nike Store,* CHI. SUN-TIMES, Apr. 19, 1998, at 10 (relaying that seventy-five demonstrators protested outside Nike's Michigan Avenue store concerning Nike's treatment of its foreign workers). Following media revelations of forced labor in China and child labor in Southeast Asia, major retailers and apparel and footwear manufacturers adopted policies and codes of conduct concerning forced labor, child labor, and worker health and safety. Firms with such codes and policies include Levi Strauss, Sears, J.C. Penney, Walmart, The Gap, Starbucks, Timberland, Nike, and Reebok. Some firms, including Levi-Strauss and

Timberland, have gone so far as to pull out of entire countries where there are pervasive human rights violations. *See* Douglass Cassel, *Corporate Initiatives: A Second Human Rights Revolution?*, 19 FORDHAM INT'L L.J. 1963, 1973 (1996).

10. For critiques of the substitution of the market for the government, see ROBERT KUTTNER, EVERYTHING FOR SALE: THE VIRTUES AND LIMITS OF MARKETS 328–61 (New York: Knopf 1997); STATES AGAINST MARKETS: THE LIMITS OF GLOBALIZATION (Robert Boyer & Daniel Drache eds., New York: Routledge 1996); THE GROUP OF LISBON, LIMITS TO COMPETITION xi–xii (Cambridge, MA: MIT Press 1995).

11. Richard L. Pierce, Jr., *Reconciling Chevron and Stare Decisis*, 85 GEO. L.J. 2225 (1997).

12. Jost Delbruck, *Exercising Public Authority beyond the State: Transnational Democracy and/or Alternative Legitimation Strategies*, 10 IND. J. GLOBAL LEGAL STUD. 29 (2003).

13. Janet McLean, *Government to State: Globalization, Regulation, and Governments as Legal Persons*, 19 IND. J. GLOBAL LEGAL STUD. 173, 175 (2003) (arguing that "[i]nternational and contract law both tend to conceive of the government actor as a determinate legal person: a single authority representing all branches of the state and able to make commitments on behalf of the whole.").

14. *Id.*

15. PAUL C. LIGHT, THE TRUE SIZE OF GOVERNMENT 1 (Washington, DC: Brookings Institution 1999).

16. *Id.*

17. 5 U.S.C. § 551, *et seq.* (2000).

18. The APA applies to federal agencies only. Section 551(1) applies to agencies, which it defines as "each authority of the Government of the United Sates. ..." 5 U.S.C. § 551.

19. For an excellent analysis of the state-actor doctrine and some of its ambiguities, see Ronald J. Krotszynaski, Jr., *Back to the Briarpatch: An Argument in Favor of Constitutional Meta-Analysis in State Action Determinations*, 94 MICH. L. REV. 302 (1995).

20. 5 U.S.C. 551 (1) (1994) (defining agencies as authorities of the "Government of the United States").

21. For an excellent discussion of these theories and their relationship to U.S. and U.K. constitutional and administrative law, *see generally*, P. P. CRAIG, PUBLIC LAW AND DEMOCRACY IN THE UNITED KINGDOM AND THE UNITED STATES OF AMERICA (New York: Oxford Univ. Press 1990).

22. *Id.* at 58–63.

23. *Id.* at 63–67.

24. Cass R. Sunstein, *Interest Groups in American Public Law*, 38 STAN. L. REV. 29, 31 (1985); *see also* Christine B. Harrington, *Regulatory Reform: Creating Gaps and Making Markets*, 10 J. L. & POL'Y 293 (1988) (arguing that regulatory

negotiation substitutes an informal process for meaningful political debate over the values of regulation and that the silence of the state in such negotiation is actually "an expression of state power and an aspect of the minimalist state").

25. *See generally,* Freeman, *supra* note 3, at 572; THE PROVINCE OF ADMINISTRATIVE LAW (Michael Taggart ed., Oxford, UK: Hart Pub., 1997).

26. Freeman, *supra* note 25, at 597.

27. *See* CRAIG, *supra* note 21, at 148–53; *see generally,* ALAN CAWSON, CORPORATION AND POLITICAL THEORY 22–46 (New York: Blackwell 1986).

28. Philippe Schmitter has defined corporatism in the following way: Corporatism can be defined as a system of interest representation in which the constituent units are organized into a limited number of singular, compulsory, noncompetitive, hierarchically ordered and functionally differentiated categories, recognized or licensed (if not created) by the state and granted a deliberate representational monopoly within their respective categories in exchange for observing certain controls on their selection of leaders and articulation of demands and supports.

Philippe C. Schmitter, *Still the Century of Corporatism, in* TRENDS TOWARD CORPORATIST INTERMEDIATION 7, 13 (Philippe C. Schmitter & Gerhard Lehmbruch eds., London, UK: Sage Press 1979). Though the new governance, with its emphasis on networks rather than hierarchy, would seem to undercut this view, the combination of the relatively few groups involved in providing some of the services, such as private prisons, coupled with the narrowing of the discourse to largely economic terms and the state's need to be as efficient as possible, all militate in favor of bargaining relationships between the state and the interest groups selected to undertake the public tasks at hand. *But see* Robert H. Salisbury, *Why No Corporatism in America?, in* TRENDS TOWARD CORPORATIST INTERMEDIATION 213 (Philippe C. Schmitter & Gerhard Lehmbruch eds., London, UK: Sage Press 1979).

29. *See* CAWSON, *supra* note 27, at 35.

30. *See, e.g.,* J. H. H. Weiler et al., *European Democracy and Its Critique, in* THE CRISIS OF REPRESENTATION IN EUROPE 4, 32–33 (Jack Hayward ed., London, UK: Frank Cass 1995).

31. *See infra* text accompanying note 76.

32. CRAIG, *supra* note 21, at 150.

33. CAWSON, *supra* note 27, at 35.

34. *Id.*

35. For a critique of technocracy in this sense, *see* Weiler et al., *supra* note 30, at 33 ("The technocratic and managerial solutions often mask ideological choices which are not debated and subject to public scrutiny beyond the immediate interests related to the regulatory or management area.").

36. *Id.*

37. *See generally,* PETER DICKEN, GLOBAL SHIFT: THE INTERNATIONALIZA-
TION OF ECONOMIC ACTIVITY (New York: Guilford Press 2d ed. 1992).

38. For a general discussion of the private involvement in relation to administrative accountability, *see* Aman, *supra* note 2; *see also* Freeman, *supra* note 3,
at 672 (analyzing "the reality of the extensive private role in every dimension of
administration and regulation").

39. *See* Edward L. Rubin, *Getting Past Democracy,* 149 U. PA. L. REV. 711
(2001).

40. Alfred C. Aman, Jr., *Globalization, Democracy, and the Need for a New
Administrative Law,* 49 UCLA L. REV. 1687 (2002); Alfred C. Aman, Jr., *Proposals for Reforming the Administrative Procedure Act: Globalization, Democracy and the Furtherance of a Global Public Interest,* 6 IND. J. GLOBAL LEGAL
STUD. 397 (1999) [hereinafter Aman, *Proposals*]; Alfred C. Aman, Jr., *The Globalizing State: A Future-Oriented Perspective on the Public/Private Distinction,
Federalism, and Democracy,* 31 VAND. J. TRANSNAT'L L. 769, 816–19 (1998)
[hereinafter Aman, *Globalizing State*]. Many of the proposals for reform in this
chapter are based on the reforms advocated in these articles. For perspectives on
democracy and administrative law in Eastern Europe, see Paul H. Brietzke, *Democratization and . . . Administrative Law,* 52 OKLA. L. REV. 1 (1999) (stressing
that a well-structured administrative state is crucial to the democratization
process). Randall Peerenboom has conversely proposed that deregulation and involving private actors in rule making and implementation may actually serve to
reduce the Chinese "democracy deficit" by inviting shared governance. Randall
Peerenboom, *Globalization, Path Dependency and the Limits of Law: Administrative Law Reform and Rule of Law in the People's Republic of China,* 19
BERKELEY J. INT'L L. 161, 253–58 (2001). Because China maintains a vast administrative bureaucracy that is inaccessible to citizens, reform is seen to encourage accountability, even though Peerenboom recognizes that private actors also
have accountability concerns. *Id.* at 257.

41. *See* HINDY LAUER SCHACTER, REINVENTING GOVERNMENT OR REINVENT-
ING OURSELVES: THE ROLE OF CITIZEN OWNERS IN MAKING A BETTER GOVERN-
MENT 7–9 (Albany, NY: SUNY Press 1997); Aman, *Globalizing State, supra*
note 40, at 799.

42. *See, e.g.,* Tumey v. Ohio, 273 U.S. 510, 532 (1927).
[T]he requirement of due process of law in judicial procedure is not
satisfied by the argument that men of highest honor and the greatest self-
sacrifice could carry it out without danger of injustice. Every procedure
which would offer a possible temptation to the average man as a judge to
forget the burden of proof required to convict the defendant, or which
might lead him not to hold the balance nice, clear, and true between the
State and the accused, denies the latter due process of law.

43. 5 U.S.C. § 557(d)(1)(B) ("[N]o member of the body comprising the agency, administrative law judge, or other employee who is or may reasonably be expected to be involved in the decisional process of the proceeding, shall make or knowingly cause to be made to any interested person outside the agency an ex parte communication relevant to the merits of the proceeding").

44. *See, e.g.,* United States Steel Workers of Am. v. Marshall, 647 F.2d 1189 (D.C. Cir. 1980).

45. Enron had much to do with GATT rules involving energy. See Paul Krugman, *In Broad Daylight,* N.Y. TIMES, Sept. 27, 2002, at A31; see also Marianne M. Jennings, *A Primer on Enron: Lessons from a Perfect Storm of Financial Reporting, Corporate Governance, and Ethical Cultural Failures,* 39 CAL. W. L. REV. 163 (2003); Richard A. Oppel, Jr., *U.S. Regulators Are Requiring Full Details of Energy Sales,* N.Y. TIMES, May 15, 2002, at C1.

46. See Joseph E. Field, Note, *Making Prisons Private: An Improper Delegation of a Governmental Power,* 15 HOFSTRA L. REV. 649, 662–63 (1987) ("The presence of a profit motive results in private prisons substituting the goal of the general welfare of society with the goal of profit maximization. In this manner, cost considerations may hamper, if not totally override, society's interest in correctional policy.").

47. As Lester Salamon has noted with regard to the many tools of governance now employed, each has its own "political economy" and each "imparts its own 'twist' to the operation of the programs that embody it." Lester M. Salamon, *The New Governance and the Tools of Public Action: An Introduction, in* THE TOOLS OF GOVERNMENT: A GUIDE TO THE NEW GOVERNANCE 1, 2 (Lester M. Salamon ed., New York: Oxford Univ. Press 2002).

48. *Id.* at 1.

49. *See e.g.,* Bonsor v. Musicians' Union, 1 Ch 479 (1954); R. V. Monopolies and Mergers Comm. Ex. P. Argyll Group Plc 2 All E.R. 257 (Court of Appeal 1986).

50. Section 553 of the APA provides exemptions from its general rule-making procedures. Among these is one granted for "matter[s] relating to contract." 5 U.S.C. § 553(a)(2) (2000). This exemption has, however, generally been construed narrowly by the courts.

51. Alfred C. Aman, Jr., *Privatization and the Democracy Problem in Globalization: Making Markets More Accountable through Administrative Law,* 28 FORDHAM URB. L.J. 1477, 1502 (2001).

52. Robert L. Fischman, *Stumbling to Johannesburg: The United States' Haphazard Progress toward Sustainable Forestry Law,* 32 ENVTL. L. REP. 10,291 10,304 (2002).

53. *Id.*

54. *Developments in the Law: The Law of Prisons: III. A Tale of Two Sys-*

tems: Cost, Quality, and Accountability in Private Prisons, 115 HARV. L. REV.
1868, 1869 (2002).

55. *See, e.g.,* N.Y. CORRECT. LAW § 72(1) (McKinney 2003) (requiring the
department to house and care for all inmates); ARK. CODE ANN. § 12-50-106(a)
(Michie 2002) (authorizing contracts for construction, financing, and operating
facilities).

56. Charles W. Thomas & Sherril Gautreaux, *The Present Status of State and
Federal Privatization Law,* available at http://web.crime.ufl.edu/pcp/html/
statelaw.html (last updated Mar. 19, 2000).

57. *Id.*

58. *Id.*

59. COLO. REV. STAT. ANN. § 24-50-501 (West 2003).

60. MASS. GEN. LAWS ANN. ch. 7, § 52 (West 2003).

61. Alfred C. Aman Jr., *Privatization and the Democracy Problem in Globalization: Making Markets More Accountable through Administrative Law,* 28
FORDHAM URBAN L.J. 1477, 1481 (2001).

62. See ROBERT B. REICH, THE WORK OF NATIONS: PREPARING OURSELVES
FOR 21ST-CENTURY CAPITALISM 301–15 (New York: Knopf 1991).

63. *See, e.g.,* Fox Butterfield, *Hard Times, A Special Report: Profits at a Juvenile Prison Come with a Chilling Cost,* N.Y. TIMES, July 15, 1998, at A1 (stating
that

> inmates of the privately run prison regularly appear at the infirmary with
> black eyes, broken noses or jaws or perforated eardrums from beatings by
> the poorly paid, poorly trained guards or from fights with other boys.
> Meals are so meager that many boys lose weight. Clothing is so scarce that
> boys fight over shirts and shoes. Almost all the teachers are uncertified, in-
> struction amounts to as little as an hour a day, and until recently there
> were no books.

> From the beginning, the company . . . pursued a strategy of maximizing
> profit from the fixed amount it received from the state for each inmate[.]
> The plan was to keep wages and services at a minimum while taking in as
> many inmates as possible[.]).

64. For example, the deregulation of electricity rates at the generation level
has turned out to be more complex than first imagined. It is, therefore, important that there be public input into both the creation and continuation of these
markets. The trade-offs involved are, essentially, public questions that require
public input. *See, e.g.,* Nancy Vogel, *How State's Consumers Lost with Electricity Deregulation,* L.A. TIMES, Dec. 9, 2000, at A1; *see also, e.g.,* Richard B. Stewart, *Environmental Regulation and International Competitiveness,* 102 YALE L.J.
2039 (1993) (discussing toxic dumping); Bill Maurer, *Cyberspatial Sovereignties:*

Offshore Finance, Digital Cash, and the Limits of Liberalism, 5 IND. J. GLOBAL
LEGAL STUD. 493 (1998) (discussing money laundering); Geoffrey W. Smith,
*Competition in the European Financial Services Industry: The Free Movement of
Capital Versus the Regulation of Money Laundering,* 13 U. PA. J. INT'L BUS. L.
101, 124 (1992) (noting that the banking laws of countries such as Switzerland,
Austria, Monaco, Hong Kong, the Cayman Islands, Uruguay, Gibraltar, and the
Bahamas tend to provide secrecy and tax havens that attract money launderers
as well as legitimate business).

65. *See generally,* Katherine Cox, *The Inevitability of Nimble Fingers? Law,
Development, and Child Labor,* 32 VAND. J. TRANSNAT'L L. 115, 128–29 (1999).

66. *See generally,* JEAN DREZE & AMARTYA SEN, INDIA: ECONOMIC DEVELOP-
MENT AND SOCIAL OPPORTUNITY 13–16 (New York: Oxford Univ. Press 1995).

67. *See* SASKIA SASSEN, THE MOBILITY OF LABOR AND CAPITAL: A STUDY OF
INTERNATIONAL INVESTMENT AND LABOR FLOW (New York: Cambridge Univ.
Press 1988).

68. *See also* Pam Belluck, *As More Prisons Go Private, States Seek Tighter
Controls.* N.Y. TIMES, Apr. 15, 1999, at A1 (describing the private prison industry's recent practice of building "speculative prisons" in economically depressed
areas):

[A] company arranges to build a prison and promises to fill it with inmates, instead of contracting in advance with the state for a prison that
state officials have decided they want.

[T]he company usually negotiates directly with a town or city, often one
desperate for jobs and corporate taxpayers because its factories or mines
have dried up. . . . There is often no contract outlining the prison's responsibilities to that city or its state; the prison's only contract is with the supplier of the inmates.

The prison company buys land on the cheap (in some cases, it's free) in exchange
for providing jobs, but local officials are given no control over prison conditions.
Id. "It's sort of like hazardous waste. . . . When you bring in something that is
potentially dangerous, which inmates are, what, if any, obligations do states
have to regulate them?" *Id.*

69. *See, e.g.,* KY. REV. STAT. ANN. § 197.510(13) (Banks-Baldwin 1998) (requiring at least 10 percent savings); TENN. CODE ANN. § 41-24-104(c)(2)(B)
(2002 Supp.) (requiring at least 5 percent savings); OHIO REV. CODE ANN. 9.06
(A)(4) (West 2002) (requiring at least 5 percent savings); FLA. STAT. ANN. 957.07
(West 2003 Supp.) (requiring at least 7 percent savings).

70. COLO. REV. STAT. ANN. § 24-50-501 (West 2003).

71. D.C. CODE ANN. § 2-301.05(d)(2)–(4) (2003).

72. COLO. REV. STAT. ANN. § 24-50-501 (West 2003).

73. 117 S. Ct. 2100, 2106 (1997).

74. ARK. CODE ANN. § 12-50-106(d) (Michie 2002).

75. OHIO REV. CODE ANN. 9.06 (A)(1) (West 2002).

76. JAMES AUSTIN & GARRY COVENTRY, EMERGING ISSUES ON PRIVATIZED PRISONS 4 (Bureau of Justice Assistance 2001).

77. Simon Domberger & Paul Jensen, *Contracting Out by the Public Sector: Theory, Evidence, Prospects,* OXFORD REV. ECON. POL'Y, Winter 1997, at 67, 68.

78. TENN. CODE ANN. § 41-24-104 (2002 Supp.).

79. *Id.*

80. *Id.*

81. *Id.*

82. *Id.*

83. IDAHO CODE § 20-241A (Michie 1997).

84. MONT. STAT. ANN. § 2-8-302 (2002).

85. KY. REV. STAT. ANN. § 197.510(7) (Banks-Baldwin 1998).

86. *Id.* at § 197.515 (Banks-Baldwin 1998).

87. MICH. COMP. LAWS ANN. § 791.220g (West 2001).

88. COLO. REV. STAT. ANN. § 17-1-202(f) (West 2003)

89. *See, e.g.,* Colorado General Assembly's Homepage, *available at* http://www.state.co.us/gov_dir/stateleg.html (last modified Sept. 2, 2003); Arizona @ Your Service, http://az.gov/webap/portal (last modified Sept. 5, 2003).

90. Colorado General Assembly's Homepage, *available at* http://www.state.co.us/gov_dir/stateleg.html (last modified Sept. 2, 2003).

91. FLA. STAT. ANN. § 957.03 (West 2001).

92. *Id.* at (1).

93. *Id.* at (2).

94. *Id.* at (4)(c).

95. U.S. v. Morrison, 529 U.S. 598, 621 (2000). *See also* discussion in ch. 2, at 000–000.

96. ROBERT POLLIN & STEPHANIE LUCE, THE LIVING WAGE: BUILDING A FAIR ECONOMY (New York: New Press 1998).

97. *See, e.g.,* Robert B. Reich, *Working Principles, in* MAKING WORK PAY vii, x (Robert Kutter ed., New York: New Press 2002) (stating that before passage of the last minimum wage increase 80–85 percent of Americans supported the raise).

98. David Moberg, *Martha Jernegon's New Shoes, in* MAKING WORK PAY 108, 111 (Robert Kutter ed., New York: New Press 2002). State and local global-warming initiatives are also being spurred by the absence of federal action in that area. Several rural states have passed legislation to capitalize on greenhouse-gas emission trading, if such a system is developed. New England states and Canadian provinces entered into an agreement to limit greenhouse emissions, while California, Oregon, and Washington have agreed to collaborate to

combat global warming. Governor Pataki of New York is attempting to establish a regional carbon dioxide trading network. Overall, in 2003 "24 states have introduced 90 bills that would build frameworks for regulating carbon dioxide." Jennifer Lee, *Warming Is Global, but the Push for Legislation in U.S. Is Local,* INT'L HERALD TRIBUNE, Oct. 30, 2003, at A2.

99. Scott Adams & David Neumark, *Living Wage Effects: New and Improved Evidence* 1 (NBER Working Paper no. 9702, May 2003).

100. *See, e.g.,* Georgiana Vines, *Candidates for Mayor Differ over Living Wage,* KNOXVILLE NEWS-SENTINEL, Aug. 17, 2003, at B1 (discussing mayoral candidates' views on living-wage proposal rejected the previous year by the city council); *Bloomington to Consider Mandatory Living Wage* (Assoc. Press, Sept. 16, 2003) (discussing living-wage campaign in Bloomington, Indianapolis, Lafayette, and South Bend, Indiana).

101. Rachel Gordon, *Survey Gives Impetus to Raise Minimum Wage; Few Businesses in S.F. Would Be Affected,* SAN FRANCISCO CHRONICLE, May 8, 2003, at A25.

102. *See e.g.,* Tennessee House Bill 421, 2003 (amending TENN. CODE ANN., Tit. 50, Ch.2, pt.1 to read "local government shall possess no authority to require a private employer to pay its employees any wage that is not required to be paid by such employer under applicable state or federal law.").

103. POLLIN & LUCE *supra* note 96, at 10–12.

104. Adams & Neumark, *supra* note 99, at table 1.

105. *Id.* at 5.

106. Florida Senate Bill 54, 2003. Tennessee House Bill 421, 2003, states that such ordinances "are . . . detrimental to the business environment of the state and to the citizens, businesses and governments of the various political subdivisions."

107. Florida Senate Bill 54, 2003.

108. Moberg, *supra* note 98, at 114.

109. POLLIN & LUCE, *supra* note 96, at 90.

110. *See supra* ch. 2, at 000–000.

111. Lane Kensworthy, Stewart Macaulay & Joel Rogers, *"The More Things Change . . .": Business Litigation and Governance in the American Automobile Industry,* 21 LAW & SOC. INQUIRY 631, 674 (1996).

112. Note, *Like Oil and Water: The WTO and the World's Water Resources,* 19 CONN. J. INT'L L. 183, 185 (2003).

113. Public Citizen, *How New "Global Trade" Talks Threaten Municipal Water Services in the U.S., at* http://www.publiccitizen.org/ID=9237 (last visited Feb. 2, 2004). Recently, many communities have been privatizing waterworks on their own accords. *See* Douglas Jehl, *As Cities Move to Privatize Water, Atlanta Steps Back,* N.Y. TIMES, Feb. 10, 2003, at A14 (stating that "over the last five years, hundreds of American communities . . . have hired private companies to

manage their waterworks"). However, not every experience with water privatization was a positive one. Atlanta officials canceled a private service contract with United Water, a subsidiary of the French company Suez, because of "service they call poor, unresponsive and fraught with breakdowns, including an epidemic of water-main breaks and occasional 'boil only' alerts caused by brown water pouring from city taps." *Id.* One Atlanta customer noted a problem with current privatization efforts discussed in this book: "if you have a political problem in your city, you can vote in a new administration. If you have a private company with a long-term contract . . . then it gets a lot more difficult." *Id.*

114. Lori M. Wallach, *Accountable Governance in the Era of Globalization: The WTO, NAFTA, and International Harmonization of Standards*, 50 KAN. L. REV. 823 (2002).

115. *See* Sidney A. Shapiro, *International Trade Agreements, Regulatory Protection, and Public Accountability*, 54 ADMIN. L. REV. 435, 444–45 (2002); *see also* AM. BAR ASS'N. HOUSE OF DELEGATES RECOMMENDATION NO. 107C, HARMONIZATION RECOMMENDATION (Aug. 2001), *available at* htpp://www.abanet.org/leadership/2001/107c.pdf.

116. Shapiro, *supra* note 115, at 458.

117. World Trade Organization, Agreement on Application of Sanitary & Phytosanitary Measures, art. 4.1, *available at* http://www.wto.org/english/tratop_e/sps_e/spsagr_e.htm (last visited Feb. 8, 2004).

118. Public Citizen, *The WTO Comes to Dinner: U.S. Implementation of Trade Rules Bypasses Food Safety Requirements* 10, *at* http://www.publiccitizen.org/documents/EQUIVALENCYFINALREPORT.PDF (last updated July 17, 2003).

119. 9 C.F.R. § 381.94 (2002).

120. Public Citizen, *supra* note 118, at 10.

121. *Id.* at 12.

122. *Id.*

123. *Id.*

124. *Id.* at iii.

125. Cindy Skrzycki, *Now, You May Never Know Where That Broccoli Has Been*, WASH. POST, Feb. 3, 2004, at E1.

126. *Where Your Food Comes From*, N.Y. TIMES, Jan. 23, 2004, at A22.

127. Gardiner Harris, *Pfizer Moves to Stem Canadian Drug Imports*, N.Y. TIMES, Aug. 7, 2003, at C1.

128. Sarah Gay Stolberg & Gardiner Harris, *Industry Fights to Put Imprint on Drug Bill*, N.Y. TIMES, Sept. 5, 2003, at A1.

129. *Id.*

130. Chart, N.Y. TIMES, *available at* www.nytimes.com/imagepages/2003/09/04/business/05MEDI.chart.jpg.html (posted Sept. 4, 2003).

131. H.R. 2769, 108th Cong. §§ 1,2(b) (2003).

132. Ceci Connolly, *An Unlikely Pair Fights for Cheaper Medications; Congressmen Support Drug Reimportation Plan,* WASH. POST, Sept. 5, 2003, at A3.

133. Elizabeth Becker, *Drug Industry Seeks to Sway Prices Oversees,* N.Y. TIMES, Nov. 27, 2003, at A1.

134. Elizabeth Mehren, *Boston Looking to Canada for Drugs,* L.A. TIMES, Dec. 10, 2003, at 21.

135. *Id.*

136. *Id.*

137. Christopher Rowland, *Canadian Pharmacy Group Warns of Supply Problems,* BOSTON GLOBE, Dec. 18, 2003, at C3.

138. *Id.*

139. Mehren, *supra* note 134.

140. *Id.*

141. Monica Davey, *Illinois to Seek Exemption to Buy Drugs from Canada,* N.Y. TIMES, Dec. 22, 2003, at A27.

142. *Id.*

143. Claire Kittredge, *Seniors See Hope in Limiting Drug Prices,* BOSTON GLOBE, Dec. 18, 2003, at A3.

144. Harris, *supra* note 116.

145. *Id.*

146. *Id.*

147. Rowland, *supra* note 137.

148. Becker, *supra* note 133.

149. *Id.*

150. *Id.*

151. *Mass. Lawmakers Propose Publicizing Prices of Canadian Prescription Drugs,* CONG. DAILY, Aug. 4, 2003, at 9.

152. Stolberg & Harris, *supra* note 127.

153. Connolly, *supra* note 132.

154. Katharine Seelye, *Study Confirms "Stakeholders" Gave Advice to Energy Panel,* N.Y. TIMES, Aug. 26, 203, at A16.

155. *But see* In Re Cheney, 334 F.3d 1096, 1117 (D.C. Cir. 2003) (Randolph, J., dissenting) (stating that "[a]lready the government has voluntarily produced some 36,000 pages of documents" relating to the taskforce).

156. Walker v. Cheney, 230 F. Supp. 2d 51, 67 (D.D.C. 2002).

157. 230 F. Supp. 2d 12,15 (D.D.C. 2002).

158. Judicial Watch, Inc. v. Nat'l Energy Pol'y Dev. Group, 230 F. Supp. 2d 12, 16 (D.D.C. 2003).

159. *Id.*

160. In Re Cheney, 334 F.3d 1096, 1104 (D.C. Cir. 2003) (citations omitted).

161. *Id.* at 1105 (citations omitted).

162. *Id.*

163. *Id.* at 1117 (citations omitted).
164. 5 U.S.C. App. 2 § (2)(a).
165. 997 F.2d 898 (D.C. Cir. 1993).
166. In Re Cheney, 334 F.3d at 1114–15.
167. *Id.* at 1115 (decision pending before U.S. Supreme Court).
168. 123 S. Ct. 2374 (2003).
169. *Id.* at 2379.
170. CAL. INS. CODE ANN. § 13801 (West Cum. Supp. 2003).
171. Garamendi, 123 S. Ct. at 2382–83.
172. *Id.* at 2381 (citation omitted).
173. *Id.* at 2382 (citation omitted).
174. *Id.* at 2395.
175. *Id.* at 2400.
176. *Id.* at 2401.
177. *Id.*
178. Moreover, as the dissent pointed out, international diplomacy—and the German agreement in particular—was not very successful in getting insurance contracts from the Holocaust era paid. The dissent noted that "[f]or over five decades, untold Holocaust-era insurance claims went unpaid." *Id.* at 2395 (citation omitted). The dissent also stated that the commission that the agreement with Germany relies upon (the ICHEIC) for the payment of insurance claims was created in response to litigation against insurance companies in the United States. *Id.* at 2395–96 (stating that "the litigation propelled a number of European companies to agree on a framework for resolving unpaid claims outside the courts."). The dissent further asserted that ICHEIC had done a poor job of getting Holocaust-era policies paid: "ICHEIC has thus far settled only a tiny proportion of the claims it has received"; "although ICHEIC has directed its members to publish lists of unpaid Holocaust-era policies, that non-binding directive had not yielded significant compliance at the time this case reached the Court"; and "it remains unclear whether ICHEIC does now or will ever encompass all relevant insurers." *Id.* at 2396. Justice Ginsburg also implies that the California law indirectly improved the performance of ICHEIC by creating this lawsuit: "[s]hortly after oral argument, ICHEIC-participating German insurers made more substantial disclosures." *Id.*
179. 530 U.S. 363 (2000). While Justices Scalia and Thomas concurred in the judgment only, this action was based upon their objection to the majority's analysis of factors beyond the language of the statute at issue itself, and not upon any disagreement with the result of majority's interpretation.
180. *Id.* at 365.
181. Terry Collingsworth, *The Key Human Rights Challenge: Developing Enforcement Mechanisms*, 15 HARV. HUM. RTS. J. 183, 184 (2002).

182. Crosby, 530 U.S. at 375 (citation and internal quotation omitted).
183. *Id.* at 378.
184. *Id.* at 392–83.
185. Stuart Auerbach, *46-Year-Old CAB Goes Out of Existence; Chairman Bangs Final Gavel at Bittersweet Session,* WASH. POST, Jan. 1, 1985, at D1.

Index

About the Author

Alfred C. Aman, Jr., is the Director of the Indiana University Institute for Advanced Study and the Roscoe C. O'Byrne Professor of Law at Indiana University School of Law. From 1991 to 2002 he was the Dean of the Indiana University School of Law–Bloomington. Dean Aman has held a Distinguished Fulbright Chair in Trento, Italy, and visiting professorships in England, France, and Italy. He is the author of four books, including *Administrative Law in a Global Era* (Cornell Univ. Press, 1991), and numerous articles on administrative and regulatory law, especially as it relates to the global economy. He is the faculty editor of the *Indiana Journal of Global Legal Studies*. Dean Aman earned his A.B. from the University of Rochester (1967) and a J.D. from the University of Chicago (1970). He was the Executive Editor of the *University of Chicago Law Review*. After law school, Dean Aman was a law clerk for the Hon. Elbert P. Tuttle, U.S. Court of Appeals, Eleventh Circuit (1970–72); an Associate at Sutherland, Asbill & Brennan in Atlanta and Washington, D.C. (1972–77); and a member of the Cornell Law School faculty (1977–91). Dean Aman stepped down from the deanship in 2002 and then spent the following year as a Visiting Fellow in the Princeton University Law and Public Affairs Program and Visiting Professor in the Woodrow Wilson School.